Yevgeny Vakhtangov

Yevgeny Vakhtangov was a pioneering theatre artist who married Stanislavsky's demands for inner truth with a singular imaginative vision. Directly and indirectly, he is responsible for the making of our contemporary theatre: that is Andrei Malaev-Babel's argument in this, the first English-language monograph to consider Vakhtangov's life and work as actor and director, teacher and theoretician.

Ranging from Moscow to Israel, from Fantastic Realism to Vakhtangov's futuristic projection, the Theatre of the "Eternal Mask," *Yevgeny Vakhtangov: A critical portrait*:

- considers his input as one of the original teachers of Stanislavsky's system, and the complex relationship shared by the two men;
- reflects on his directorship of the First Studio of the Moscow Art Theatre and the Habima (which was later to become Israel's National Theatre), as well as the Vakhtangov Studio in Moscow (currently the Vakhtangov Theatre and Institute), the institution he established; and
- examines in detail his three final directorial masterpieces, *Erik XIV*, *The Dybbuk*, and *Princess Turandot*.

Lavishly illustrated and elegantly conceived, *Yevgeny Vakhtangov* represents the ideal companion to Malaev-Babel's *Vakhtangov Sourcebook* (2011). Together, these important critical interventions reveal Vakhtangov's true stature as one of the most significant representatives of the Russian theatrical avant-garde.

Andrei Malaev-Babel is an actor, director, and scholar, a graduate of the Vakhtangov Theatre Institute in Moscow. He serves as an Associate Professor of Theatre at the FSU/Asolo Conservatory for Actor Training, and on the board of the Michael Chekhov Association. He is the editor of *The Vakhtangov Sourcebook*.

Figure 0.1 Yevgeny Vakhtangov, 1915. Courtesy of Vakhtangov Theatre Museum.

Yevgeny Vakhtangov
A critical portrait

Andrei Malaev-Babel

LONDON AND NEW YORK

First published 2013
by Routledge
2 Park Square, Milton Park, Abingdon, Oxon OX14 4RN

Simultaneously published in the USA and Canada
by Routledge
711 Third Avenue, New York, NY 10017

*Routledge is an imprint of the Taylor & Francis Group, an
informa business*

© 2013 Andrei Malaev-Babel

The right of Andrei Malaev-Babel to be identified as author of
this work has been asserted by him in accordance with
sections 77 and 78 of the Copyright, Designs and Patents
Act 1988.

All rights reserved. No part of this book may be reprinted or
reproduced or utilised in any form or by any electronic,
mechanical, or other means, now known or hereafter
invented, including photocopying and recording, or in any
information storage or retrieval system, without permission in
writing from the publishers.

Trademark notice: Product or corporate names may be
trademarks or registered trademarks, and are used only for
identification and explanation without intent to infringe.

British Library Cataloguing in Publication Data
A catalogue record for this book is available from the British
Library

Library of Congress Cataloging-in-Publication Data
Malaev-Babel, Andrei.
Yevgeny Vakhtangov: a critical portrait / Andrei
Malaev-Babel.
    p. cm.
  Includes bibliographical references and index.
  1. Theater—Production and direction.   2. Vakhtangov,
  Evgenii, 1883–1922—Criticism and interpretation.
  3. Theater—Philosophy.   4. Acting—Study and teaching—
  Russia.   I. Title.
  PN2053.M35 2012
  792.02′33—dc23

                                        2012011958

ISBN: 978-0-415-46586-1 (hbk)
ISBN: 978-0-415-46587-8 (pbk)
ISBN: 978-0-203-85285-9 (ebk)

Typeset in Sabon
by RefineCatch Limited, Bungay, Suffolk

Printed and bound in Great Britain by
TJ International Ltd, Padstow, Cornwall

This publication was made possible by a generous grant from the Dolores Zohrab Liebmann Fund.

I dedicate this book to the memory of my grandmother, Antonina Pirozhkova (1909–2010), who truly looked forward to this book. A pioneering Moscow metro designer, and the widow of Russian-Jewish author Isaac Babel, she was introduced to her future husband as "Princess Turandot"—a nickname she received after Vakhtangov's most popular production. The independence and strength of Antonina's character, apparent from this nickname, were supplemented, through the years, with patience, wisdom, and compassion. I took full advantage of these qualities as I was growing up, and well into my adulthood. My grandmother always supported my work on Vakhtangov, and she encouraged me to carry it forward, no matter what. For that, and for numerous other gifts I received from Antonina, I am forever grateful.

Contents

Illustrations and plates

Illustrations

Plates
Plates can be found between pages 110 and 111.

Acknowledgements

This book would not have been possible without the support from many generous, dedicated and talented individuals. At Routledge, I would like to acknowledge Talia Rogers, Ben Piggott and Sam Kinchin-Smith.

I am greatly indebted to Franc Chamberlain, whose insightful comments and suggestions helped me better express my thoughts and clarify my ideas.

Florida State University and its Council on Research and Creativity provided me with a generous award in support of my work on this book. I am thankful to them and to those people who supported my application: Dr. Sally McRorie, Vice President for Faculty Development and Advancement, Theatre and Dance; Dr. C. Cameron Jackson, Director of the School of Theatre; Professors Terry Lynn Hogan and Martha Cooper. I would also like to thank Kirby Kemper, Vice President for Research and Jan Townsend of the Council on Research and Creativity.

The Dolores Zohrab Liebmann Fund gave a generous gift in support of *The Vakhtangov Sourcebook*. I would like to thank the Liebmann Fund, and especially Edward L. Jones and Mr. M. Haigentz, for their contribution to this pioneering Vakhtangov edition.

My wife, Lisa Eveland Malaev, has proofread every word of my writings for the past 19 years. I want to thank her, my son Nicholai and my mother Lidiya for their tremendous patience and support during my Vakhtangov saga. My deep gratitude goes to Steven Ross Evelend, who has patiently edited every word I have penned for the past 16 years.

I am forever indebted to the noted Russian scholar Vladislav Ivanov, who demonstrated an unprecedented generosity of spirit by sharing with me the manuscript of his fundamental two-volume edition, *Yevgeny Vakhtangov, Documents and Evidence*, prior to its Russian publication in February 2011. This groundbreaking Vakhtangov collection restored the material removed in Soviet-era censorship cuts to the major Vakhtangov texts, and introduced many new, previously unpublished materials by Vakhtangov and on Vakhtangov. Thanks to Mr. Ivanov and the Moscow INDRIK publishers, Vakhtangov's heritage appeared uncensored and uncut in my recent publication, *The Vakhtangov Sourcebook*, thus allowing English-language readers around the globe to appreciate Vakhtangov as a futuristic, highly spiritual thinker and artist.

I also want to thank Dr. Pavel Dmitriev of the St. Petersburg State Theatre Library and noted St. Petersburg theatre scholar Margarita Laskina for the unique opportunity they gave me to become acquainted with the theatrical heritage of Vakhtangov's contemporary, director and teacher Nikolai Demidov. Demidov's rare insight into the Stanislavsky System, and his own unique school of acting, allowed me a better understanding of Vakhtangov's heritage.

I am especially grateful to Galina Remizova, the Moscow actress and daughter of my teacher Aleksandra Remizova, for her selfless support of my work. I am indebted to the Moscow theatre director and photographer Sergei Tuptalov for magically restoring several of the key illustrations to this book. Moscow literary agent and copyright specialist Vladimir Kozyrev helped me to communicate with archives and museums, and for that I would like to thank him. I am also grateful to Anna Callander of Routledge, to Paula Clarke, and to Kevin Eaton of Refinecatch for seeing *Yevgeny Vakhtangov* seamlessly through production.

Several generous and patient individuals were instrumental in helping me identify and secure illustrations for this collection. My deep gratitude goes to the Vakhtangov Theatre Museum's curators Irina Sergeyeva and Margarita Litvin for their generous support, and for the research they conducted on my behalf. I also would like to thank the talented photographer Vitaly Myasnikov, who is associated with the Vakhtangov Theatre and Museum in Moscow.

I am indebted to Roza Zaripova, the head of Arsis Design, for supplying unique images for this publication.

I am deeply indebted to the Director of the Israel Goor Theatre Archives and Museum Luba Yuniverg for sharing the Goor Archives' collection with me, and connecting me with other organizations in Israel. I also would like to thank the talented photographer Gregory Khatin, who is associated with the Goor Archives.

I am grateful to Marfa Bubnova, Director of the Moscow Art Theatre's Museum for her invaluable help and advice.

Last but not least, I would like to thank my colleagues and students at the Florida State University/Asolo Conservatory for Actor Training and at the New College of Florida. I learn from them daily.

Andrei Malaev-Babel

Special thanks to the Florida State University's Council on Research and Creativity for their support through the COFRS grant award.

Introduction

Vakhtangov in the twentieth and twenty-first century theatre context: justifying theatre and liberating the actor

In October 1922, Russian theatre critic and scholar Pavel Markov wrote an article entitled "Princess Turandot and the Contemporary Theater".[1] Reading Markov's article today highlights how deeply some of Vakhtangov's contemporaries understood his intentions, and how hopelessly Vakhtangov's heritage has been forgotten and misunderstood in the years since. Eight months after the opening of Vakhtangov's final production—Carlo Gozzi's *Princess Turandot*—Markov wrote:

> Vakhtangov gave to the theater the truth about the actor; this truth became the truth of this performance [*Turandot*].
>
> The actor was asserted as the creative origin of the performance; [. . .] The character did not absorb the actor; the character's weight did not bend the actor's individuality to its will; the actor— master and histrionic—revealed its simple, but personal essence (large or small, significant or insignificant). This essence was intrinsic and distinctive to him alone. [. . .]
>
> Vakhtangov justified theater's existence that was on the verge of becoming fruitless, and annihilated its ethical and moral contradictions.
>
> (Markov in *Printsessa Turandot* 1923: 49–50)

For several decades, Vakhtangov's theatrical concepts, as outlined in his *Turandot*, influenced Western Theatre more than they did the theatre of "socialist realism." Bertolt Brecht studied Vakhtangov's approach closely, and he had every reason to do so. Vakhtangov's

---

1 This article was printed in an exclusive book collection, *Printsessa Turandot* [*Princess Turandot*] (Moscow-Petrograd: State Publishers, 1923), and it has never been reprinted.

principle of transformation, utilized in *Turandot, created the illusion of a gap between the character and the actor.* This *illusion* allowed for an actor's point of view on the character to resonate more clearly onstage, thus foreshadowing Brechtian "alienation."

Markov's statement that, in his *Turandot*, Vakhtangov "justified theater" and "liberated the actor" was accurate. On the most obvious level, *Turandot* actors (as well as the audience members) were freed by Vakhtangov from subordination to the reality of the play. Audiences were no longer eavesdropping on the character's life, as invisible witnesses. The actors no longer had to merely embody the life of the character. Unlike in a Stanislavskian production where the audience was supposed to find itself "visiting with the Prozorov family" (Ivanov 2011 vol. I: 219), Vakhtangov openly invited his spectators "into the midst of actors, doing their theatre work" (*Sourcebook*, Malaev-Babel 2011: 149; hereafter referred to as *Sourcebook*).

Vakhtangov made the actor's mastery and creativity a cornerstone of the theatrical process, thus *morally justifying* the element of lie and pretense intrinsic to the very nature of theatre. (Such a justification appeared especially timely in the 1920s, when the Russian theatre actively entered the so-called formalistic stage; it remains timely today.) Vakhtangov's *Turandot* became a hymn to creativity—both of the actor and of the audience. Ultimately, *Turandot* was the hymn to human creativity, and to theatre *as a place where the creative spirit can be evoked nightly.*

In 1922, when Vakhtangov premiered his *Turandot*, he was unanimously pronounced the leader of the Russian theatre—the one and only artist capable of leading the way to the Theatre of the Future. These proclamations came from recognized heads of the two opposing theatrical camps. The following is a short list of statements, issued by the leaders of the Russian theatre in 1922:

> This performance [*Turandot*] is a festive holiday for the entire collective of the Art Theatre. [. . .] I am proud of such a student, if he is my student.
>
> In the twenty five-year history of the Moscow Art Theatre such victories were few. You found what many theatres sought long and in vain.
>
> (Konstantin Stanislavsky[2] quoted in Gorchakov 1957: 183–84)

---

2   The inscription on the photograph Stanislavsky gave to Vakhtangov in April 1922 reads: "To the hope of the Russian art, to the future head of the Russian theater" (Vendrovskaya and Kaptereva 1984: 429).

Yes, the creator of this performance knows what among the old must be demolished, and what is inviolable. And he knows how to do so. Yes, a noble and courageous hand acts here by the will of intuition, splendidly feeling the way of the theatre of tomorrow. In some things this master will reject the delusive novelty, and in other things he will strike us, elders, on the head even harder. Even today we feel "pain and bliss", joy and fear. My soul is full of gratitude to the master himself, as well as to his collaborators.

(Vladimir Nemirovich-Danchenko 1984a: 427)

Stanislavsky was right in his definition of Vakhtangov's image: "The Leader." "It is not so difficult to prepare a director, but how do you find a leader?"

[. . .]

Vakhtangov's final works showed us that [. . .] at the Third Studio [of the Moscow Art Theatre] and at The Habima, where he worked,—the new experiments that were conducted truly helped the art of theater to move forward.

(Vsevolod Meyerhold 1984: 447)

There was not a single problem of the contemporary theatrical form that would not be touched upon and resolved one way or another by the performance of *Turandot*.

(Pavel Markov 1923: 46)

Vakhtangov's triumphs, and the acknowledgements of his genius, were bitter-sweet, as they came too late. Yevgeny Vakhtangov died of cancer in May 1922, at the age of 39. For decades following Vakhtangov's death, his disciples intentionally distorted Vakhtangov's ideas. They did so in order to preserve the theatre company named after Vakhtangov during the communist reign. Consequently, throughout the history of the twentieth century, all of Vakhtangov's achievements were appropriated, although unintentionally, by practitioners with longer careers, who lived under more fortunate historic circumstances. The fact that some of the defining innovations currently attributed to theatre artists such as Antonin Artaud, Bertolt Brecht, and Jerzy Grotowski[3] were preceded by Vakhtangov's experiments escapes the contemporary theatrical community.

3 In the mid-1950s Grotowski studied Vakhtangov's heritage in Moscow, where he trained under Vakhtangov's direct disciple Yuri Zavadsky.

4 *Introduction: Vakhtangov in context*

In the meantime, the influence of Vakhtangov upon today's theatrical horizon is inestimable. One cannot find a significant theatrical figure of the twentieth and twenty-first century theatre who did not study Vakhtangov, write about him, tackle his heritage, and/or see his productions[4] (see Figure 0.2). Directly or indirectly, Vakhtangov is responsible for the making of our contemporary theatre. Most importantly, Vakhtangov's heritage still holds the keys for the Theatre of the Future or, as Vakhtangov called it, the Theatre of the Eternal Mask.

4 On Vakhtangov's influence on the key twentieth-century theatrical figures, see *Sourcebook* (2011: 3–6).

Figure 0.2 Gordon Craig with the cast of Vakhtangov's production of *Princess Turandot*, 1935. Courtesy of Vakhtangov Theatre Museum.

Part I

Vakhtangov's theatrical youth

1 The city of Vladikavkaz
Fathers and sons

When trying to fathom the roots of some of his younger contemporaries' art—the art that seemed to have distorted the world—Konstantin Stanislavsky wrote:

> I think that organically I can no longer understand much in the aspirations of present-day-youth. One must have courage to admit this. [. . .]
>
> We spent our youth in a Russia that was peaceful; in which there was plenty for few. The present generation has grown up in the midst of war, hunger, world upheavals, transitional era, mutual misunderstanding and hate. [. . .] The new generation almost does not know the joy that we knew, it seeks and creates joy in new environments, and tries to make up for those years of youth that it has lost.
>
> (Stanislavsky 1953: 464–65)

Yevgeny Vakhtangov's childhood and youth fell in the period of Russian history when the dividing line of the revolution was sensed in every aspect of society's life. Vakhtangov himself will speak of this fateful line in one of his articles:

> The red line of the Revolution divided the world into the "old" and the "new." There is no corner of human life through which this line has not passed, and there is no person who has not felt it in one way or another.
>
> (*Sourcebook* 2011: 165)

Needless to say, the dividing line of the revolution did not bypass a Russian family, creating a dramatic gap between "fathers and sons." Vakhtangov's family was not an exception. Vakhtangov belonged to the generation of the theatre artists born in a turbulent time when art, theatre, was no longer considered the domain of wealthy connoisseurs. The dividing line of the revolution made art a powerful weapon in a struggle between the new and the old. At that time, art almost exclusively became a domain of the new progressive middle class, or rather of a "social stratum," known as the Russian intelligentsia.

Yevgeny Bogrationovich Vakhtangov was born on February 13, 1883, in the southern Russian City of Vladikavkaz[1] into the family of wealthy Armenian tobacco manufacturer Bograt (Bogration)[2] Vakhtangov. Bograt came into his tobacco factory and his fortune through his marriage to Yevgeny's mother Olga (née Lebedeva).

Vakhtangov's biographers disagree on the atmosphere of Vakhtangov's childhood. One thing is certain—Bograt Vakhtangov was a tyrannical person, accustomed to being the master, both in his business and in his home. Bograt's harsh treatment of his own father Sarkis, Yevgeny's grandfather, led to the proud old man's suicide—this tragic childhood memory must have left a deep imprint on Vakhtangov. A house painter, proud of his background and of his Armenian heritage, Sarkis could not accept his son's *rusification*—the price of doing serious business in the Russian empire.

In his childhood and youth, Vakhtangov seemed to be more sympathetic with his father's factory workers than he was with his father's business. He became a member of *Arzamas*—a secret circle, named after the progressive Russian author Maxim Gorky. (The tsarist government sentenced Gorky to exile in the southern city of Arzamas.) Members of the circle gathered at a private home to further their social, political and philosophical education. Together they read and discussed the works of Gorky, Tolstoy, Nietzsche, Schopenhauer, Marx and Lenin.

Much to his father's disappointment, Yevgeny showed no interest in learning to manage the family tobacco factory, and dedicated all his time free from studies to amateur theatricals. Bograt disapproved of his son's theatrical aspirations; in fact, he did not accept them until after Vakhtangov won his acclaim as the famed Moscow Art Theatre's director and actor.

1   Currently the capital of the Russian Republic of North Ossetia-Alania—the neighboring region of the ongoing Russian-Georgian and Chechen conflicts.
2   Another possible spelling of Vakhtangov's father's name is Bagrat, spelled with an "a." This would make Vakhtangov's patronymic "Bagrationovich"; in fact, Vakhtangov did use this spelling in his younger years.

Some of Vakhtangov's biographers (Smirnov-Nesvistsky 1987: 13) insist that there is no evidence that Bograt's actual treatment of Yevgeny was cruel (see Figure 1.1). Despite the old man's frequent threats and open disapproval, the young Vakhtangov, this Prince Royal, still enjoyed freedom and the means to do what he wanted. Trying to avoid angering his father, however, he undertook some of his theatre projects in secret (or under an assumed name).

Vakhtangov's literary talents became apparent rather early. Besides poetry and articles written for his high school newspaper, he wrote several autobiographical sketches. Two such sketches, written by a 19-year-old Yevgeny, give us insight into the Vakhtangov family atmosphere. They describe an unalterable routine of family life, where every activity, every relationship and even every conflict are reenacted with ritualistic precision.

One of Vakhtangov's sketches describes a family gathered for a traditional noontime coffee. In the sketch, the high school student Yasha (recognizably Vakhtangov) revolts against the senseless and onerous gathering. Even this revolt, however, appears to be routine and predetermined. Vakhtangov-the-author stresses that all the partic-ipants in the family scene, including his rebellious self, play perma-nently established roles.

Characters' behavior, as described by Vakhtangov, appears programmed—every human impulse steeped in the forever routine. Members of the family seem to be deprived of free will—wound-up mechanical toys that think and feel:

> In the next instant, Yasha's sister will appear from the next room, wearing her long loose housecoat. Silently, she will sit at the table . . . Having sat there for awhile, she will get up, and then bring a book. She is nearsighted, and she holds the book close to her eyes, and never hunches.
>
> Yasha waits for his other sister, Nina, to come in. He waits angrily, while biting his cigarette holder.
>
> "Let her come ahead of me, so that not to disrupt the routine domestic harmony, created by our family"—he thinks, while holding himself to his chair.
>
> (Ivanov 2011 vol. I: 36)

In another sketch, we encounter a father delivering "a daily talk" to his son. The father, recognizably Bograt, reproaches Yevgeny for avoiding his duties as an heir. He accuses his son of acting a role. In the father's view, Yevgeny is only *preaching* "non-exploitation," and

Figure 1.1 Vakhtangov's family, 1895. Vakhtangov standing next to his father Bograt, second from the left. Courtesy of Vakhtangov Theatre Museum.

neglecting to help the factory workers in practice, while eating their bread. Once again, the theme of the social role-acting appears in the sketch:

> Yasha's father pretends that he is reading a lecture on worldly wisdom in front of an entire audience of youth, who are lost, and whose life forces are going to waste.
>
> (Ivanov 2011 vol. I: 37)

Vakhtangov's sketches give us more than a glimpse into his youth. They provide an understanding of the origins of Vakhtangov's model of theatre, and his acting methods. At the essence of Vakhtangov's observations of life, there lies a perception that people are seldom free to fully express their true selves in their daily life. Instead, they hide behind social masks (progressive or regressive) and engage in senseless social rituals. Their true, essential life remains a secret, almost entirely buried behind daily disguises. Already at the age of 19, Vakhtangov was capable of perceiving the deathly, mechanical essence of human routines. He felt the stagnant, constricting nature of "social masks" worn by everyone.

Vakhtangov's father remains alone at the end of the sketch—his son just made his theatrical exit. "The audience" is gone, and the mask of the "educator of youth" is shed. Bograt becomes his real self—he withdraws into his bedroom to *nonchalantly* read his Stock Exchange Journal; he thinks his sacred, deep thoughts about his son. A completely different, real man looks out from behind the mask.

Vakhtangov's writings of the period reveal the many-layered, multifaceted personality of the author. The theme of social protest appears next to insightful and witty psychological observations. Elegant humor and irony, including self-irony, is juxtaposed against the theme of complicity with the sufferings of those less fortunate. Dreams of a great destination, of rising above the earth, are found alongside the sense of utter despair, of the futility of human existence.

At this youthful stage of his development, Vakhtangov can not foresee the deathly horror in the mundane—the characteristic tendency of some Russian authors, such as Pushkin, Gogol and especially Dostoyevsky. Instead he describes the *tedium* of the pointless daily routine; in that, he is closer to Chekhov's perception. As late as 1910, having watched rehearsals for Dostoyevsky's *The Brothers Karamazov* at the Moscow Art Theatre, Vakhtangov wrote in his diary:

There is a reality of Dostoyevsky, and then there is a reality of Chekhov, for example—yet the same life served as a source [for both of these realities]. Everything I saw on the stage from *Brothers Karamazov*, is still further removed from the life I understand than what Chekhov gave us.

(Ivanov 2011 vol. I: 205)

Even in the Dostoyevskian soul, "wrecked by today's time and conditions," "sunk into baseness and perversion," Vakhtangov longs to see the "bright spots," the inner "tenderness" (Ivanov 2011, vol. I: 205). Romantic perception of the earthly life as essentially tragic, and yearning for the creative realm, are present in Vakhtangov's youthful poetry. Earthly existence, as perceived by the young Vakhtangov, may be futile, cruel. However, a man is capable of shedding his vulgar earthly skin in the higher spheres of creativity:

To kick away the earthly sphere, to step into the new world, to embrace the mysterious beauty.

Cursed be the flowers, cursed be the sun, cursed be the fruits, cursed be the ice.

To embrace beauty—the mysterious beauty that is beautiful with its mystery.

To plunge my thought into the creative sea. To adorn the Thought's regal head with the immortal crown; to create, and, having created—to fall down at the feet of your creation. To soar in the realm of free thought, to glide among the stars, to caress the particles of light. To tear out my heart, to squeeze out my brain . . .

The thought of my soul! My life belongs to you. Take it and live. Extinguish the earthly hell with your mighty hand.

(Ivanov 2011 vol. I: 83)

Vakhtangov's literary experiments reveal a powerful inner life, with a mind and heart capable of reconciling seemingly opposing phenomena. Polarities, such as life and death, the singular and the global, the comical and the tragic, the heroic and the mundane, were embraced by Vakhtangov as opposite parts of one entire whole. As an example, a literary portrait of a high school Greek teacher betrays Vakhtangov's ability to perceive tragedy behind the pathetic mask. At the same time, this portrait is clearly written by a man with a sensitive heart, capable of complicity.

The influence of the Russian literary tradition, with its compassion toward "the little man," is evident in the sketch. The Greek teacher, who is perpetually disobeyed, mocked and humiliated by his students, because of his meekness, resembles the low clerk Bashmachkin—the main character of Gogol's tale, *The Overcoat*. As Vakhtangov projects his teacher's thoughts, one can almost hear Bashmachkin's heart-wrenching cry: "Why do you offend me?"

> What is going on in his soul? What does this little man feel? What does he think of, as he nervously fiddles with his watch chain? He does not hear the noise, yelling, and witty remarks . . . He is deaf . . . He thinks how little they understand him, and how little they respect his human dignity . . .
>
> (Ivanov 2011 vol. I: 41)

A human face, and an aching heart peep from under the impenetrable mask of an educator. Vakhtangov exhibits a gift, rare for his age, to see the human being in "an authority." Similarly, the glimpse of his father Bograt's inner self, evident in Vakhtangov's youthful literary portrait, reveals a mature understanding. The old man's loneliness, his inability to connect with his own family, the misunderstood heart behind the mask of a despot—all this is present in a short sketch.

Vakhtangov will continue "reaching" to his father through several of his theatrical works, including the character of the family patriarch from Hauptmann's *The Festival of Peace* (Vakhtangov's first professional production). In 1913, Vakhtangov will create the role of Dickens' cruel toy manufacturer Tackleton in the First Studio of MAT's production of *The Cricket on the Hearth*. In the role, he will rise to the art of the psychological grotesque by revealing the lonely soul behind the rough external characterization. Vakhtangov will play the inner tragedy behind the mask. Several of Vakhtangov's close colleagues and scholars (Khersonsky 1940a: 117) will recognize Bograt Vakhtangov in this role.

2 Freedom and nature

In October 1901, Vakhtangov met his future wife, Nadezhda Baytsurova, at a rehearsal for his high school's benefit performance. At rehearsals, Vakhtangov hardly gave her a glance. The young girl fell in love with Vakhtangov at first sight and patiently waited to be noticed. Following the performance, Vakhtangov suddenly invited Nadezhda to a waltz at the benefit ball. Years later, Mrs. Vakhtangov recalled this event as a not so happy experience:

> I was hurt. At my finishing school, I spent seven years studying dance, and I considered myself a good dancer. While waltzing with Vakhtangov, however, I understood that my dancing was stupid. I danced diligently, in earnest, while Zhenya danced with full ease, as if he could do it in his sleep. He danced as though he wanted to *demonstrate* how one must dance—lightly, freely and joyfully. His dance was artistic and, even at that early date, it subconsciously contained an element of a directorial demonstration.
>
> (Vakhtangova 1959: 333)

The culture of freedom is at the core of a directorial demonstration. Moreover, the quality of freedom is the foundation for any creative process. Vakhtangov's grasp of inner and outer freedom was an inborn quality. His closest colleague, Michael Chekhov, gave the following explanation for this psychological phenomenon:

> The capacity to *demonstrate* was particularly well developed in him [Vakhtangov]. A person who is merely *demonstrating* is experiencing an entirely different psychological state from when he is *actually performing*. The *demonstrator* has a certain confidence and lightness, and he is not burdened with the responsibility that

rests on the one who is *doing* the job. [. . .] Vakhtangov had the psychology of the *demonstrator* down to perfection.

(Chekhov 2005: 70)

The future Mrs. Vakhtangov also became a star of Vakhtangov's directorial debut—she played two female leads in his amateur production, based on Anton Chekhov's comedic one-acts *The Marriage Proposal* and *The Bear*. Baytsurova's memoir depicts the atmosphere of Vakhtangov's debut production:

> The performance took place in the open air, in the courtyard of a house that belonged to the family of one of the actors. A few pieces of furniture (only those essential to the plot . . .) were placed on a wooden stage platform with a curtain of printed cotton. No artificial lighting was featured. The performance began before dark, and it ended by sunset.
>
> (Vakhtangova 1959: 334)

One cannot help but trace similarities between the early stage of Vakhtangov's personal and artistic biography, and that of his future mentor, Konstantin Stanislavsky. Both men became fascinated with theatre in their childhood; both staged their first performance on a domestic stage. These similarities, however, point to drastic differences in the social, psychological and aesthetic makeup of the two artists of Russian Theatre. Stanislavsky's father built his son a theatre on the familial Lyubimovka estate—a spacious building equipped with a double-lighting system, a gallery, a stage, and four dressing rooms (Stanislavsky 1953: 490). Vakhtangov, like Konstantin Treplev from Chekhov's *The Seagull*, built himself an outdoor theatre, merging it with the breathtaking mountainous landscape of the Caucasus.

Stanislavsky's productions of Chekhov's plays featured detailed "natural" sound effects and settings. Chekhov himself protested against the constant background of barking dogs, chirping crickets and croaking frogs. The author felt that naturalistic details distract the audience from the essence of his plays.

Vakhtangov's first production was synchronized with the natural rhythms. His directorial debut anticipated the quest for the organic technique that models nature's *creative* laws, without literally *copying* nature. Years later Vakhtangov insisted that theatrical concepts, such as stage rhythm and plasticity of movement, must be absorbed from nature. In his first Chekhov production, Vakhtangov, while featuring bare settings, allowed his actors to breathe freely and joyfully, in harmony with the natural world.

3 Vakhtangov's early theatrical influences

The Brothers Adelgeim

Vakhtangov's first theatrical "teachers," according to his own admission, were the famous tragedians the Brothers Adelgeim (see Figure 3.1), who traveled Russian provinces in the late nineteenth and early twentieth century. The Adelgeim Brothers were among the most cultured and enlightened traveling tragedians of their time. They relied on the solid external technique they trained in Europe. They studied their roles carefully, and their productions were better "organized" composition-wise than those of many of their colleagues. The Adelgeim Brothers' psychological system of training was based on careful observation and recollection of life, as well as on self-observation. In fact, the Adelgeims' technique was somewhat similar to Stanislavsky's, as witnessed by some of their students (Speranskaya 1987: 79).

By the 1920s and 1930s, the Adelgeim Brothers traveled with their own troupe. They conducted regular classes and rehearsals with their actors. In this, the Adelgeim Brothers also favorably contrasted with most of their fellow travelers. At the time when Vakhtangov saw the Adelgeim Brothers perform in Vladikavkaz, however, they still had to rely on an "accidental" company of players. Such a company was either assembled for the tour in one of the larger cities, or selected out of the local talent pool. Such practices often resulted in rather uneven and eclectic ensembles—a mere background to the traveling stars' brilliant performances.[1]

---

1 Some of the most talented tragic actors of the time were able to "pull their ensembles together" in performance due to the piercing truthfulness of their own acting. By the power of their contagious performances, they "directed" less talented and experienced partners; such a hands-on approach to ensemble building, however, was an exception from the rule. Most of the traveling performers did not strive to achieve ensemble acting in their productions.

Figure 3.1 The Brothers Adelgeim, late nineteenth/early twentieth century. Courtesy of Andrei Malaev-Babel.

The Adelgeim Brothers' repertoire was of excellent taste and included plays such as Schiller's *The Robbers*, Gutzkow's *Uriel Acosta* and Shakespeare's *Hamlet* and *King Lear*. Vakhtangov did not formally study with the Adelgeim Brothers, but he frequently saw their performances at the Vladikavkaz Theatre. Vakhtangov's initial theatrical education included the very plays that "suffered" in the Moscow Art Theatre's interpretation. The MAT was at home in the realm of "feelings that seem true."[2] The tragic repertoire, however,

2 A formula, borrowed by Stanislavsky from Russian poet and playwright Alexander Pushkin, demanded "truth of passions" or "feelings that seem true" from an actor (Stanislavsky 2009: 103).

demanded the theatre of heightened emotions and elevated artistic truth. It called an actor to fill larger-than-life language and characters with "the truth of the passions."

At the foundation of the Adelgeim Brothers' school of acting was laid an elaborate technique of breathing, intrinsic to the art of the nineteenth-century tragedians. At the end of his career, Vakhtangov also put special emphasis on breathing in his own technique. In Vakhtangov's practices, however, breath was approached not only as a part of external technique, but as a psychological device. The breathing technique ultimately aimed at connecting the actor with their passions. The Adelgeim Brothers were also aware of the psychological aspects of breathing. Nevertheless, they trained their students exclusively in the conscious aspects of the breathing technique. The Adelgeims' teaching put an emphasis on long and deep breath—the tragedians considered such a breath essential for lengthy heroic monologues.

The Adelgeims' breath technique was rigid and prescriptive, probably at the expense of subtlety and nuance. While acknowledging the power of the subconscious, the brothers also believed that without constant conscious awareness, the subconscious will do more harm than good. They called their students to develop a certain state of split, where the conscious side would control and correct the subconscious (Speranskaya 1987: 88–89). Subsequently, the Adelgeim Brothers' approach to plays, as well as their training methods, erred on the analytical side. This approach distinguished the Adelgeim Brothers as consistent and reliable tragedians; however, they never achieved the flights of inspiration characteristic of their intuitive contemporaries—Duse, Giovanni Grasso, Komissarzhevskya, Yermolova.

Vakhtangov must have admired the Adelgeim Brothers' culture. Most importantly, their technique was accessible for observation—at least to a sharp and insightful observer, such as Vakhtangov. (This distinguished the Adelgeim Brothers from many of their fellow tragedians, whose technique was purely subconscious and, therefore, difficult to grasp.) The very same qualities that initially attracted Vakhtangov to the Adelgeim Brothers' acting eventually caused him to reevaluate his own views. Around 1907, Vakhtangov became disillusioned with the Adelgeim Brothers' art (Ivanov 2011 vol. I: 110).

4 To Moscow! To Moscow!

In 1903, at the age of 20 (see Figure 4.1), Vakhtangov left his hometown for Riga, presumably to embark upon a reliable career as an engineer. Vakhtangov-the-elder insisted that his son avoid Moscow, one of Russia's major political and cultural centers; he considered it "safer" for Yevgeny to study in quiet provincial Riga. Vakhtangov deliberately flunked his Riga Technical School exam, but the same year he was accepted by Moscow University's Natural Science Department. (Anton Chekhov graduated from this department in 1882.) Vakhtangov's move did not please his pragmatic father. In 1905, Vakhtangov, on his own accord, transferred to the School of Law.

Throughout Vakhtangov's time in Riga and Moscow, and during his summer trips back to Vladikavkaz, amateur theatre remained his main focus. At Moscow University, Vakhtangov, a Southerner, closely associated himself with the northern Smolensk and Vyaz'ma regions' student community. With his northern peers, Vakhtangov shared both progressive political views and the need for artistic expression through theatre.

Vakhtangov was also an active participant in the organization of the Theatrical Circle of the Moscow University studentship. Together with his fellow students, he participated in the events of the failed Russian Revolution of 1905. During the December workers' uprising, Vakhtangov found himself in the streets of Moscow, building barricades and organizing medical help for the wounded workers.

Vakhtangov's natural wholeness caused him not to separate between social, political and artistic callings. The Theatrical Circle was closely connected with an underground revolutionary students' circle. The Theatrical Circle's plays often spoke to the burning issues of the day. Among these plays was Maxim Gorky's *Summer Folk*, staged by Vakhtangov in 1906. Vakhtangov performed the role of the revolutionary Vlas in his own production.

Figure 4.1 Vakhtangov as a high school student, 1903. Courtesy of Vakhtangov Theatre Museum.

In 1908, Vakhtangov staged Gorky's *The Lower Depths*, where he also performed the role of the Baron. Not all of Vakhtangov's youthful repertoire, however, was based on social drama. Lighthearted, comedic plays helped the students to relieve psychological stress. In fact, these performances celebrated life in the face of self-sacrifice, danger and conflict with the establishment. Both sides of the Theatrical Circle's repertoire, dramatic and lighthearted, came naturally to Vakhtangov.

Memoirs of the period, left by Vakhtangov's friends, describe the young man's dual personality. Vakhtangov-the-student could spend hours on top of his bed in silence, fully clothed, absorbed in a dark and depressive mood. In such moments Vakhtangov appeared to be carrying the woes of the world on his shoulders. Was this a premonition that his life on this earth would be short?

Episodes of deep melancholy, however, were abruptly followed by bursts of joyful enthusiasm. A different side of Vakhtangov—an impromptu poet, impersonator, comedic storyteller, singer of satirical songs, improviser on a piano or mandolin, and overall the soul of the company—was completely unlike his sad and reclusive self. At these moments, Vakhtangov appeared as being connected with everything living on earth.

What seemed to be a split, or a contradiction, were ultimately the two parts of one whole. Two universal origins of life—the dead and the living—coexisted in Vakhtangov's soul. His personality was never split. At any given moment, he was capable of *fully* delving into one of the two states—the joyful or the tragic—remaining completely at one with himself. In fact, Vakhtangov's acute sense of tragedy and death originated from his love of life, while his love of life, and the desire to fully enjoy it, became even more ardent at the thought of the neighboring death.

In Moscow, Vakhtangov took full advantage of the city's rich theatrical life. He attended all of Moscow's major theatres, such as the imperial Maly and Bolshoi, as well as the private Korsh and Nezlobin. As for the Moscow Art Theatre, Vakhtangov would not miss a single production. At the MAT, he carefully studied the work of his favorite actors and the innovative directorial compositions.

Vakhtangov was not alone in his fascination with the Moscow Art Theatre. All of educated Russia, and especially the Russian intelligentsia (doctors, teachers, engineers, artists, military officers, etc.), considered the Moscow Art Theatre the quintessence of Russia's cultural and social life. Any member of the Russian intelligentsia visiting Moscow felt it a spiritual necessity to attend a performance at the MAT. Together with the enthusiastic Maxim Gorky, they would exclaim: "The Moscow Art Theatre—it is as good and significant as the Tretyakovsky Gallery, St. Basil's Cathedral[1] [. . .]. One cannot help but love it" [. . .](Gorky 1954 vol. XXVIII: 131–32).

In eventful 1905, in October, Nadezhda Baytsurova (see Figure 4.2) and Yevgeny Vakhtangov were married in Moscow, in secret from Vakhtangov's father. The newlyweds celebrated the day of their marriage by attending a matinee performance of Anton Chekhov's

---

1   Symbols of Russian culture and architecture.

Figure 4.2 Nadezhda Vakhtangova, née Baytsurova, 1905. Courtesy of Vakhtangov Theatre Museum.

The Seagull at the Moscow Art Theatre. The MAT captivated Vakhtangov as a bearer of the new truth. Most of the contemporary actors seemed false and full of affectation, in comparison with the MAT's modest, intelligent style.

Vakhtangov observed the classical nineteenth-century theatre tradition degenerate in Russia and elsewhere. Things were dire in the provinces. With the exception of the few true artists and traveling stars, the provincial stages were populated with cheap imitators. These imitators did not inherit the subconscious inner technique of their idols and instead tried to achieve emotionally heightened results using an amateur, "domestic" approach. Instead of high passions, Vakhtangov saw artificial declaiming, the clenching of fists and the loud thunder of empty bellowing. Instead of selfless dedication to the art, he saw cynicism, craft, routine and bohemian pursuits.

The remaining great tragedians, such as Komissarzhevskaya, experienced a spiritual crisis. Vakhtangov could not help but observe it when he apprenticed with Komissarzhevskaya's visiting troupe in 1909. Komissarzhevskaya, who instinctively felt that the time of pure tragedy was over, was torn between realism, on one hand, and symbolism, on the other. During his apprenticeship, Vakhtangov, for the first time, witnessed the art of the avant-garde director Vsevolod Meyerhold, whose work Vakhtangov followed throughout his career. Komissarzhevskaya, following her scandalous artistic divorce with Meyerhold, nevertheless, kept his production of *A Doll's House* in her repertoire.[2]

Komissarzhevskaya was one of the few noted tragedians who dared to engage in formal experimentation. This was seen as a director's domain. Stanislavsky explored symbolist forms in 1905, when he sponsored the Studio at Povarskaya Street. At that studio, Vsevolod Meyerhold, together with the artists Ulyanov, Sapunov and Sudeykin and composer Sats, staged Maeterlinck's *The Death of Tintagiles* and Hauptmann's *Schluck and Jau*. Stanislavsky did not risk sharing Meyerhold's experimental productions with the audience. He closed the Studio the same year. At that point Meyerhold moved his symbolist search to Komissarzhevskaya's Theatre in St. Petersburg.

Some of the tragedians, such as Komissarzhevskaya and Yermolova, gravitated toward a constant troupe. Others, such as Duse, Salvini and Shalyapin, preferred to travel. However, in general, the theatre of the tragedians was never the theatre of the ensemble. It was built around one or even several stars, surrounded by a relatively mediocre background of players. Vakhtangov, who was drawn to creative individualities, nevertheless could not justify the theatre of the stars. On one occasion, he told his students: "One genius actor is not theatre; it is a monster, a miracle. To prefer one good actor over a good ensemble is to deny the very essence of theatre; the concept of theatre includes the notion of the collective" (*Sourcebook* 2011: 87).

In the meantime, Modern Drama (Chekhov, Ibsen, Strindberg, Hauptmann) demanded from the theatre an organized ensemble, a production composed and arranged by an intelligent interpreter-director. The Moscow Art Theatre provided such an ensemble and

---

2 For further information on Komissarzhevskaya and Meyerhold, please see *Sourcebook* (2011: 29–30).

such a director. These achievements, however, came at the detriment of the tradition of Russia's great tragedians. While sharing their ideals, rooted in the secrets of the subconscious creative nature, Stanislavsky developed a very different technique—the one of a mildly emotional and predominately *intellectual* actor.

The art of the tragedians was alien to the Moscow Art Theatre, whose sizable troupe encountered only one tragic actor—Leonid Leonidov. This actor, who made his fame playing Dmitry in Nemirovich's production of *Brothers Karamazov*, was to become one of Vakhtangov's teachers at the Adashev Theatre School. Leonidov was also one of the two Moscow Art Theatre actors ever to be directed by Vakhtangov, the other one being Anton Chekhov's widow—Olga Knipper-Chekhova.

MAT's most successful productions, based on Chekhov's plays, featured the everyday life of the Russian intelligentsia. According to "the truth of life," MAT portrayed these people as tactful and somewhat restrained individuals, who contained their passions and seldom expressed them outwardly. And yet it was Chekhov who, in the words of his character Konstantin Treplev,[3] pronounced the verdict on naturalism, and on the art of "physical characterization," favored by MAT:

> The curtain goes up, the lights come on, you're in a room with three walls, and here they are, these servants of art, and all they do is show us how people eat, drink, make love, walk and wear clothes! And then they try to draw some kind of moral, some nice *easy* little moral, something you wouldn't mind having around the house. You go, they give you the same stuff over and over and over . . . and it makes me sick! I want to run away from it all, the way Maupassant ran away from the Eiffel Tower, he thought it was so ugly and vulgar.
>
> (Chekhov 1997: 114)

The passing of the torch from the tragic solo-performers, surrounded by a mediocre ensemble, to the intelligent ensemble of "equally talented," but emotionally restrained, players is also depicted in *The Seagull*. When steward Shamrayev proclaimed: "The theatre is in a decline [. . .] There were giants back then! Nothing left now but

---

3 How symbolic it is that the role of Treplev was originated on the Moscow Art Theatre stage by the theatrical innovator Vsevolod Meyerhold.

pygmies!" another Chekhovian philosopher Doctor Dorn replied: "There aren't all that many geniuses nowadays, true, but I think acting in general has improved. In the smaller roles, I mean" (Chekhov 1997: 117).

The deeper meaning of the split of the century's theatre tendencies could not entirely escape Vakhtangov. The great nineteenth-century tragedians were taking their art and technique to their graves. These great actors often refused to share their professional secrets, earned by sweat and blood, with less dedicated young colleagues. More often the technique was lost because the natural actors of old did not possess the scientific objectivity required to recognize one's own subconscious technique. Some of the greatest actors of the time, such as Yermolova, simply underestimated their technique because of its seeming simplicity. They thought it too obvious to be taught.

It took Vakhtangov some ten years to see the true origin of the school of experiencing, associated with Stanislavsky. In his quest for "instant inspiration," Vakhtangov ultimately turned to the heritage of the tragic actors of the past. After all, Vakhtangov's ideal was similar to the one of the tragedians. He dreamed of an actor, who would be an intuitive improviser, guided by the creative subconscious. Most importantly, Vakhtangov strove to develop an actor capable of stage life that was truthful and passionate, "confessionally" sincere and unrestricted in its expression.

5 Vakhtangov before the MAT

The "prehistoric time"—this is how one of Vakhtangov's students, poet Antakolsky (Vakhtangova et al. 1939: XVI), referred to his teacher's pre-MAT period. Nevertheless, it is important to picture Vakhtangov as a director and actor before he entered the MAT circle. It is evident that prior to 1908 Vakhtangov did not pay serious attention to the naturalistic details of setting, character behavior and physicality. His performances as an amateur actor are described as being psychologically mobile and sincere. Moreover, since his early steps as an actor, Vakhtangov appears to have been a master of expressive external form, capable of justifying it intuitively. This form did not come as a result of careful work on body and voice. The expressivity of Vakhtangov's acting originated from his unrestricted inner life, as it freely manifested in his external behavior.

The accounts of Vakhtangov's performance of the character of Vlas, from Gorky's *Summer Folk*, confirm Nikolai Demidov's (2007: 19) theory that a gifted actor develops *organically*, if left to his own devices. Vakhtangov's partner in the Gorky production, Nadezhda Yeryomenko, left the following recollection of Vakhtangov's performance:

> It seems to me that Vakhtangov, as he performed Vlas, was not aware of any responsibility of truthful experience onstage; he did not make such demands of himself. The truth of emotions and high demands toward his art, however, *organically belonged to his actor's nature*. This fact reflected upon his performance. Acting with him as a partner was easy, because both thoughts and the emotional state of the character he portrayed, were so apparent.
>
> (Yeryomenko 1959: 347)

Psychological expressiveness and articulateness of Vakhtangov's acting was also stressed by his other partner in the production, the future noted Russian director Boris Sushkevich. Some 30 years following Vakhtangov's performance in *Summer Folk*, Sushkevich reread the play in preparation for his own production:

> I did not recognize the text of my own role, and did not remember anything about my partners' acting in the production. When it came to the text of Vakhtangov's role, however, I suddenly clearly remembered the entire role, one line after another, and all the details of Vakhtangov's performance. His Vlas was an undoubtedly gifted man, deeply intelligent, a bit broken-hearted and sarcastic.
>
> (Sushkevich 1959: 366)

A few accounts of Vakhtangov's early directorial work that have come to us allow us to suppose that the form of his productions was not just a result of his keen observation of life. Elements of this form were created by Vakhtangov, however intuitively, based on his artistic agenda. Vakhtangov, like Chekhov-the-writer, had the gift, through minute behavioral detail, to peer into the very essence of a person's soul. Similarly, he could perceive the hidden essence of every spiritual, psychological or social phenomenon.

Unlike early Stanislavsky, Vakhtangov was extremely selective in his choice of naturalistic details he brought to the stage. Like Chekhov, he only employed those details that spoke to the essential. Already at the very start of his directorial career, Vakhtangov was a realist, not a naturalist. Later on, Vakhtangov would make a step towards "fantastic realism"—the kind of art where the form is improvised (created through purely artistic means). The form of such a performance is never blindly copied, or even carefully selected, from life. This form is fantasized, imagined; the process of fantasizing, however, is governed by natural creative laws.

In the early 1920s, during Vakhtangov's rehearsals for his final production, Vakhtangov's students marveled at his ability to animate any objects onstage (*Sourcebook* 2011: 299–300). At the same time, Vakhtangov demanded a different kind of psychological experience from his actors—an ability to mold their emotions instantly and achieve sweeping transitions from one psychological moment to another—without any external motivations. Apparently, Vakhtangov already possessed this gift of physical and emotional "plasticity" in the time of his amateur youth. Nadezhda Yeryomenko left us the following description of Vakhtangov's performance in a one-act comedy *On the Run:*[1]

> Lightness of step, rhythmical movements and instantaneous transitions from suffering to hope and joy made the character of the husband "on the run" extremely expressive. When playing this role, Vakhtangov treated stage props with amazing dexterity—they lived in his hands.
>
> (Yeryomenko 1959: 351)

By the year 1909, however, Vakhtangov—like many provincial directors and actors of his generations—began to imitate the Moscow Art Theatre. One of the participants of Vakhtangov's summer 1909 season in Vladikavkaz, Georgy Kazarov (interviewed in Khersonsky 1940a: 199), remembered that "sets, blockings, interpretation of the roles, the way of working on the roles in rehearsals, sound effects, technical details—everything was 'according to the Moscow Art Theatre'." Even in those plays never produced at the MAT, Vakhtangov used the approach, characteristic of the early Stanislavsky and Nemirovich productions. For example, Vakhtangov's script of Nedolin's play *Zinochka*, surviving in the director's archive, indicates an elaborate development of every blocking, and an exaggerated attention to the naturalistic details. The list of props, featured in the script, is so detailed, it resembles a shopping list, and the external characterization of every character is indicated with painstaking scrupulousness.

In his own roles, Vakhtangov imitated the MAT actors, such as Stanislavsky, Kachalov and Leonidov. And yet, according to Kazarov (interviewed in Khersonsky 1940a: 199), this was an unusual imitation:

> During one of the student evenings, Zhenya performed the title part monologue from Andreyev's play *Anatema*, after Kachalov.
>
> And yet this was not a mere imitation. Zhenya's performance of the monologue left his audience emotionally moved. There was an artist before us.

Vakhtangov, when imitating, managed to permeate *the inner essence of the object of his imitation*, thus bringing true life into the performance. Imitation that is mostly understood as a mechanical copy from

---

1   A comedy-vaudeville by S. Rassokhin and V. Preobrazhensky.

the original, appeared to be inwardly justified—thus ceasing to be an imitation.

Vakhtangov's adherence to the MAT's naturalistic forms was short-lived. So was his tendency to imitate the MAT actors. Blind imitation, in general, was foreign to Vakhtangov's gift. As early as 1907, he made an entry in his diary, criticizing Moscow's Maly Theatre – a company known to cling to old traditions – for its lack of "freedom in staging plays" (Ivanov 2011 vol. I: 106). By the time of Vakhtangov's 1909 audition for the MAT-affiliated Adashev Theatre School, he seemed to have completely outgrown his fascination with the MAT style, and had a new goal. Vakhtangov's imitations of the MAT actors vanished from his serious work; however, they found a new life on the cabaret stage.

6 Vakhtangov at the Adashev Theatre School

The influence of Leopold Sulerzhitsky

In 1909, six years after his arrival in Moscow, Vakhtangov entered the theatre school founded by Aleksandr Adashev. A Moscow Art Theatre actor, Adashev employed the MAT's greats, such as Kachalov and Leonidov, to teach at his school. Vakhtangov entered the professional theatrical path decisively and abruptly, although he did not formally withdraw from Moscow University for another two years.[1]

Can acting be taught? Vakhtangov always answered this question negatively. Acting *as a creative process* cannot be taught. There are natural-born actors, who seem to be in touch with their creative process subconsciously, or intuitively. There are also those actors who do not have easy access to their creativity. For such individuals, an experienced teacher of the inner technique can create conditions conducive to their creative process. (Alternatively, they could discover these conditions on their own—consciously and/or subconsciously—through theatrical practice.)

Only one theatre personality in Russia of the period was searching for such conditions, and this was Konstantin Stanislavsky. At the same time, Stanislavsky did not teach his discoveries at any school. Neither did he teach them at the Moscow Art Theatre. For five years, he applied his new principles in rehearsals, but that was it. Stanislavsky did have a trusted colleague, Leopold Sulerzhitsky (see Figure 6.1). Sulerzhitsky did teach at the Adashev Theatre School. This made Vakhtangov's choice.

---

1 Officially, Vakhtangov maintained his status of Moscow University student through the fall of 1911. Upon entering the Adashev School, however, university studies clearly took second place to the theatre.

Figure 6.1 Leopold Sulerzhitsky, 1911. Courtesy of Moscow Art Theatre Museum.

Following his first semester at the school, Vakhtangov was moved to the second year. Even prior to that, however, Vakhtangov spent most of his time at the school with the second year group taught by Sulerzhitsky. The teacher took an immediate liking to his "stowaway" student, and he would not start a class without Vakhtangov.

In the spring of his first year, Vakhtangov was moved to the third year. That very summer Vakhtangov was invited to join the MAT by its co-founder Nemirovich-Danchenko; Vakhtangov refused the temptation and finished the Adashev School instead. Sulerzhitsky's laboratory seemed to be more important to him than the practical work at the MAT.

Sulerzhitsky's role in the development of the Moscow Art Theatre, and his influence upon Stanislavsky, have been greatly underestimated. Moreover, Sulerzhitsky had a critical impact on the artistic formation of the significant twentieth-century Russian directors and actors— Yevgeny Vakhtangov, Michael Chekhov, Richard Boleslavsky, Maria Ouspenskaya, Aleksey Dikiy, as well as many others.

Sulerzhitsky's horizon was wider than most of his theatre colleagues'. He changed occupations several times before he became a theatre director and teacher at the age of 34. Sulerzhitsky traveled the world as a sailor. A convinced follower of Tolstoy's pacifist philosophy, Sulerzhitsky refused to be drafted in to the Russian army. For his refusal, he was persecuted by the authorities—Sulerzhitsky was first confined to a psychiatric ward and later spent time serving in the desert, at the frontier post of Kushka, the utmost southern point of the Russian empire. He answered Tolstoy's call and organized the resettlement to Canada of the members of the Russian *dukhobory* religious sect, as well as their families. He was one of the few Russians of the time who visited America.

A close personal friend of Tolstoy's, but also of many significant authors of the time, Sulerzhitsky himself was a gifted writer. Like Vakhtangov, he possessed the gift of leadership and the skill of an organizer. He took his MAT colleagues, as well as his students, to Ukraine and to the South of Russia, to the Crimea, where he "treated" them to a healthy diet of outdoor labor and improvisational performance-parties. In fact, Sulerzhitsky was famous in artistic circles for initiating improvised concerts and entertainment. Moreover, he constantly instigated acting improvisations in the streets, in restaurants and other public places—this was his way of extending the creative process, of transforming the dullness of everyday life into a theatrical festival.

Like Vakhtangov, Sulerzhitsky must have possessed a natural talent for acting. He had a mobile inner world, a gift for plasticity and physical expression. His demonstrations to actors were brilliant. They are described by Michael Chekhov in his book *Life and Encounters* (Chekhov 1995 vol. I: 161–62). Sulerzhitsky's improvised dances were even admired by Isadora Duncan. Like Vakhtangov, Sulerzhitsky found theatre a medium in which he could synthesize all of his varied gifts.

Sulerzhitsky shared Stanislavsky's quest for the new theatre, and for the discovery of the organic acting technique. Between 1907 and 1911, Stanislavsky, assisted by Sulerzhitsky, explored the forms of symbolism, expressionism and the fantastic. (For Stanislavsky, this was a "return engagement" following the 1905 closing of the Studio at Povarskaya Street.[2]) In collaboration with Stanislavsky, Sulerzhitsky staged the MAT 1907 productions of Hamsun's *The Drama of Life* and Andreyev's *A Life of a Man*. In 1908, together with Stanislavsky, he staged the world premiere of Maeterlinck's *The Blue Bird*. These productions also revealed the talents of the designer Egorov and the composer Ilya Sats. Echoes of the Povarskaya Studio's experiments, present in these productions, produced a significant effect upon Vakhtangov.

Finally, it was Sulerzhitsky who collaborated, as a director, with Stanislavsky and Gordon Craig on the historic MAT production of *Hamlet*. This production took about two years to produce, and opened at the MAT in 1911. The final phase of *Hamlet* rehearsals coincided with Vakhtangov's arrival at the MAT.

Sulerzhitsky's contribution to the Art Theatre's history goes beyond the search for symbolist forms. The deviation from realism observed in his three co-productions with Stanislavsky of 1907–8, as well as in *Hamlet*, had a deep meaning. Sulerzhitsky's symbolism was rooted in his belief that theatre should not portray the peripheral, naturalistic layer of a man's life, but rather convey its hidden spiritual essence.

The deviation from naturalism, in the minds of Sulerzhitsky and Stanislavsky, was not a deviation from truth, but rather a search for a deeper and greater existential truth. Similarly, *Blue Bird* author Maeterlinck, in a private conversation with Stanislavsky, protested against being labeled a symbolist. "I am an ultra-naturalist of the exalted feelings," exclaimed Maeterlinck (Demidov 2004 vol. I: 115).

Vakhtangov later shared his own Method of Fantastic Realism with Stanislavsky/Sulerzhitsky's co-productions of 1907–11. Moreover, Vakhtangov considered Sulerzhitsky's theatrical ethics and aesthetics responsible for Stanislavsky's deviation from realism during this period.

Vakhtangov, who avoided classical and symbolist plays as an amateur director and actor, saw his Adashev School training as an opportunity to venture into this new, desired territory. He strove for the theatre of mystery that speaks of the deeper layers of the human psyche. At the same time, he was convinced that for the moment he was not fit, or technically equipped, to approach such plays and roles. Vakhtangov looked at the Moscow Art Theatre school, and specifically at Sulerzhitsky, as guides into the realm of the Theatre of Mystery.

2 See p. 25.

Every comedic or character actor, including Vakhtangov, dreamed of becoming a tragedian. He ultimately achieved this goal—partially through the help of the MAT, but also through his own struggle with the MAT influence. The kind of tragedy Vakhtangov eventually discovered was different from the one practiced by the classical trage-dians, and it was different from the symbolist experiments conducted inside, or outside, the MAT.

The kind of tragedy that evolved out of Vakhtangov's productions absorbed many influences. It was symbolic and realistic, and it combined the inner fire of a tragedian with the subtleness of comedic touch. Vakhtangov's tragedy was individual—just as Vakhtangov's gift was individual and unique. A complex spiritual life, hidden passion, creative ingenuity, beauty and ease, unpredictability, even strangeness—such were the qualities characteristic of Vakhtangov's new type of tragedy. All these qualities, inherent in Vakhtangov's orig-inal theatrical gift, were cultivated and further revealed by a true magician of theatre pedagogy—Leopold Sulerzhitsky.

Vakhtangov's expectations connected with Sulerzhitsky and the Adashev School were not immediately met. Instead of approaching the Theatre of Mystery directly, as Vakhtangov envisioned it, he had to submit to a very different kind of school. At the Adashev School, Sulerzhitsky offered him, first and foremost, the sense of a greater meaning behind the art of theatre.

Sulerzhitsky saw theatre as the festival of goodness. Like Tolstoy, he saw every human being as essentially good and kind, and he urged his collaborators to reveal this goodness in men. According to Sulerzhitsky, theatre was "not just a spectacle, not merely an artistic reproduction, and not the beauty alone; the theatre has and must have yet another goal—God. An actor is not just an artist, but a high priest" (*Source-book* 2011: 239).

The idea of the Theatre of Mystery, where both the actor and the audience find themselves in communion with a higher being, became Sulerzhitsky's mission. This type of theatre called for a specific psychology of acting, and for a new "spiritual technique." The search for such technique, grounded in truth and sincerity, was undertaken by Stanislavsky and Sulerzhitsky at the MAT.

This collaboration began as early as 1906—Sulerzhitsky was the first of Stanislavsky's associates in the development of the System. Stanislavsky, who never taught his technique in a classroom, traced its origins back to 1904. That was the year Stanislavsky introduced his methods at the MAT in his directorial work on Turgenev's play, *A Month in the Country*. Sulerzhitsky, as a teacher of the Adashev

School, worked with the Stanislavsky System in application to acting training.

It was Sulerzhitsky, and not Stanislavsky, who can be called the first formal teacher of the Stanislavsky System. Sulerzhitsky is also responsible for the philosophy, both creative and ethical, behind the System. At the same time, Sulerzhitsky, whose contribution to the System is difficult to overestimate, always remained in the shadows, yielding the place in the spotlight to those less selfless colleagues who desired it.

Every so often, Sulerzhitsky would write a bitter letter to Stanislavsky on the subject, but then he would continue to remain in the shadows for years—perhaps voluntarily. As a result of this selfless "policy," one of the most original and influential Russian theatre thinkers and practitioners of the twentieth century, Leopold Sulerzhitsky, remains an obscure figure to this very day. Those reading Stanislavsky's *My Life in Art* cannot help but wonder why the master dedicates so many passages to Sulerzhitsky and what he means when he writes: "This remarkable man of exceptional talent [Sulerzhitsky] played a large part in our theatre and in my artistic life" (Stanislavsky 1953: 363).

What was the essence of Sulerzhitsky's theatrical magic, and why was he so influential to Vakhtangov's formation? Sulerzhitsky's main gift was to recognize the unique creative individuality that belonged to an actor, or a student, and—without distorting this individuality—facilitate its development. Sulerzhitsky saw that Vakhtangov possessed a natural, organic sense of truth, reinforced by his prior stage experience. He also saw Vakhtangov's inner protest against his own type (a character actor), and his impatient longing for the theatre of tragedy.

Sulerzhitsky knew, however, that Vakhtangov was not a natural-born tragedian, and that his path toward tragedy, toward the theatre of the heightened emotions, would not be an easy one. Vakhtangov's volcanic inner temperament was not happily married with the physicality (voice, figure, face) of a classical tragedian. Most importantly, volcanic passion constituted only one side of Vakhtangov's individuality. Sulerzhitsky was determined to facilitate Vakhtangov's development, while capitalizing on the very gifts he naturally possessed. Sulerzhitsky's job, therefore, was to allow Vakhtangov, at the Adashev School, to verify "the truth he nurtured—through practice" (Luzhsky 1959: 363).

At Sulerzhitsky's insistence, Vakhtangov's classroom work differed from that of his fellow students. To imagine the kind of training offered to the Adashev School students, one needs to address Stanislavsky's *An Actor's Work*. The so-called *études*, or improvisational exercises, performed in the Stanislavsky-based classroom dealt with frantic activity and heightened emotional situations—it was typical for such études to feature a madman who escaped from an insane asylum and terrorizes the participants, or an unfortunate mother accidentally drowning her child in a bathtub.

In hindsight, the highly melodramatic *études* offered to beginning actors were meant to provoke them into overacting. These themes successfully served their purpose, causing young actors to fake great passions—at which point the wise guru could teach his guilty students (now entirely in his power) the lesson of truth. Similarly, many of the Stanislavsky early exercises in concentration of attention, imagination, etc., were openly setting students up for failure. Their goal was to prove to the student that, in their present state, they know nothing, and can do nothing—thus making them obedient clay in the teacher's hands.

Having proven to his students that they are not capable of truthfully living (thinking, hearing, acting, or even walking) onstage, the teacher broke the process into *elements* and led his students toward mastery one by one. The fact that such a tactic destroyed one of the most important qualities in an actor—the sense of confidence in their own creative powers—must have escaped the teachers. Neither did they realize that the unnecessarily high level of difficulty of the tasks, as well as the authoritative demeanor of the teacher, were making the beginner students tense, thus setting them up for failure.

Guided by Sulerzhitsky at the Adashev School, Vakhtangov developed distaste for Stanislavsky's improvisational *études*—he did not perform them, and he never asked his future students to perform such études. Vakhtangov's own Adashev School études were surprisingly *passive*. Sulerzhitsky insisted that Vakhtangov, in his training, avoid heightened emotional situations. Instead, Vakhtangov's études dealt with *the most complex and finest psychological currents*:

> Suddenly Vakhtangov would demonstrate, naturally and simply, the subtlest experience of a man, who is yearning without any visible motivation. There is such a yearning—unmotivated, inconsolable and uncertain. Other students considered such emotional experience unreachable. This was some new aspect, a new stage of the actor's work.
>
> (Khersonsky 1940a: 58)

At the Adashev School, Vakhtangov reinforced his natural tendency to delve into a psychologically subtle and refined sphere of the human psyche. This became possible thanks to Sulerzhitsky's guidance. Unlike most of the Stanislavsky System teachers, Sulerzhitsky absorbed the very essence and foundation of the System. His teaching was grounded in what Stanislavsky himself referred to as "the fundamentals of the creative act and the organic laws of nature" (Stanislavsky 2008: 21).

In his own directing practice, as well as in his writings, Stanislavsky often deviated from the methods of the organic technique, and concentrated more on rational analysis and imperative activity. As for Sulerzhitsky's approach, the rational and imperative elements in his training were limited. He only used these with students, who, according to their creative type, were inclined toward rationality and the imperative. Therefore, Sulerzhitsky's training put the stress onto the student-actor's *creative individuality*.

Vakhtangov learned many of his teacher's lessons. For example, he understood that, when working with actors, a teacher should insure their *immediate* success. Vakhtangov became convinced that setting impossible tasks, and demanding truth in a heightened emotional situation, is a sure way to distort a young actor's creative process. This process should first be *originated* in relatively calm circumstances. Once the actor's process, and the formation of the character, has been established under normal conditions, the heightened moments take care of themselves, just as they do in life, when the heightened circumstances present themselves.

Sulerzhitsky's spiritual cultivation of Vakhtangov's gift

In parallel with the stage training, Sulerzhitsky engaged in scrupulous cultivation of Vakhtangov's character, his inner world—both inside and outside of the studio. Vakhtangov's personality at the time of his arrival at the Adashev School was well described by his peer Lidiya Deykun (2011: 163): "He could be tender and caring, at times even sentimental and, simultaneously, harsh, even rude. Quite self-assured, he despaired at the slightest hint of failure. And he was tireless when it came to creative work."

The job ahead of Sulerzhitsky was not an easy one. He had to help Vakhtangov defeat his own fits of despair, to educate his feelings and, therefore, make them deeper and more intelligent. During the early stages of his training at the Adashev School, Vakhtangov often tried to dazzle his teacher, failing miserably at each attempt. Sulerzhitsky had to assist Vakhtangov in developing greater patience with himself, and teach him not to wish for an immediate result.

Another difficult task standing before Sulerzhitsky was cultivating Vakhtangov's leadership qualities, without encouraging the dictatorial aspects that came with the territory. Vakhtangov's tendency to be unnecessarily categorical, and his quick eastern temper, were often subjects of Sulerzhitsky's observation and, if need be, ridicule. Shortly before his death, Sulerzhitsky confessed to Stanislavsky that he was not able to effectively confront Vakhtangov's dictatorial tendencies.

The work of cultivating Vakhtangov's character took place in class, but also outside of classes—Sulerzhitsky spent a great deal of time with his students in "private life." Gatherings at his flat were frequent; on such occasions participants discussed life, social events, acting technique, contemporary theatre, as well as theatre at large. Sulerzhitsky's apartment was open for visitors; Sulerzhitsky's wife and son also welcomed guests. Students were always fed at the Sulerzhitskys'. Since most of the students, including Vakhtangov,[3] were of meager means, Sulerzhitsky considered it his duty to make sure that they were well nourished. On top of it all, Suler (as he was known in the MAT circles) shared with his students the incredible tales about his foreign travels and his friendships with Tolstoy, Chekhov and Shalyapin.

Spiritual and physical health were inseparable for Sulerzhitsky. The idea behind the summer commune Suler eventually organized for his students, first in Ukraine, on the banks of the Dnepr River, and later in Crimea, rested on three cornerstones—communion with nature, improvisational play, and manual labor. Strict discipline permeated every aspect of the communal life. According to Stanislavsky, who sponsored the communal enterprise, it was a part of Suler's plan to create a "spiritual order of actors"—people of "lofty views and ideas, of wide horizons, who knew the human soul and [. . .] who were willing to sacrifice themselves for art" (Stanislavsky 1953: 410).

Of Sulerzhitsky's three cornerstones, Vakhtangov easily embraced nature and play; however, it took him some time to embrace labor. Much to his teachers' displeasure, he flunked the work. Sulerzhitsky's persistence prevailed. Vakhtangov and his fellow actors returned to Moscow "energetic, strong, brown-skinned and joyful, boasting of their biceps, blistered hands and suntan" (Vendrovskaya and Kaptereva 1984: 165) (see Figure 6.2).

In 1914, Sulerzhitsky moved his summer commune to the steaming hot Crimean town of Yevpatoriya, where it soon came to an end. During the summer of 1915, Vakhtangov felt so ill from the

---

3   Vakhtangov, while in Moscow, could not always count on support from his father.

Figure 6.2 Vakhtangov at Sulerzhitsky's Dnepr River commune, summer of 1913. Courtesy of Vakhtangov Theatre Museum.

"invigorating" Crimean regime, he begged one of his friends to rent him a room in a country house, back in central Ukraine with its milder climate, where he could recuperate after his time at Sulerzhitsky's "resort."

Overall, Sulerzhitsky's discipline, applied both in and outside of the classroom, helped Vakhtangov develop his will. Vakhtangov's future tragic masterpieces had a lot to do with his perfect inner control. This does not mean that Vakhtangov controlled his passions, but rather that Vakhtangov's will allowed him to control the non-involvement in his subconscious inner life. As a result, Vakhtangov was able to reconcile, in his acting, the different sides of his talent. The inner passion, external ease and mobile, expressive physicality happily synergized in Vakhtangov's acting.

Vakhtangov's life onstage remained subtle, nuanced, refined and full of external ease. He never raised his voice, and yet his acting radiated condensed energy. According to one of the most insightful of Vakhtangov's biographers, Smirnov-Nesvitsky (1987: 87) "the most essential part of Vakhtangov's acting individuality was his fiery passion that remained secret, hidden." Nesvitsky insisted that Vakhtangov's passion "did not burst onto the surface, even in the most dramatic moments; instead it was concentrated in gesture, mimicry and in the overall pattern of the role."

Cabbage parties

Suler continually encouraged his students' multiple talents. Among Vakhtangov's qualities stimulated by Suler were his sense of humor and gift for astute observation. Vakhtangov was perfect for the cabaret stage. Since his time at the Vladikavkaz high school, he had performed in benefit concerts, playing mandolin, guitar, reciting poetry, performing humorous monologues and scenes, and singing in a choir. Back in Vladikavkaz, Vakhtangov also organized cabaret performances; his directorial talent helped him create the overall composition of the program. Vakhtangov's literary gifts allowed him to contribute to the cabaret repertoire.

The cabaret tradition, practiced at the Adashev School, was born within the MAT walls. One of the MAT company members, Balieff, was a questionable actor, but a genius cabaret entrepreneur. Balieff involved the MAT directors and actors, including Stanislavsky himself, in humorous sketches, parodies, and burlesques on the theme of the day. These semi-improvised shows were given late at night, after a regular MAT performance.

Cabaret parties, or, as they became known, *kapustniki* (cabbage parties), soon became hugely popular not only among the MAT members, but among the Moscow artistic elite. In fact, Balieff's *kapustniki* became so popular that they soon outgrew the MAT walls. A professional company, Chauve Souris, was formed by Balieff. This company enjoyed a long illustrious life both inside Russia and abroad.[4]

Vakhtangov's talent for imitation, and his ability to localize his creative energy in a comedic cameo role, made him an immediate hit at the first Adashev School *kapustnik* of the 1909–10 season. When

4   On Vakhtangov's affiliation with Chauve Souris please see *Sourcebook* (2011: 46).

the MAT star Kachalov, in the audience, heard "his own voice" from backstage, he demanded that an actor, responsible for uncanny mimicry, immediately appear on the stage. Vakhtangov's appearance drew applause. That very evening, Vakhtangov was also noticed by the MAT elder in a silent cameo role he performed in one of the sketches.

Clearly, Sulerzhitsky encouraged this lighter side of Vakhtangov's gift. His musicality, improvisational talent, feeling of style and form, as well as his feeling of rhythm—all these qualities, exercised in the *kapustnik* evenings, found their expression in Vakhtangov's final masterpiece *Princess Turandot*. In Sulerzhitsky's mind, these qualities also happily counterbalanced Vakhtangov's tendency for soul searching, his despotic intensity, and his brooding, depressed moods.

7   Vakhtangov's trips abroad

Sulerzhitsky is also responsible for giving Vakhtangov a wider perspective of the world. Vakhtangov was one of the most cosmopolitan of the early twentieth-century Russian theatre directors, with a repertoire almost exclusively concentrated in Western drama. If not for Sulerzhitsky, however, Vakhtangov may never have traveled outside of Russia. In the winter of 1910–11, Sulerzhitsky took Vakhtangov to Paris as his assistant in the staging of the European premiere of Maurice Maeterlinck's new play *The Blue Bird*. (The world premiere of the play was entrusted by the author to the Moscow Art Theatre and directed by Stanislavsky and Sulerzhitsky.) This was one of Vakhtangov's two trips outside of Russia.

Vakhtangov set off for Europe in the company of a friend, on December 27, 1910. On his way to Paris, he stopped in Berlin. In the less than two days Vakhtangov spent in the German capital (December 30 and 31, 1910) time was dedicated to major museums and architectural masterpieces. Cultural education was Vakhtangov's main occupation on his trip.

In Paris, Vakhtangov spent very little time at the Réjane Theatre,[1] where Maeterlinck's *The Blue Bird* was rehearsed. Assisting Sulerzhitsky was a mere pretext for giving Vakhtangov a chance to see Europe. Rehearsals for *The Blue Bird*, conducted by Sulerzhitsky, depressed Vakhtangov—his teacher was reduced to having to demonstrate to the French actors their blocking and the form of their roles. To Vakhtangov's disappointment, the actors appeared completely satisfied with this method of work.

---

1   The noted French actress Gabrielle Réjane (1856–1920) opened the Théâtre Réjane in Paris in 1906. The European premiere of Maeterlinck's *The Blue Bird* was one of the highlights of the theatre's history.

Vakhtangov, who did not have a cent to his name, spent part of his time in Paris reconnecting with a Moscow University friend. Vakhtangov's friend immigrated to Paris, having escaped from a Moscow jail, where she was imprisoned for her revolutionary activity. While in Paris, Vakhtangov also went to listen to Lenin speak on Tolstoy. Most of his time, however, was spent in museums and art galleries, and strolling the city and its suburbs.

Vakhtangov was drinking in the art, the atmosphere of Paris, the rhythms of its many inhabitants. Years later, in the mid-1920s, when Vakhtangov's production of Maeterlinck's *The Miracle of St. Anthony* came to Paris, the critics noted Vakhtangov's familiarity with the types of French provincial bourgeois—the main characters of the play. And yet, Vakhtangov never visited the French provinces. His tremendous intuition helped him to complete the picture of the French provincial way of life from his accidental Paris observations.

Vakhtangov's Parisian theatrical impressions are few. A Belgian troupe, performing at the Réjane Theatre, impressed him with their "ease of dialogue." He was puzzled by the interpretation of the part of Mephistopheles in the Paris Opéra's production of Charles Gounod's *Faust*. The singer, whose name Vakhtangov did not mark, interpreted his character as a buffoon.

Vakhtangov left Paris on January 31 (February 13, according to the Gregorian calendar)[2] of 1911. After five days of traveling through Switzerland, Germany and Austria, Vakhtangov returned to Moscow on February 9 (22) of 1911. The next day he already had rehearsals scheduled at the Adashev Theatre School.

Vakhtangov's second trip abroad took place in the second summer of his work at the Moscow Art Theatre. In March 1912, he was forced to turn down an invitation from Sulerzhitsky to co-direct Baring's play *Double Game* in London.[3] Nemirovich-Danchenko would not allow the new associate a leave of absence. Two months after, with the start of his summer vacation, Vakhtangov took an independent trip to Sweden. He sailed for Stockholm from St. Petersburg via Helsingfors (Helsinki) on June 15, 1912 with exactly 17 rubles in his pocket. On June 17, Vakhtangov arrived in Stockholm. The difference in the rhythms of Stockholm and Paris immediately struck Vakhtangov:

---

2 The Gregorian calendar was introduced in Russia on February 14, 1918.
3 A play by Maurice Baring (1874–1945), English author and playwright.

Life in Paris flies, you miss every day that goes by, and how difficult it is to part with the boiling stream of Parisian life.

In Stockholm, you count days and save up your health.
Unthankful thought keeps creeping into your head (but how
can one help it?)—"Patience, I will soon be going back to free
life".

Here they love the sun for sunbathing, the sea—for medicinal
salts and forests—for the shade.

No exaltation, no poetry.

Although, at the Olympic games, I did see passionate Swedes.

(Ivanov 2011 vol. I: 310)

Vakhtangov did attend the 1912 Stockholm Olympics. Other than
that, he spent most of the time "saving up his health" in Stockholm
and its suburbs. On his trip to the theatre, the Swedish audiences and
actors impressed him:

What an audience!

They won't drop a word, they are sensitive to pauses; they sit
stock-still, not a single cough is heard. And what good actors;
how good they are at coming out to take their bows when they are
called before the curtain. Carnations and roses with white cards
attached fly onto the stage. An actor is happy as a boy to receive
them; he joyfully catches them with no affectation—sincerely,
with natural facial expression, he bows to the audience that
applauds as one man.

(Ivanov 2011 vol. I: 315)

Vakhtangov finds the Swedish actors' art to be "amazing in its
simplicity, ease and elegance." These very qualities, and this very
model of the relationship between the audience and the actors, will
serve as a foundation for Vakhtangov's masterpiece *Princess Turandot*.

On June 20, a few days prior to leaving Stockholm, in a letter
to his wife, Vakhtangov described his plans for his return to
Russia. He plans to buy a cheap round ticket for a cruise—Stockholm—Christiania (Oslo)—Copenhagen (see Figure 7.1)—Malmö—
Stockholm—St. Petersburg. At the end of his letter, Vakhtangov
exclaimed:

My dream is to travel the world.

We must put aside the money for the next summer.

Let's save up.

London, and New York, and Chicago!
I will die, but go.

How can one live on this earth and not see it? If I sat under my papa's wing—I would not see or know anything . . .

(Ivanov 2011 vol. I: 312–13)

London, New York and Chicago saw Vakhtangov's production of *The Dybbuk*. As for Vakhtangov himself, this was his second and final trip abroad. According to Michael Chekhov, in the spring of 1922, a few weeks before his untimely death, the bed-bound Vakhtangov invited a photographer to take his picture for an international passport. (The First Studio of MAT, where he was a leader, was planning a European

Figure 7.1 Vakhtangov in Copenhagen, 1912. Courtesy of Vakhtangov Theatre Museum.

tour.) Vakhtangov's final photo was tragic, indeed. Its look passes a grim sentence—not only on Vakhtangov's trip abroad, but also on his life. The more important is Sulerzhitsky's role in Vakhtangov's "cultivation," for allowing the young director to experience Ibsen, Strindberg, Maeterlinck, and Hauptmann's respective cultures.

Part II
Vakhtangov at the Moscow Art Theatre

8   First meeting with Stanislavsky

On March 4, 1911, one week prior to his graduation from the Adashev Theatre School, Vakhtangov (see Figure 8.1), accompanied by Adashev himself, appeared in the office of the MAT co-founder, Nemirovich-Danchenko. During the short conversation, Nemirovich acted as if he forgot that the previous summer he had invited Vakhtangov to join the MAT. Nemirovich's pride must have been hurt by the young man's refusal, so he was now conducting a "formal" interview:

NEMIROVICH: Please take a seat. Well, what would you like to receive from us, and what would you like to give us?
VAKHTANGOV: I would like to receive everything I can; as for giving— I never even thought about that.
NEMIROVICH: What exactly do you want?
VAKHTANGOV: I want to learn the work of the director.
NEMIROVICH: Just in the directing field then?
VAKHTANGOV: No, I will do everything you let me.

(*Sourcebook* 2011: 227)

It was Nemirovich-Danchenko, not Stanislavsky, who accepted Vakhtangov into the Moscow Art Theatre. Vakhtangov came as a student of the Adashev School, where Stanislavsky's closest collaborator, Sulerzhitsky, took Vakhtangov under his special patronage. Nemirovich, whose relationships with Stanislavsky and Sulerzhitsky were complex, nevertheless immediately recognized Vakhtangov's talent, and Vakhtangov never forgot that. Shortly after his acceptance to the MAT, Vakhtangov was introduced to Stanislavsky.

In April 1921, at the time of the ten-year anniversary of his work at the MAT, Vakhtangov recalled the trajectory of his relationship with Stanislavsky (see Figure 8.2), as it developed after each of Vakhtangov's First Studio of MAT directorial works:

Figure 8.1 Vakhtangov seated second from right among teachers and graduating students of the Adashev School, 1911. Standing Sergei Glagol', Leopold Sulerzhitsky, Alexander Adashev, Leonid Leonidov, Nilolai Massalitinov, Vasily Kahalov, Vasily Luzhsky, Antonina Shalomytova, [?] Smirnova. Vakhtangov sitting second from the right. Courtesy of Vakhtangov Theatre Museum.

Figure 8.2 Vakhtangov and Stanislavsky at the Vakhtangov Studio, January 30, 1921. Photo's date as appears in its first publication (Vakhtangova et al. 1939). According to other sources (Ivanov 2011), photo was taken on November 13, 1921, when Vakhtangov's studio was granted the name of the Third Studio of MAT. Courtesy of Vakhtangov Theatre Museum.

Leopold Antonovich [Sulerzhitsky] introduced me to K.[onstantin]
S.[tanislavsky]:
—I am quite happy to know you,—and he left.
[. . .]
At the end of my work on *The Festival of Peace*, K.S. said:
I am getting to know you. Quite happy.
After *The Deluge*:
I got to know you quite well. I am happy.
After *Rosmersholm*:
Quite . . .
After *Erik XIV*:
—Happy.

(Vendrovskaya and Kaptereva 1984: 357)

Vakhtangov's first meeting with Stanislavsky took place on March 11,
1911, during Stanislavsky's talk with the Moscow Art Theatre's
youth. Vakhtangov took this talk down verbatim, thus attracting
Stanislavsky's attention. (The latter asked Vakhtangov to stenograph
his future talks on the System, as well as the Moscow Art Theatre's
rehearsals of *Hamlet*.) At the start of the talk, Stanislavsky drew a
decisive line between the two theatres—Theatre of the Mystery and
the Popular: "One theatre originated in a temple (mysteries). It went
forward and, somehow, was lost. Another one [the Popular] in a form
of morality play, pastoral, etc., transformed into market square
performances, into a spectacle" (Ivanov 2011 vol. I: 218).
   During the talk, Stanislavsky explained the meaning, the greater
reason behind his System. Its principles and exercises were supposed to
serve a higher goal. Sulerzhitsky's concept of theatre, where both the
performer and the audience share in the act of communion with a higher
being, suddenly took concrete shape in the words of Stanislavsky:

Immobility is needed.
Different qualities of voice are needed.
The audience must forget the impression of the eye.
Audience must be transformed into a third creator.
Just think of the power this theatre has.
It can move one to do anything.
In such a theatre, all of the arts combined act simultaneously.

(Ivanov 2011 vol. I: 220)

Vakhtangov's record conveys Stanislavsky's anxiety at sharing his
ideas with the young generation of actors, as he thought, somewhat

prematurely, before they were fully formed. However, Stanislavsky felt that he had no choice but to start the battle for the new theatre. Every once in a while, he would stop and address Sulerzhitsky: "What shall I tell them next, Leopold Antonovich?" (Ivanov 2011 vol. I: 222). During the first talk with the MAT youth, Stanislavsky outlined the history of the MAT's aesthetic and its perspectives:

> During the last decade, a lot has changed in the goals, means and conditions of our art.
> We felt restricted by the old boundaries. The revolution took place.
> We rushed to destroy convention in theatre.
> We had to substitute the old artistic means with the new. New possibilities opened up.
> First and foremost, we rushed toward what's graphic—that is toward external realism.
> Therefore, a great deal of falseness concentrated in the inner technique, and in the means to experience the role.
> We went through several stages: stylization, impressionism, etc.
> Finally we returned to refined realism. This is not the old realism of the mundane, of the external life.
> This is the realism of the inner truth that exists in the life of the human spirit. This is the realism of the natural inner experience.
> This realism is externally simplified, down to a minimum, for the sake of spiritual deepening.
>
> (Ivanov 2011 vol. I: 223)

The concept of the Theatre of Mystery, as explicated by Stanislavsky, inspired Vakhtangov. He dedicated the next eight years of his life to implementing this ideal. The implementation often had to be carried forward in a bitter struggle with Stanislavsky himself. At times, Vakhtangov felt that his teacher was betraying his own ideals. Leopold Sulerzhitsky, whose creative philosophy stood behind the Mystery concept, was often stuck between the two artists, constantly trying to reconcile their creative geniuses.

9 Gordon Craig and *Hamlet* at the MAT

At the time of Vakhtangov's arrival at the Moscow Art Theatre, the company entered the final phases of its collaboration with the English director, stage designer, and theoretician Edward Gordon Craig. Craig was invited to the MAT in 1909 to direct and design a production of *Hamlet*.[1] In reality, *Hamlet* at the MAT was a child of three directors—Gordon Craig, Stanislavsky, and Sulerzhitsky. Gordon Craig introduced the overall concept of the show, facilitated through costumes and sets. Stanislavsky and Sulerzhitsky worked with the actors, in constant dialogue with Craig's ideas.

A future famous Georgian director, Mardzhanov, assisted with the technical aspects of the show that were complicated. Vakhtangov, at the request of Stanislavsky and Sulerzhitsky, fulfilled several jobs on this production—together with Mardzhanov, he conducted some of the technical rehearsals, and he also contributed as an acting coach. Finally, Vakhtangov participated in the 1911 *Hamlet* premiere as an actor.

According to Craig's concept, the Moscow Art Theatre production of *Hamlet* was supposed to be realized as a mono-drama (Bachelis 1983: 242–45). The events and characters of the play were to be presented on the MAT stage as if seen through the prism of its central character—Hamlet. The execution of this groundbreaking concept was not entirely fulfilled on the MAT stage, because of the artistic differences between Stanislavsky and Sulerzhitsky on one hand, and Craig on the other. At the same time, Craig's concept of mono-drama clearly influenced Vakhtangov; its echoes are heard in his productions from the early 1920s.

---

1 This was done at the advice of the influential American modern dancer Isadora Duncan, whose own experiments in the realm of movement and dance fascinated both Sulerzhitsky and Stanislavsky.

Hamlet rehearsals also gave Vakhtangov his first opportunity to witness Stanislavsky-the-director in action. Moreover, he could compare Stanislavsky's methods and philosophies with those of Sulerzhitsky, and even Nemirovich-Danchenko, who was also present at some of the rehearsals. Finally, Vakhtangov could witness Stanislavsky's interaction with several generations of MAT actors, including the leads, such as Kachalov and Leonidov.

This experience taught Vakhtangov to distinguish between Stanislavsky and the rest of the MAT environment. He saw that, at the MAT, Stanislavsky often had to compromise by adjusting to the stagnant environment. The MAT "elders"—successful, distinguished actors, who enjoyed international reputations—for the most part were hostile to Stanislavsky's new methods. Stanislavsky, in turn, began to look more intently toward the Moscow Art Theatre youth— he now connected his hopes for the development of his System with the younger generation. During the March 17, 1911 *Hamlet* rehearsal, for example, Vakhtangov recorded the following words by Stanislavsky:

> In the last five years, our theatre aged. Money—only those things are now considered artistic that bring money.
>
> I will separate [from the rest of the theatre] with a special group, and form an opposition, with the goal to restore the former conditions. I want a studio for the theatre; I want to bestow a blemish on my beloved theatre's face, right on the nose.
>
> A pure attitude is needed (discipline).
>
> Results in three years.
>
> [. . .]
>
> Vl.[adimir] I.[vanovich Nemirovich-Danchenko]—Theatre has been infested at birth.
>
> It is time to disinfect it. This requires a school.
>
> (Ivanov 2011 vol. I: 233)

A little less than a month later, on April 12, 1911, Vakhtangov made the following entry in his own diary:

> I want to form a studio where we could learn. The main principle—we must accomplish everything on our own. Everyone is a leader. We must test the Stanislavsky System on ourselves. Accept it, or reject it. Correct, complete (add on, supplement), or take out the false.

From day one, I plan to institute lessons in plasticity, voice, and fencing. Lectures in the history of art and costume. Once a week we will listen to music (invite musicians). Here we will bring all the fruits of our thoughts, all our exciting discoveries: humorous sketches, musical pieces, short plays.

(*Sourcebook* 2011: 229)

The interesting fact about this entry is that, because of the time when it was written, it is frequently associated with the formation of the First Studio of the Moscow Art Theatre. And yet, Vakhtangov dreams about *his own* Studio, or *their own* studio, meaning the younger generation of MAT associates. Another important detail: Vakhtangov sees the Stanislavsky System as grounds for an experiment, not as ultimate truth.

To the System, Vakhtangov adds disciplines commonly associated with the Popular Theatre spectacle, such as plasticity of movement, voice, and fencing. It is not quite clear how these disciplines were supposed to aid the "Stanislavsky" Studio's quest for inner truthfulness. What is the connection between plasticity and fencing and the inner technique of spiritual realism? Vakhtangov's own talent, however, did not distinguish between psychological and physical plasticity. His inner life was mobile and full of spontaneous emotional transitions. At the same time, Vakhtangov boldly channeled his inner energy into the body, thus making his physical life coined, expressive, and condensed.

Plasticity was a universal quality for Vakhtangov, a symbol of everything living in nature, while fencing was a way to develop inner courage. Where Stanislavsky (1953: 406) insisted that "the young actor should not strain his rather weak voice, temperament and technique," Vakhtangov dealt with these challenges decisively—he took the bull by the horns.

Vakhtangov's early program for the Studio was much deeper than is typically understood. In his "manifesto," Vakhtangov puts special emphasis on the spiritual, providing cultural food for the actors—lectures in the history of art and costume, and music. Vakhtangov's program calls for the formation of a creative collective, engaged in regular spiritual communion (cultural gatherings outside of training and rehearsals).

After Sulerzhitsky, Vakhtangov sought ways to stimulate and channel humor, as a historically integral part of an actor's life and creative process. (Think of irreverence and jokes as being constant elements of an informal actor's ritual, aimed at exercising an inner jester that lives in every actor.) Finally, Vakhtangov introduced the idea of self-governance, where "everyone is a leader" and, therefore, responsible for the entire Studio family. Vakhtangov's quest for his own Theatre of Mystery, as well as Sulerzhitsky's lessons, can be heard in this manifesto.

10 Novgorod-Seversky enterprise

The art of the provocation

Stanislavsky soon had a chance to witness Vakhtangov's potential. The same summer, a fellow by the name of Anatoly Assing, a lover of theatre, organized the Adashev School graduates' performances in his provincial hometown of Novgorod-Seversky. Vakhtangov headed this trip; he also directed most of its repertoire. In his directing work, Vakhtangov used Stanislavsky's principles and techniques, as he received them from Sulerzhitsky. The repertoire of the Novgorod-Seversky troupe included plays and adaptations of Ibsen, Hamsun, Maupassant, Chirikov, and others. Out of 12 performances, Vakhtangov directed all but Stanislaw Przybyszewski's play *The Snow*. From Novgorod-Seversky, Vakhtangov sent detailed accounts to Sulerzhitsky in Moscow:

> July 8, 1911
>> Novgorod-Seversky
>> [. . .]
>> We performed nine times (six plays). Three more plays to go. If you saw *The Fire*,[1] you would remain satisfied with the tempo, pauses, definition, and feeling—there was a lot of feeling. The rest is worse. But still good.
>> All plays, with the exception of *The Snow*,[2] were performed honestly and cleanly. The audience is pleased.
>> (Vendrovskaya and Kaptereva 1984: 93)

---

1 *The St. John's Eve Fire*, a 1900 play by Hermann Sudermann (1857–1928), German playwright and author. Please see p. 64 for Vakhtangov's notebook entry from August 6, 1911, that refers to the performance of the play given for Stanislavsky at the Moscow Art Theatre.
2 *The Snow*, a 1903 play by Stanisław Przybyszewski (1868–1927), Polish symbolist author and playwright.

Not reflected in Vakhtangov's accounts of the Novgorod-Seversky escapade are the daily details of the enterprise. These details, not published until very recently, shed important light on how Vakhtangov orchestrated the success of the trip, and achieved the "Stanislavskian" sincerity and truthfulness of life onstage.

Due to Vakhtangov's tactics, the financial and organizational hardships of the trip further solidified the bond between the members of the Adashev School family. A tight interpersonal collective that began to form through common training—or, as Vakhtangov would put it, "common cultivation"—became even tighter during the difficult journey to Novgorod-Seversky. After an exhausting trip in a third-rate train carriage, the Adashev troupe had to rehearse and perform an extensive repertoire, while struggling to obtain proper costumes and sets, and to adjust to the conditions of a dilapidated barn-like theatre space.

On top of it all, Vakhtangov, the leader of the group, would sink into one of his depressive moods throughout the journey, and upon arrival. Interestingly enough, Vakhtangov's despair did not produce a paralyzing effect upon his company—quite the opposite. Knowing their leader's tendencies of dealing with the threat of failure, the troupe's impulse was to counterbalance Vakhtangov's passive mood, and spring into action. All challenges were finally met, due to the company's resourcefulness, as well as the devoted help of the Novgorod-Seversky theatre amateurs and art patrons.

It would not be impossible to assume that Vakhtangov, facing a difficult situation, intentionally amplified the size of his own depression. Downplaying the hardships, offering sympathy to the collective, or acting as a cheerleader in a difficult situation—all these means would have produced the wrong effect upon the company. They would cause self-pity and delusions quite dangerous in the Novgorod-Seversky situation. Instead Vakhtangov used different "devices" in order to mobilize his troupe.

The whole ensemble knew that Vakhtangov was susceptible to defeatism, and that Sulerzhitsky fought these tendencies in Vakhtangov. This battle was unfolding in front of the Adashev collective. Vakhtangov skillfully used this fact as a way to breathe energy, confidence, and enthusiasm into his actors. For example, upon arrival in town, the director issued the following compliments to his three female leads: "Actresses must be pretty; the audience must feast their eyes on them, but you are so ugly!" (Ivanov 2011 vol. I: 255). The effect produced by Vakhtangov could not be obtained through any other means. Actress Serafima Birman, who truly could not be called a classic beauty, responded with indignant laughter: "Not true, Val'da is nice-looking, Lida is charming and nice, and I—I am original and unique!" (Ivanov 2011 vol. I: 255).

No preaching or praise could have breathed the kind of confidence and energy into Vakhtangov's actresses as his seemingly tactless statement. Vakhtangov's tactlessness had plenty of tactics behind it! Having seen the desired response, Vakhtangov immediately dropped the depression, sprung to life and began entertaining his actresses, singing some silly songs and accompanying himself on a mandolin.

Vakhtangov utilized the intimate personal knowledge he had of each of the Adashev School graduates as a vehicle toward success. He used this knowledge in order to *provoke* the company into successful action. Similarly, Vakhtangov's casting principles, and his directorial devices, were also based on the principle of *personal provocation*. This device was grounded in the close personal familiarity among the company members.

At the Adashev School, each of the students intimately knew the other students' characters. This familiarity and closeness within the theatrical family was one of the main sources of Vakhtangov's "provocative" directorial means. The life of the theatrical family, its plots and themes, its relationships, its ups and downs—such was the true psychological content (and true material) of Vakhtangov's productions.

Vakhtangov's tendency to capitalize on the actual life of the theatrical collective was not fully revealed until his final masterpiece— *Princess Turandot*. His fascination with the actual, ultra-realistic backstage life, however, was evident from his first steps both in literature and in theatre. It is this particular tendency of Vakhtangov's that caused him, for years, to shy away from a formal theatrical establishment, and stick to the informal family of the amateur troupe (see Figure 10.1). This peculiarity of Vakhtangov's gift, and of his theatrical aesthetics, will be discussed at length later in the book.

At present, it will suffice to say that Vakhtangov's inability to fit within the formal establishment of the Moscow Art Theatre, and his dedication to the *informal* structures, such as the First Studio of MAT, and other similar studios inside and outside the MAT, have a deep artistic and philosophical meaning. The intimate knowledge of every company member, and openness in their relationships, constituted for Vakhtangov the precious energy he harnessed and used in every production. At the MAT where Stanislavsky (2009: 557) insisted that

Figure 10.1 Vakhtangov (seated on the table) among the members of the
amateur Mikhailovsky Theatre Circle, 1913. Vakhtangov sitting
on the table. Courtesy of Vakhtangov Theatre Museum.

the actors leave "all the dirt of their daily lives" at the stage door,
before proceeding to the rehearsal hall, Vakhtangov would have been
deprived of his strongest creative material.

11 The formation of the First Studio of the Moscow Art Theatre

The news of the Novgorod-Seversky trip reached Stanislavsky. He was delighted with the trip's success. Moreover, he shared with his close circle the news of the young group that worked with his methods. Upon the troupe's return to Moscow, Vakhtangov was suddenly able to realize his plans—he could test the Stanislavsky System inside the collective of young MAT peers. Vakhtangov's diary reflects the lightning-quick speed of this development:

> August 3, 1911
> K.[onstantin] S.[tanislavsky] asked me to form a group among the Moscow Art Theatre troupe and start training them in his system.
> August 4, 1911
> K. S. suggested that I develop training exercises.
> August 5, 1911
> K. S. promised a space for the training, and the required finances. He assigned me to stage a few scenes [. . .] and show him.
> *(Sourcebook* 2011: 229)

Stanislavsky also expressed his desire to see the Novgorod-Seversky troupe perform. On August 6, 1911, Vakhtangov made the following entry in his diary:

> Following the excerpt from *The Fire*, K.[onstantin]. S.[tanislavsky] spoke a lot about my work. He was satisfied with the excerpt. So was Nemirovich.[1]
> (Ivanov 2011 vol. I: 265)

1 The excerpts from one play from the Novgorod-Seversky repertoire (namely *The St. John's Eve Fire* by Hermann Sudermann) were presented for Stanislavsky and Nemirovich upon the troupe's return to Moscow. Vakhtangov played the role of Plotz in this performance.

The following events, as recorded in Vakhtangov's diary, developed in the atmosphere of secrecy:

> August 9, 1911
>
> K. S. told me, "Work. If anyone says a word, I will tell him: goodbye. I need a new theatre. Let's act in secret. Don't mention my name."
>
> August 14, 1911
>
> Stanislavsky told me, "Every theatre has its intrigues. They should not scare you. On the contrary, it will be a good school for you. Work. Take those who trust you. If the theatre administration asks what it all means, tell them, 'I don't know, I am acting on Stanislavsky's orders.' I will provide the money you need. Don't worry where it comes from. You will have a salary of 60 rubles."
>
> August 20, 1911
>
> Stanislavsky told me, "I made a mistake of explaining my system in one lesson. Many don't get it. I am afraid this will cause conflicts. Beware." I replied, "I have my own method of teaching."
>
> K. S.: "Do you want me to come to your first class?"
>
> Me: "No, that would make me self-conscious."
>
> (*Sourcebook* 2011: 230–31)

Vakhtangov asserted his independence "from day one." It sounds like a paradox—Vakhtangov, still in his first year at the MAT, does not want Stanislavsky's guidance in teaching the Stanislavsky System. He has his "own method" of teaching, and he does not want Stanislavsky to get in the way. It appears that, already at this early date, Vakhtangov shared the basic principles of the Stanislavsky platform, but not his methods of teaching, or his techniques—at least not all of them.

Like Stanislavsky himself, the young Vakhtangov in the early 1910s was in search of a creative laboratory. A chance to realize his theatrical ideas and to complete his artistic search was important to Vakhtangov. At the same time, he knew that only an informal theatical formation could serve his goal. Only a group united by the need of spiritual communion, a desire to associate with art through theatre, or to discover a new truth in art, interested Vakhtangov. This conviction of his did not change, to his dying day. This is why Vakhtangov always felt himself a stranger at MAT-the-institution.

Moreover, Stanislavsky interested Vakhtangov insofar as he was at odds with MAT-the-establishment.[2]

Stanislavsky attracted Vakhtangov as an experimenting artist, an innovator, a theatrical revolutionary, and a seeker. Vakhtangov's own search, fearless and radical, eventually led Vakhtangov toward the theatre that differed from Stanislavsky's. Through his independent practices, Vakhtangov began to recognize the absolute values of theatrical play and developed (on the practical as well as theoretical levels) his own artistic philosophy. Like Anton Chekhov, he created his own theatrical world that was, in many ways, similar to Chekhov's. Vakhtangov's method of Fantastic Realism shared some of the basic Stanislavsky principles and ideals, and yet it illuminated the mysteries of the theatrical creativity unresolved in the Stanislavsky teachings.

Back in 1911, however, Stanislavsky—guided by generosity, or by an idealistic naiveté (or perhaps both)—once again provided the platform for a generation of new artists (as he already had done once with Meyerhold at the Povarskaya Street Studio). During the 1911–12 season, training, headed by Vakhtangov and Sulerzhitsky, continued informally, often in secret, at the MAT and at the actors' private flats.

In July 1912, Stanislavsky convinced his co-artistic director, Nemirovich, to designate the MAT funds toward renting a large apartment in the center of Moscow, on Tverskaya Street, to house the new laboratory. At that time, the formation of the select young artists received the name of the First Studio of the MAT. New staff lines were established—for Sulerzhitsky as the Studio's Head, for Vakhtangov as its chief instructor, as well as for several actors, eager to work with the Stanislavsky System. Among these actors were Lidiya Deykun, Grigory Khmara, Serafima Birman, Boris Sushkevich, Richard Boleslavsky, and the new arrival in the MAT troupe in 1912, the nephew of Anton Chekhov—Michael Chekhov.

---

2 Such was also Meyerhold's point of view on Stanislavsky. Meyerhold, who always separated Stanislavsky-the-searcher from Stanislavsky-the-artistic-director at the MAT, in 1921 co-authored an article entitled *Stanislavsky's Solitude*. In this article, Meyerhold spoke of Stanislavsky being misunderstood at the MAT.

12 Hauptmann's *The Festival of Peace*

Vakhtangov's debut as the First Studio of MAT director

When it came to training the First Studio of MAT actors, Stanislavsky did not interfere with Vakhtangov's work. Vakhtangov, in his daily activities, collaborated more with Sulerzhitsky than with Stanislavsky. The latter eventually proclaimed Vakhtangov the most effective teacher of the Stanislavsky technique. This statement did not undermine Stanislavsky's ego; after all, he never taught his own technique in a classroom (*Sourcebook* 2011: 6–8).

Stanislavsky was hurt, however, by the First Studio's tendency to transform into a theatre company. The Studio gradually deviated from its status as the Stanislavsky System laboratory. The young actors desired proper roles they could not receive at the MAT. On top of it all, three directors emerged from the First Studio troupe—Boleslavsky, Sushkevich, and Vakhtangov. Behind all three stood the harmonizing force of Leopold Sulerzhitsky.

Vakhtangov's choice of the play for his First Studio directorial debut fell upon Hauptmann's *The Festival of Peace*. Vakhtangov had staged this play before, back in 1904, upon his return to Vladikavkaz[1] from Moscow. According to Nadezhda Vakhtangova (interviewed in Khersonsky 1940b: 209–10), the 1904 production was motivated by Vakhtangov's recent exposure to the MAT. In the Vladikavkaz production, he strived to achieve "psychological truth within the acting ensemble, and careful artistic elaboration" of every detail. Moreover, the theme of the dysfunctional family resonated with

---

1 Back in Vladikavkaz, Vakhtangov directed Hauptmann's *Festival* . . . under the title *Sick People*, quite characteristic of the young director's take on the play's characters.

Vakhtangov, in view of his own family atmosphere and his strained relationship with his own father.

The Festival of Peace deals with the abnormal closeness between the Scholz family members. This pathological closeness makes the fear of separation unbearable. Incapable of facing the inevitable, the Scholzes turn their life into living hell—a kind of deathwatch, or life as a continuous anticipation of death. Their nerves are wound tight; family quarrels become a norm, and, during one such eruption, one of the sons, Wilhelm (see Figure 12.1), raises his hand to his father Fritz Scholz.

Determined to break the vicious circle, the elder Scholz challenges his family's deathly order. He undertakes a kind of a "preemptive strike"

Figure 12.1 Richard Boleslavsky as Wilhelm in *The Festival of Peace*, 1913. Courtesy of Vakhtangov Theatre Museum.

and swiftly leaves his own house. Scholz does the unthinkable, and disrupts *the established order of things*—surely, it is Wilhelm who should leave. Wilhelm does run away from home the same day, scared, and not even aware of his father's departure. The remaining two children stay with the mother—miserable together, and yet unable to separate.

At the start of the play, father and son Scholz return to the family house on Christmas Eve—as independently from each other as they left. A terminal illness brings the elder Scholz back, while his son Wilhelm returns at the insistence of his young bride, Ida Buchner, and her mother, Frau Buchner.

The elder Scholz, who now looks like an outcast and a drunkard, rather than a respectable bourgeois, seems to have reconciled with his impending death. At the same time, with his arrival, the very force of death—the inevitable force the family could not bear to face—enters the house. Scholz's old servant Friebe seems to be the only person in the household who remains unshaken by the arrival of death. This old man, as wise as he is ugly, takes his dying master into his tender care, acting more like a parent to him, than a servant.

Such are the events that bring the forever battling Scholzes together by the Christmas tree. The Buchners, mother and daughter, orchestrate this "festival of peace." The old Friebe also supports it in any way he can, while remaining inwardly skeptical. Perhaps the wise old servant instinctually feels that the same fear of separation and death that made Scholz's life hell, and caused the family war, now unites them in a forced reconciliation? Friebe's skepticism is confirmed: the false festival of peace does not last—the family erupts in a new conflict soon after the reconciliation.

In the final scene of the play, Wilhelm stands paralyzed on the threshold of the room where his father now lies dead. His bride, Ida, urges her fiancé to enter the room, and they finally do so, together. The philosophic idea of Hauptmann's play is revealed in this final scene. There will be no peace for anyone unless they free themselves from the fear of death.

The theme of unity in the face of disaster was present in Hauptmann's play. For the studio head, Sulerzhitsky, such a unity was inspired by the character's inner goodness. A variation upon this theme can be found in most of the Studio's early productions, including Heijermans' *The Wreck of Hope* (1913) and Berger's *Deluge* (1915). In many ways, the Studio itself was seen by Sulerzhitsky as a spiritual gathering meant to inspire goodness and God in the audience and in the actors. As noted before, Sulerzhitsky even attempted to structure the "outside life" of the Studio members, including their summer vacations, according to his communal ideal.

Sulerzhitsky's successes as a director and teacher should not be attributed to his professionalism as a man of theatre, but chiefly to his enormous and all-penetrating *love* for his students. It was Sulerzhitsky's ability to fully merge with his students, to become each and every one of them through empathy, that made him effective. Complete affinity with the actor's creative individuality enabled Sulerzhitsky to say to his actors just the right words, to suggest to them what already brewed, unconsciously, within their own souls. By doing so, Sulerzhitsky facilitated the actors' own creative process. Complete affinity with the creating actor was yet another lesson Vakhtangov learned from Sulerzhitsky.[2]

Vakhtangov's colleague-actors were ultra-sensitive, exalted, and nervous people. "Nervous," in the eyes of the Russian intelligentsia, equaled sensitive—nervousness was a sign of talent, of being able to take the world close to one's heart. For example, Anton Chekhov, when, for the first time, he saw his little four-year-old nephew, Michael, wrote to his sister: "[. . .] Misha is an incredible boy as far as his intelligence is concerned. His eyes glitter with nervousness. I think that he will turn into a talented person" (Chekhov 1974–83 vol. XVI: 211).

Members of the new generation of the Russian intelligentsia, those who "did not know joy," the First Studio actors deeply felt the conflict between the fathers and the sons. They heard the grinding music of the Revolution. They saw its dividing line, about to run them over. The tragedy of the Russian intelligentsia was in their inability to find themselves on either side of the barricade, to fully subscribe to any of the battling camps. On one hand, they propelled the Revolution as a force of progress, and an answer to the longstanding social injustice. On the other hand, they could not embrace the violence Revolution carried. Simultaneously, they could not help but sense that the revolutionary wave was going to destroy them first.

Precisely because of the Russian intelligentsia's inability to wear a definitive social mask, and find their place within either of the two battling camps, they were doomed. They would be the first to perish in the crossfire. Delicate spiritual constitution, constant tendency for soul-searching, acute moral sense—these were not the qualities needed for survival—quite the opposite. These qualities, and heightened sensitivity toward the great divide, caused Vakhtangov's actors to live in a constant conflict with themselves, and with the people around them. Needless to say, this conflict could be especially harsh within an

2   On the concept of Creative Individuality please see *Sourcebook* (2011: 10–16).

intimate family circle—be it an actual family, or a family of fellow artists, Studio members. All of these spiritual and social currents were present in Hauptmann's play, directly or indirectly.

In *The Festival of Peace* Vakhtangov-the-director, for the first time, teamed up with his two favorite actors—Michael Chekhov and Grigory Khmara. For Vakhtangov, Chekhov and Khmara were the quintessence of the Russian intelligentsia—they were especially sensitive and vulnerable, and therefore talented. In the foreseeable future, both of the actors will leave Russia (by then the Soviet Union). Their exile will be more than an inability to cope with the aftermath of the Revolution. Khmara and Chekhov won't be able to fit within the new commune, where every member is considered a replicable cog in a big machine—not an individual being.

In Vakhtangov's *Festival of Peace*, Michael Chekhov played the servant Friebe, while Grigory Khmara played the old Scholz. These two characters constituted one single whole, in the director's vision. Their relationship was portrayed in Vakhtangov's production as an unsentimental union between the two old men, who reached out toward each other across the social barriers. The old Scholz and his servant Friebe (see Figure 12.2) stood together on the verge of a special knowing, thus becoming the moral center of Vakhtangov's production.

Some of the production's most perceptive spectators, such as the Russian author Maxim Gorky, an admirer of Vakhtangov's talent, recognized Michael Chekhov's Friebe as the main character of the play. His ugliness, deliberately exaggerated at Vakhtangov's insistence, made Chekhov's Friebe into "the crooked mirror" (Smirnova 1982: 10) of this sick world—a jester's mirror. In a way, Friebe resembled a Shakespearian jester—a faithful, yet impartial servant, and a loving nanny to his old master. At the same time, the old Scholz resembled King Lear, who left his cruel family to wander the world, himself mad as a jester. These images—a declassed pilgrim and his honest servant-jester—will later reappear in several of Vakhtangov's productions, often merged with one another. They represented Vakhtangov's Shakespearian answer to the tragedy of life.

Deprived of a social mask, standing between the two camps, completely exposed to the battle of good and bad—Vakhtangov's "declassed" heroes lost their fear of death, because they had nothing to lose. They celebrated their own festival of peace—not a Sulerzhitskian communal gathering in the name of goodness, but an ecstatic beggars' feast. Theirs was an ugly, thrilling feast of ultimate freedom and ultimate knowing—on a chasm's threshold. It was a desperate, final feast of the honest sinners—not a deserved and decorous feast of the righteous.

Figure 12.2 Grigory Khmara as Fritz Scholz and Michael Chekhov as servant Friebe in *The Festival of Peace*, 1913. Courtesy of Vakhtangov Theatre Museum.

Can spiritual naturalism have a theatrical form? Stanislavsky's reaction to Vakhtangov's *The Festival of Peace*

Shortly before *The Festival of Peace* was shown to Stanislavsky for his approval, the First Studio received an upgrade. From its Tverskaya Street apartment, it relocated to a three-story historic mansion (circa 1812) overlooking Moscow's central Skobelevskaya Square. *The Festival of Peace* was meant to open the new space in a publicized event. This event, however, was almost cancelled.

Upon watching *The Festival of Peace* closed dress rehearsal, Stanislavsky proclaimed Vakhtangov's production naturalistic. Such an accusation sounds fantastical—in light of the popular reputation these two artists enjoy today. The future star of the Moscow Art Theatre II, Sofia Giatsintova, who played the role of Ida Buchner (see Figure 12.3) in the production, wrote in her 1981 memoir:

> To say that Konstantin Sergeyevich did not accept the perform-
> ance is to say nothing. He roared so that Zeus, the thunder-bearer
> himself envied him at that moment. He accused us of naturalism—
> we probably truly became too zealous in our striving for the truth

Figure 12.3 Sofia Giatsintova as Ida Buchner in *The Festival of Peace*,
1913. Courtesy of Vakhtangov Theatre Museum.

of life in its most heavy and ugly expressions,—Stanislavsky could no longer notice anything good and worthy in the production.

Words like "hand-wringing," "hysteria" and other vicious words fell onto our poor heads like stones. Hiding behind each other's backs, we quietly wept. In conclusion, Stanislavsky announced to Vakhtangov that he can only be a director who prepares actor's material, in other words, a teacher. Having proclaimed that Vakhtangov does not feel the form of the performance and therefore, unlike Boleslavsky, will never become a director who can build a production, Konstantin Sergeyevich left the theatre.

Devastated, hurt, upset, Vakhtangov kept turning to us his large eyes, filled with woe and humiliation.

—Why did he define it this way? Do explain to me, where are the signs that I cannot be a director? Not true, I do know, I do feel the form,—he repeated persistently.

(Giatsintova 1989: 121–22)

Running somewhat ahead, we must note that some of the audiences were also overwhelmed by the Vakhtangov production and reacted hysterically. Perhaps the hysteria in the audience was brought on by the faithful following of the Stanislavsky System—by pushing it to the limit? Did Vakhtangov remain true to the Stanislavsky platform and to the author? The noted critic of the time, Sergei Yablonsky gave the following account of Vakhtangov's premiere:

There is hardly any set.

Three walls and a ceiling—all made out of gray unpainted canvas. Two doors, a window, covered in snow; iron stove, divan, table and a few chairs. Over the doors and the window—deer horns. A lamp. I think, that's about it. Only the very necessary. The Moscow Art Theater youth performs the play. The "Studio's" first performance for the paying audiences.

[. . .]

The curtain opened.

I don't know, perhaps this is not art.

They do say that the art must excite us in a pleasant and peaceful way.

Art is aesthetics, refinement; art is always "deliberate", always somewhat striking, always a pose, always somewhat artificial.

Not here . . .

They took a scary Hauptmann play *The Festival of Peace*. The play is not at all German, because a German is methodical, well-tempered, well-behaved, and here we have our Slavic hell. Everyone in the family is a decent human being, they all love each other, and every second they all torture each other, humiliate, mock one another, wear out each other's nerves. Horror, convulsion, hysteria, anatomical theatre.[3]

Perhaps, the very play is not art: does art hit you with a stick over your head? Does art torment? This is veritable torment. Assuming this is not art, why did the author crawl into my soul, your soul, and the souls of the gentlemen sitting to your right, and the soul of the lady sitting to your left?

He must have taken it from us, for it is us, half broken, crippled, wretched (the tortured and the torturers all at once).

(Yablonsky 1984: 126–27)

Vakhtangov achieved his goal. The Russian intelligentsia of 1913 recognized itself in *The Festival of Peace*. They looked into Friebe's crooked mirror and became horrified at the grim prediction of their faith. Years later, Vakhtangov would formulate his principle of the contemporary in theatre: "one should sense 'today' in the day to come and 'tomorrow' in the present day" (*Sourcebook* 2011: 152). *The Festival of Peace* fulfilled this formula.

The rare breed of the Russian intelligentsia, represented by the actors and the audiences of the First Studio, became both Vakhtangov's material, and his target. In 1913, the Russian intelligentsia was standing on the verge of the cataclysm that eventually destroyed it as a social group. Stanislavsky in his classic productions of Chekhov's plays lulled the intelligentsia into believing that their sufferings were beautiful. His productions eulogized the intelligentsia's tragic sacrifice. They revealed an elegiac Turgenevian melody of their lives, while striving to inspire their inner goodness. According to Russian psychologist Lev Vygotsky (1936: 205), "*The Three Sisters'* yearning, as recreated on the MAT stage [. . .] was the crystallized shaping of the moods of the wide social circles; these moods, as expressed on the stage, became the means for these circles to comprehend and artistically refract themselves."

Vakhtangov, who considered Chekhov a "comfortless, cruel author" (Gorchakov 1957: 42), disagreed with Stanislavsky's interpretation of Chekhov's plays:

---

3 As early as the seventeenth century, anatomical theatres were built at European universities, for the purpose of teaching anatomy. They represent an amphitheatre-type room with a dissection table in its center.

In Chekhov's plays we find tragedy rather than lyricism. When a man shoots himself, this is not lyricism. This is either an act of triviality or heroism. Neither triviality nor heroism has ever had anything to do with lyricism. Both triviality and heroism have their tragic masks.

Lyricism, however, has had everything to do with triviality.

(*Sourcebook* 2011: 133)

Similarly, in *The Festival of Peace*, Vakhtangov employed a psychological strategy quite opposite from Stanislavsky's aesthetics—he exposed the intelligentsia's open sores to them. In Vakhtangov's production, the Russian intelligentsia heard from the stage that living as they lived was impossible, and that something must change. Maxim Gorky, who was among ardent proponents of Vakhtangov's *Festival of Peace*, saw the "art of protest" (Vendrovskaya and Kaptereva 1984: 131) in the production. As for Vakhtangov, it is quite doubtful that he thought of any revolutionary messages; more likely, he remained faithful to his own individuality, the one of his cast and, finally, the one of the author. Above all, Vakhtangov remained true to the individuality of his time, and the harsh future it carried.

The First Studio actors, inspired by Vakhtangov, achieved a new, hitherto unknown level of sincerity and self-revelation in their acting. This too was reflected by the critic Yablonsky:

The Moscow Art Theater youth went ahead and split their souls in this play.

I don't know if this will leave them unharmed. I do know that one should not do that: it is detrimental.

I repeat: I don't know if this is art or not, but I do know that in many, many years I have not experienced in the theater what I experienced yesterday at the Studio.

Fifteen years ago in Moscow an amateur performance took place that amazed Moscow by its freshness and uncommonness. The Moscow Art Theater was born. Yesterday in a tiny theater space the youth, students and apprentices, in the course of three hours held the audience at the edge of their seats in the way that only wonderful, finished actors can do in moments. No one coughed in the whole evening, no one moved.

(Yablonsky 1984: 127)

The critic's comparison of Vakhtangov's first Moscow Art Theatre Studio production with the MAT's inauguration of 1898 is significant.

The most dramatic and defining event of the MAT's inaugural season was the premiere of Anton Chekhov's *The Seagull*. It was this event, rather than the season's opening piece *Tsar Fyodor*, that ultimately determined the MAT's survival as a theatre company, and put it on a wider theatrical map.

One can trace obvious similarities between the openings of MAT's *The Seagull* and the First Studio's *Festival of Peace*. On the opening night, the MAT troupe was fearful that *The Seagull* would fail. In their minds, this failure would kill their beloved author, Chekhov, who would not survive the second consecutive flop of his play. The failure would also close the MAT, whose financial future rested on the success of *The Seagull*. The long silence at the closing of the final curtain was mistaken by the MAT troupe for a lack of appreciation of the play; the actress Knipper (the future Mrs. Chekhov), who played the role of Arcadina, fainted. The long pause, however, was followed by the ecstatic outburst of the audience, and a standing ovation.

The first public performance of Vakhtangov's *Festival of Peace*, while not nearly as legendary as *The Seagull* opening, was, nevertheless, equally dramatic for its participants. Before the critics and paying audiences could see the performance, the head of the First Studio, Sulerzhitsky, had to convince Stanislavsky to allow Vakhtangov's *Festival of Peace* to be performed at all. For reasons we won't speculate upon, Stanislavsky did allow the young troupe to show Hauptmann's play one more time to a very specific audience—the Moscow Art Theatre elders. Giatsintova offers the following recollection of *The Festival of Peace*'s closed showing:

> We applied our makeup in silence—we were saving all our will, all our powers for the performance, for yet another [. . .] leap into the unknown. . . . We began the play. Popova, who played my mother [Frau Buchner], and I stood backstage and listened how the Scholz family loses itself in another senseless fight. We also heard dead silence in the audience. We didn't know what it meant—acute interest or an absence of such. Then I myself entered the stage and stopped understanding anything that happened around me.
>
> I don't remember when, at what happy moment we understood that we won, that our victory was complete and real. Kachalov told Konstantin Sergeyevich that this is one of the best performances he had seen. The rest of "the elders" supported him "in unison", confirming that we discovered an approach toward the character through his System, that we impact the audience by exposing the

depths of the human passions. And Stanislavsky relented—he allowed us to perform the show in front of the audience.

(Giatsintova 1989: 122)

As stated earlier, both Vakhtangov's choice of Hauptmann's play, and his expressive means, served the goal of revealing the "creative individuality" of the First Studio. Hauptmann's nervous, uneasy play is inhabited by people who, like Dostoyevsky's characters, carry chaos and discord in their souls. The seed of this play fell upon the fertile soil of the young ultrasensitive generation of the MAT actors. It is significant that the same critic (Yablonsky), who evoked the echoes of MAT's inaugural *The Seagull* in relation to Vakhtangov's production, also recalled the MAT's more recent premiere. In the middle of the *Festival of Peace* review, Yablonsky suddenly addressed Nemirovich-Danchenko on his 1910 epic *Brothers Karamazov*:

> Vladimir Ivanovich [Nemirovich-Danchenko], you said that for the actors to express themselves fully you need Dostoyevsky. You did a whole lot, but, despite the help from wonderful actors and varied means of theatrical impact, your performance turned out heavy, pale in places and, in places, dull. Your excellent stage did not give a hundredth part of the impression Dostoyevsky produces in reading. And here the youth took a heavy, tedious Hauptmann play and did such a Dostoyevskian production, such a limit of anguish, that everyone wanted to scream, moan and at the same time we felt that sometimes our sores should be revealed to us, we should be lead down the dark corners of our bleeding and rotting souls.
>
> Is it art?
>
> However, if it is not achieved through screaming, waving one's arms and bulging one's eyes from their orbits—it was achieved through extraordinary simplicity of tone—such horrifying simplicity is much harder for an actor than any kind of exaltation.
>
> People speak quietly, mundanely, and "chaos moves" beneath it all.

(Yablonsky 1984: 127–28)

The combination of external lightness coupled with inner fire, characteristic of Vakhtangov's acting, became the signature style of his First Studio's directorial debut. One would have thought that Vakhtangov fulfilled the ideal of the Theatre of Mystery, as projected by Stanislavsky and Sulerzhitsky. Vakhtangov's realism in *The Festival of Peace* was "externally simplified, down to a minimum, for the sake of spiritual deepening" (Ivanov 2011 vol. I: 223).

Vakhtangov achieved the external "immobility"; he expelled the "oily" voice of an actor, and invited the new quiet, soulful voice onto the stage. He caused "the audience to forget the impression of the eye" and he "transformed it into the third creator" (Ivanov 2011 vol. I: 220). The life in Vakhtangov's production concentrated in the inward realm, and yet its fine inner currents burst onto the surface through the delicate life of the face, and of the hands. What could possibly dissatisfy Stanislavsky in Vakhtangov's production?

Stanislavsky could not accept Vakhtangov's *The Festival of Peace*—conceptually, philosophically, and ethically. The moral task Vakhtangov was to fulfill in the Hauptmann production was clearly formulated to him by Sulerzhitsky: "It is not their [the Scholz family's] wickedness that causes them to quarrel, but rather it is their essential goodness that causes them to reconcile" (*Sourcebook* 2011: 238). The force that gathered the Scholz family by the Christmas tree was supposed to be the spirit of reconciliation. In Vakhtangov's production, however, the family was drawn back together in a false union. This union was based in fear (and anxious anticipation!) of the close separation and death—the very same fear that drove the family apart in the first place.

The only aspect that could redeem the harsh content of Vakhtangov's performance, in the eyes of Stanislavsky, would have been precise theatrical form. Such a form, by overcoming the content, would provide an immediate catharsis effect, thus canceling the cruel, depressing essence of the piece. To his horror, Stanislavsky did not encounter any theatrical form in Vakhtangov's production. Can spiritual realism have a theatrical form?

Despite some Sulerzhitsky-inspired proclamations, Stanislavsky's understanding of the theatrical form was, of course, much different from Vakhtangov's. Stanislavsky understood form in theatre as physical form, expressed in precise, definite, logical, and truthful physical actions. The form of Vakhtangov's *Festival of Peace* was quite different. It was the form of spiritual naturalism, and therefore *an inner form*. On the surface it expressed itself in subtle, hardly noticeable, minuscule movements of the fingers, hands, half-glances, small, almost unfinished gestures (Markov 1925: 108).

Hellish Dostoyevskian layers of the human psyche were married in *The Festival of Peace* with the expressive means one might call

Chekhovian.[4] Moreover, *The Festival of Peace* revealed Dostoyevs-kian depths in a Chekhovian situation. Vakhtangov helped his actors to marry deep subconscious emotions with the psychological yearn-ings (like the ones Sulerzhitsky cultivated in Vakhtangov at the Adashev School). The result was quite powerful and, as paradoxical as it may seem, quite Chekhovian.

Contrary to the MAT interpretations of Chekhov, Vakhtangov achieved a different kind of realism: "People speak quietly, mundanely, and 'chaos moves' beneath it all" (Yablonsky 1984: 128). By doing so, he realized the famous Chekhovian formula seldom fulfilled in theatre: "People are sitting at a table having dinner, that's all, but at the same time their happiness is being created, or their lives are being torn apart" (Gurlyand 1904: 521). The tragic chaos that moved beneath the quiet, subtle, mundane life of the Hauptmann characters opened a new perspective on Chekhov and Dostoyevsky. This interpretation was half a century ahead of its time and, therefore, could not be embraced by Stanislavsky.

Being faced with Vakhtangov's realization of the Theatre of Mystery, Stanislavsky also must have felt that he was looking in Friebe's "crooked mirror." He saw in this mirror the reflection of his own principles and ideals, and he did not like what he saw. He stopped short of telling Vakhtangov what he would tell him, on a similar occa-sion, five years later: "One must strive for this, but one should never do this. One must move toward the truth of life, but one should give the stage truth" (Ivanov 2011 vol. I: 462).

Sulerzhitsky, who was also hurt by Vakhtangov's noncompliance with his views, nevertheless rose above the conflict. He convinced Stanislavsky to give the production another chance. In the end, Vakhtangov came out as a victor. His spirit was not destroyed by Stanislavsky's criticism. Vakhtangov was upset with Stanislavsky. He considered his teacher inconsistent, but he continued his experiments in the realm of the Theatre of the Mystery.

Vakhtangov knew that Stanislavsky and Sulerzhitsky, who both accused Vakhtangov and his cast of naturalism and hysteria, were justified. The very actors' material that seemed so suitable for the Hauptmann piece—one of the young Russian intelligentsia—ulti-mately betrayed Vakhtangov. By choosing an unbalanced psyche of a

---

4 Not in the Moscow Art Theatre's sense, as MAT never achieved this kind of subtlety in its Chekhov productions, but in Vakhtangov's sense.

First Studio actor to portray a similar psyche of a Hauptmann character, Vakhtangov miscalculated. He did not take into consideration that his actors' tendency toward peripheral nervous excitement would eventually backfire. Such is always the case when extreme sensitivity is not balanced with healthy psyche and not supported by the deep inner world.

The majority of the First Studio actors became overwhelmed by their sudden power over the audience. Their delicate inner constitution could not withstand Vakhtangov's hidden chaos (Ivanov 2011 vol. I: 364). Unable to sustain turbulent inner life, the actor substituted it with peripheral energy. In performance, they often resorted to a mere plucking of shattered nerves. The hysterics onstage caused similar hysteria in the audience, as the audience tends to psychologically imitate the actors. The actors' power over their audiences was, of course, illusionary. In actuality, the First Studio troupe was also facing the historic choice of the Russian intelligentsia—to perish, or to transform as a breed.

13 Life as creative play
The cultivation of a new man-actor

In the end, Vakhtangov could join the tragic actress Kommisarzhevskaya in saying: "we don't have the actor; he needs to be created; he cannot be created without creating a new man in him; a new man must be cultivated . . ." (Bely 1934 cited in Rybakova 1994: 458). The lessons of *The Festival of Peace* must have further confirmed for Vakhtangov the correctness of Sulerzhitsky's mission. At the Studio, they must continue cultivating a new kind of human being. For Vakhtangov this was also a cultivation of self.

Vakhtangov insisted that one of the important outcomes of the Stanislavsky System was "the knowledge of self" (*Sourcebook* 2011: 101), an actor's spiritual self-discovery. This is why even in everyday life Vakhtangov provoked his Studio peers to discover their true, creative selves. The work of cultivating a new human could not be accomplished by preaching. Together with Sulerzhitsky, Vakhtangov transformed the First Studio troupe through *creative play*.

Numerous descriptions of Vakhtangov's play in life exist in the memoir literature. Michael Chekhov's book *The Path of the Actor* contains precious examples of Vakhtangov's daily creative play. Improvisations between Vakhtangov and Chekhov could be harmless, but at times they gained cruel overtones. These improvisations often resembled contemporary status game exercises (Chekhov 1995 vol. I: 72–74).

At times, Vakhtangov's play was meant to cure Chekhov of his painful soul-searching. But first and foremost, it was supposed to serve as an exercise in refining life's instincts through improvisation. Play, improvisation, was a means of turning mundane instincts into creative by constantly exercising in spontaneous, witty, non-banal resolution of a life's task.

One of Vakhtangov's students recalled an improvised dialogue filled with dark humor, so characteristic of the Chekhov-Vakhtangov relationship. The student accidentally witnessed this dialogue in the First Studio corridor after a long rehearsal, and wrote it down:

CHEKHOV: I am looking for a coffin. Would you happen to have a cheap one?

VAKHTANGOV *(hoarsely)*: Male or female coffin?

CHEKHOV: For a small size *mamasha*.

VAKHTANGOV *(hoarsely)*: Seven rubles and fifty kopecks; ruble and a quarter for the ruche and four tassels at sixty kopecks each.

CHEKHOV: May I have a coffin with one tassel?

VAKHTANGOV *(in his own voice)*: Mishka, I'll kill you! *(Hoarsely)* For *mamashas*—with white brocade, for *papashas*—with red brocade.

CHEKHOV: And what about *pamashas*?

(Smirnov-Nesvitsky 1987: 147)

Vakhtangov and Chekhov improvised in the Moscow streets: these improvisations gathered crowds. In fact, to gather a crowd was the task of the improvisation. After several unsuccessful attempts, Vakhtangov stood in the middle of the square staring at the sky. Chekov joined in. In 10–15 minutes, all the traffic in the square came to a stop—a large crowd gathered around the two, trying to discern something significant in the sky (Butkevich 2002: 177–78).

Vakhtangov could start a solo improvisation with any object, any piece of prop really, and improvise endlessly, until he literally exhausted every possible combination in resolving a task. For example, he would improvise a drunk, trying to dispose of a used match by dropping it into a narrow neck of a wine bottle. The task was to improvise the psychology of a man, who is astonished at the fact the he always misses the bottle neck (Chekhov 1995 vol. I: 62: 150). Together with Sulerzhitsky, Vakhtangov once decided—to the horror of their dinner-guests—to improvise two drunks, who can't find their wallets to pay for dinner (Polyakova 1970: 602).

Some of Vakhtangov's "improvisations" served the purpose of cleansing himself and his colleagues of everything superficial, of all that "lumber" they assumed from life and society. (In his directorial notes on the production of *The Deluge*, Vakhtangov will compare this social mask with barnacles; he will write of "the crabs, octopi, and sea monsters" (*Sourcebook* 2011: 204) that get stuck to a human soul.) Just as Vakhtangov's rehearsal practices used the method of provocation, his play in life also often provoked the participants.

A MAT Studio actress, Pyzhova, recalled an episode during a MAT trip to St. Petersburg (Petrograd at the time) when she invited Vakhtangov and other studio members to dine at her mother's rich apartment:

> [. . .] I took an expensive white tablecloth out of my mother's chest of drawers, placed porcelain figurines, and hung beautiful golden lampshades on the chandelier [. . .]
> —Luxurious life style!—said Vakhtangov [. . .]
>
> (Pyzhova 1974: 63)

At the end of the evening, the hostess went to the kitchen to make tea. When she returned, she did not find Vakhtangov and another guest in the dining room:

> They moved to my mother's room and stretched out on the beds; one—on my mother's, another—on my sister's [. . .].
> —We are quite exhausted! [. . .] Vakhtangov, his eyes closed, said:
> —This is perfect. We will rest, and you will read to us, but only in French.
> Such impudent directorial work by Vakhtangov made me furious, and I ran back to the dining room. And here I noticed that my dear guests glued to the statue of cupid the "missing piece," molding it out of bread. And then I howled:—Get out! All of you! All! Get out of here!
> [. . .]
> The next day Vakhtangov came up to me and said, squinting his eyes: "It is excellent that you showed us the door. You have a good sense of plot."
>
> (Pyzhova 1974: 63–64)

Vakhtangov created an artistic plot in a plot-less everyday life. His everyday improvisations represented an elaborate play, meant to breathe artistic meaning into the mundane. Moreover, they awakened, or rather liberated, his colleagues and himself as free, bold, and creative humans. Every improvisation had a particular "creative task." The task of Pyzhova's improvisation was obviously to get thrown out of a respectable house.

The everyday life improvisations developed creative reflex—the actors trained how to turn into artists spontaneously, the moment they crossed the stage threshold. The problem of the threshold—being able to create "on cue," to become inspired at 8 pm sharp—this problem always haunted Vakhtangov. In rehearsals, the approach toward inspiration can be more gradual than in performance. This is why in rehearsals Vakhtangov could afford to build creative atmosphere, conducive to the ensemble's process. He safeguarded this atmosphere from any distribution—sometimes with kindness and, when necessary—with force.

For example, during the rehearsal period for *The Festival of Peace* Vakhtangov battled with the actor Boleslavsky, who constantly disrupted the rehearsal atmosphere by his tardiness, absences, and frivolous attitude toward the work. Vakhtangov's war was clearly not the war with Boleslavsky, but rather the war for Boleslavsky. It seems that the actor understood that and changed his attitude. Giatsintova wrote that "in the year of close work together" the members of the Studio engaged in Vakhtangov's *Festival of Peace* "merged into something solid, complete" (Vendrovskaya and Kaptereva 1984: 123). Achieving such unity of the theatrical collective was part of Vakhtangov's artistic method.

14 Tackleton

The Cricket on the Hearth

One of the most famous creations of Vakhtangov-the-actor was the character of a toy manufacturer Tackleton (see Figure 14.1). Vakhtangov originated this role in the 1914 First Studio production, based on Charles Dickens' Christmas tale *The Cricket on the Hearth*. Theatre audiences despised the heartless Tackleton, just as they were supposed to, according to Vakhtangov's plan. They inwardly revolted against his cruel treatment of the kindly old toy maker Caleb Plummer and his naive blind daughter Bertha.

Specialists in the audience, however, noted that Vakhtangov's style of acting differed from most of his colleagues' (Dikiy 1957: 274). All actors gave delicate and tasteful performances, and yet specialists noticed that two actors in the production, Vakhtangov and Chekhov, existed differently than the others, stylistically and psychologically. Chekhov's portrayal of Caleb was expressionistic in style; Vakhtangov's portrayal of Tackleton was graphic—full of contrast, shadow, and crisp definition (Markov 1925: 166–67). The critic Nikolai Volkov left us the following portrait of Vakhtangov's creation:

> Abrupt intonations. Squeaky voice. Croaky laughter. The click of the heel. Vakhtangov—Tackleton. One eye is half-closed. A fastidious grimace on the lips. Stripy vest. Short tails with velvet lapels. Trousers with foot straps. The figure of the toy manufacturer is drawn with a hard line. Movements are few. Gesture is reduced to a minimum. You look at Tackleton and wonder: is it a living man, or just a clockwork toy, crafted by Caleb Plummer's skillful hand? The wind-up mechanism is just about to run down, and this droll and unpleasant gentleman will freeze at half-word, half-movement. His hands will helplessly hang. His steps will come to a stop.
>
> (Volkov 1922: 13)

Figure 14.1 Vakhtangov as Tackleton in *The Cricket on the Hearth*, 1914. Courtesy of Andrei Malaev-Babel.

Vakhtangov's performance was marked by a certain precision, and the sharpness of treatment. Vakhtangov's Tackleton was harsh, and it was not a naive "fairy-tale" harshness. With the exception of Michael Chekhov, who played the role of Caleb, all other characters in the performance appeared as naive, just as they would be in a fairy tale. Vakhtangov's Tackleton breathed with irreverence and sarcasm.

From the standpoint of the First Studio's moral agenda, he became the main character of the play. Throughout the entire performance, the audience remained intrigued by Vakhtangov's character—is he really as irredeemable as he appears, or is he, as Caleb insists, just an "an odd fellow," who is good on the inside? (Dikiy 1957: 275). The audience had to wait until the play's finale, before they suddenly saw Tackleton's "fish eyes beam with bright light" and heard him address his neighbors:

> —John Peerybingle, Caleb . . . Friends . . . My house is very lonely tonight. I have not so much as a cricket on my hearth. I have scared them all away.
>
> His look is the same. So are the hinged movements.[1] So are the tails. In the meanwhile, something has happened with Tackleton. His intonations have warmed up. His voice softened. There is anguish and loneliness in his gaze. You can't help but feel that the soulless piece of wood came to life. The wind-up spring is gone. A human heart beats in its place. And the audience who, up till this point, has been receiving Tackleton—the marionette, now receives Tackleton—the human being. In the duration of the entire Christmas tale, the image of the character remained equally distinct and strongly defined.
>
> (Volkov 1922: 13)

At the end of the play, Vakhtangov's Tackleton suddenly revealed completely unexpected psychological qualities—his loneliness and melancholy created a nagging sensation in the audience and suddenly made them feel for "cruel" Mr. Tackleton. This was an entirely new, psychological, texture introduced by Vakhtangov at the end of the performance. The new texture was not prepared, or "justified" by the previous performance of Vakhtangov's. It was completely unexpected—a striking contrast to everything Vakhtangov had done up to this point. And yet, it was completely believable and it produced, as every artistically justified contrast, a strong psychological effect upon the audience.

The transformation came literally during the last few moments in the production—Vakhtangov continued "painting" his character, drawing it upon the canvas of the artistic space and time, up to the last seconds of the performance. The final image of the character, therefore, was not created onstage, but in the audience's minds, upon the drawing of the curtain. Vakhtangov's complex emotional accord continued to resonate in the audience long after the end of the perform-

---

1 Aleksey Dikiy, on the contrary, insisted that "a spring came into Vakhtangov's movements" in the finale.

ance. Vakhtangov's characters, in general, had the tendency to "linger" with the spectators.[2] For example, the Moscow Art Theatre's lead actor, Ivan Moskvin, found Vakhtangov's Tackleton "memorable" (Vendrovskaya and Kaptereva 1984: 132).

Vakhtangov's soulless toy manufacturer was a human toy, a mechanical puppet that suddenly came to life at the end of the play (see Figure 14.2). This transformation was—as it was supposed to be—the miracle of Christmas, for only a miracle can bring a wooden toy to life. Within the artistic world of a fairy-tale, such a concept was entirely motivated. Moreover, if Vakhtangov had chosen to motivate and prepare it according to the everyday laws of human psychology, the transformation would have appeared unmotivated—according to the fairy-tale laws.

An abrupt psychological transformation, however, also lies within the realms of human psychology. Caused by extraordinary, almost fantastical events, such transformation is possible in life. One should not look for it, however, in its everyday, mundane realm. Vakhtangov chose to travel into the deeper, "fantastical" sphere of the human psyche. This hidden sphere is as organic as the sphere of the mundane. At least, Vakhtangov was able to psychologically justify his character's sudden inner reversal. The audience believed the new soulful Tackleton of the finale, just as it believed its heartless "predecessor." After Dostoyevsky, Vakhtangov, in his Tackleton, pursued the art he later defined as "Fantastic Realism."

The image of a mechanical toy, hidden behind Vakhtangov's performance, was not revealed to the audience immediately. Vakhtangov was not playing a puppet, but rather he lived on the stage as a puppet-like human being. His acting was delicate and subtle; in fact, it was not even acting, but life in the circumstances of the Dickensian world.

Some of the audiences, who, unlike theatre critics and practitioners, did not care about the mechanism of the artistic impression, may not have consciously deciphered Vakhtangov's image. At the same time, every member of the audience received it subconsciously, as a universal image—a "statue, intelligible to every nation" (*Sourcebook* 2011: 156). The archetypal image of the mechanical toy that came to life

---

2 See Sushkevich's account of Vakhtangov's performance in Gorky's *Summer Folk* on p. 29.

Figure 14.2a,b,c,d Vakhtangov as Tackleton in *The Cricket on the Hearth*, 1914. Courtesy of Vakhtangov Theatre Museum.

went to the very core of the audience's soul, as it spoke of the eternal aspect of life and death.

Symbol and archetype are at the core of Vakhtangov's imagery as both director and actor. Several of Vakhtangov's productions were populated with characters who appeared as monuments, puppets, toys, and mannequins come to life. Vakhtangov's human puppet imagery was inexhaustible. Almost every performance he staged in the early 1920s, be it Chekhov's *The Wedding*, or the famous *Dybbuk*, contained a new variation on this theme.

Vakhtangov's human puppets signified death, and they were always opposed by living forces, represented by a different group of characters. Tackleton is the only example of a "dead" puppet turned into a human being in Vakhtangov's artistic world. Michael Chekhov's character of King Erik from Vakhtangov's production, at times, exhibited the elements of a broken-down puppet, whose wind-up mechanism "went astray." This, however, was an image of psycho-physical disintegration. A similar image was used by Vakhtangov for a group of relatives in *The Dybbuk* wedding scene. These human puppets were "stuck" in the same set of gestural reactions executed regardless of the emotional content they meant to express.[3]

Vakhtangov's creative variations on the puppet themes had nothing to do with the stylistic fashion of the period—they were deeply connected with Vakhtangov's artistic theme of the two origins in the world—the dead and the living.

Most importantly, Vakhtangov's archetypal images were inwardly fulfilled, or justified by the laws of the creative, non-mundane human psychology. (One could call it, perhaps, the psychology of a cataclysm.)

One of Vakhtangov's scholars guessed that the "slave driver" Tackleton, as performed by Vakhtangov, was inspired by his father Bograt.[4] In fact, performing Bograt in Tackleton was Vakhtangov's way to artistically transcend the darker aspects of his relationship with his father. Vakhtangov's chief partner in *The Cricket on the Hearth*, Michael Chekhov, once confessed that in his kindly and gentle Caleb he, in turn, played his own mother (Gromov 1970: 35). Apparently, Chekhov's love for his mother, hypertrophied to the point of obsession, also needed to be artistically refracted, or overcome.

---

3 Similarly, Vakhtangov's cabaret miniature *The Parade of the Wooden Soldiers* (staged in 1911 for Balieff's Chauve Souris) satirized the unstoppable, mechanical nature of the war machine, using the puppet theme. (See *Sourcebook*: 2011: 46.)
4 See p. 15.

15 *The Deluge*

The America of Vakhtangov's *Deluge*

Among "Vakhtangov's authors," Swedish playwright Johan Henning Berger is one of the few unknowns. Today Berger's prominence resides entirely on the fact that the First Studio of MAT once produced his play *The Deluge*. Nevertheless, in the history of the Russian theatre, Vakhtangov's 1915 production of *The Deluge* occupies a special place. Berger's play, despite its naiveté, is a work of talent. Moreover, approached by Vakhtangov as a tragic-comical parable, *The Deluge* revealed an unexpected depth.

The social spectrum of *The Deluge* is broad—it includes people from different walks of life. A group of customers held inside the bar by the natural disaster includes two businessmen, one prosperous and another ruined by his "colleague." Another customer is a prostitute— an ex-lover to the prosperous businessman. She was driven to her present condition by the businessman, who left her for the prospects of marrying a rich bride. A wealthy contractor is also a part of the group, but so are a would-be-inventor, and an unsuccessful actor. A stingy bar keeper and his black servant-waiter run the establishment.

As broad as the spectrum of characters may be, the play's action, time, and place are localized: *The Deluge* takes place inside a bar, somewhere in Mississippi or Louisiana, and its action continues almost uninterruptedly for a period of 24 hours (see Plate 1). Around brunch-time, the diverse collection of human specimens finds themselves trapped inside the bar, caught by a torrential downpour. News arrives of a flood approaching, and, like in an all too familiar scenario, there is a strong suspicion that the levees, built by the rich contractor present, are not strong enough to withstand the inflow of water.

Heavy hurricane shutters are lowered, in preparation for the disaster, and the electric light is turned on. Soon, all communications with the outside world are broken—the bar loses its telephone and telegraph connections, and the electricity is cut off last. From this sequence of events, the inhabitants of the bar assume that the water, having flooded the lower sections of town, including the telephone, telegraph, and electric stations, is gradually rising up toward the elevation where their bar stands.

By night, the basement is fully flooded, and even the front door won't open—the water must be up against it by now. In the face of impending death, the group that includes business competitors, rivals, ex-lovers, and people of contrasting social backgrounds, comes together. Led by the ruined businessman Frazer, they form a circle and, in flickering candlelight, they hold hands in a round dance, chanting the song of unity. The former rivals reconcile; the ex-lovers reunite; the social outcasts are welcomed by the rich, and even promised patronage, in the unlikely event of survival. The owner of the bar is no longer keeping tab on the booze—all drinks are on the house.

The morning arrives, but no water came inside the bar room. One by one, electricity, telephone, and telegraph come back to life. The door is opened at last (apparently, it was simply stuck) to reveal that the bar neighborhood was never flooded. The flood, as it turns out, was altogether a false alarm, as the levees stood. Life returns to normal—the newly formed friendships dissipate, ex-lovers each go their separate way, and outcasts are asked to clear the premises. The barman calculates his "damages" and presents his customers with a bill. The usual brunch-time customer, who opened the play 24 hours ago, bursts into the bar, just as every other day.

Vakhtangov's staging of *The Deluge* arguably marks the first instance of American life portrayed on the Russian stage. In 1916, America was no more concrete for most Russians than Mars. It is definite that Leopold Sulerzhitsky, one of the few Russians who traveled to the United States at the time, consulted Vakhtangov and his cast on American customs and ways of life. After all, Sulerzhitsky rehearsed *The Deluge* for a period of time, alongside Vakhtangov. It is more likely, however, that Vakhtangov relied on his own intuition in creating the world of *The Deluge*.

A couple of hints Vakhtangov received from Sulerzhitsky, and from his "research," were enough to complete the picture of American life. Vakhtangov's research was chiefly based on an 1870 book by Englishman David Macrae, titled *The Americans at Home (Pen-and-ink Sketches of American Men, Manners and Institutions)*. This book, witty but filled with stereotypes, helped Vakhtangov to shape the image of America during the industrial age. Macrae's America was the America of Wall Street, where humanity is trampled by greed.

Vakhtangov, in general, was sensitive to the rhythms of life, as well as to people's personal and national rhythms. After Macrae, he initially defined the tempo-rhythm of American business circles as extremely fast—there is no time to lose, as time is money. Later in the rehearsal process, however, Vakhtangov made a correction: "An American is prompt, but not in a hurry" (*Sourcebook* 2011: 205). As for the ferociously fast tempo of Wall Street, Vakhtangov moved it into *The Deluge*'s background, thus creating a frame for his production.

The rhythm of the American business world, synchronized with the rhythm of the stock-exchange, was created in Vakhtangov's production through the character of the "second bar-customer." In Berger's play, this character bursts into the bar at the top of the play to consume his usual brunch-time cocktail, and then makes an identical appearance 24 hours later, in the finale. According to Berger, the bar customer's reappearance is supposed to symbolize that nothing had changed in the outside world in 24 hours.

The production's spectator and participant, Aleksey Dikiy (1957: 278–79), recalled in his memoir that Vakhtangov did not spare time working on the cameo role of the customer. As a result, Vakhtangov's second customer, who "framed" the production, turned into a much larger symbol. He symbolized the spiritless ritual of the business life—the kind of ritual that reduces a human being to a programmable machine.

The opening and closing scenes of Vakhtangov's *Deluge* were almost a direct quotation from Macrae's book on America:

> The rule of doing smartly what you have to do is applied even to eating. Meals are treated as necessities of life not luxuries. People sit down at the dinner table not to talk but eat and I have seen business men in America shoot a dinner down and be off to work again in the time it would take an Englishman to sharpen the carving knife and decide where he had better begin to cut. At the Opera Restaurant in Chicago—a place much frequented by merchants—I had the curiosity to time five or six gentlemen at their dinners and found the average number of minutes taken by each to be three and three quarters. All of them had two courses—one of them had three. There were no seats; the customers swarmed in front of a long metal counter like a public house bar. A man would come in, walk briskly to the counter, order brown soup, shoot it down, order chicken and ham, give it the run of his teeth, as it flew in bits into his mouth, would snap up a blackberry tart, pay his money and be off.
>
> (Macrae 1870 vol. I: 17)

In Vakhtangov's production, the brunch-time cocktail was one of the meaningless routines that constituted a businessman's existence. In fact, the second bar-customer did not really exist outside of his daily routines. His entire life was a part of a money-making ritual where everything, including eating and drinking, was dedicated to profit.

The problem of form in *The Deluge*: definition and improvisation

Pavel Markov (1925: 132) wrote that Vakhtangov's *The Deluge* "technically outlined a new means of acting, in comparison with other [First] studio productions." The critic offered the following account of innovations, introduced in *The Deluge*:

> [The new means] consisted of increasing definition, a certain graphic quality, and in an utmost use of the characteristic features and details that stamped these characters with hyperbolic, exaggerated qualities. Such focus on a single detail and exaggeration was present in [Michael] Chekhov's Frazer [see Figure 15.1], as well as in other *Deluge* actors.
>
> (Markov 1925: 132)

Vakhtangov considered *The Deluge* as a parable (Ivanov 2011 vol. I: 381). Such an approach required that the characters of the play appear even more vivid and singular than those of *The Festival of Peace*. After all, the emotions consuming the characters of *The Festival* were subtler and more intimate (if not to say pathologically sophisticated) than those of *The Deluge* characters. The new author, Berger, and the new time dictated to Vakhtangov a different approach to inner and outer characterization.

Despite an obvious difference between *The Festival of Peace* and *The Deluge*, both of these performances appear to be in harmony with Vakhtangov-the-artist. The energy of Vakhtangov's *The Festival of Peace* concentrated in the realm of actors' emotions. According to Pavel Markov (1925: 130), in *The Festival* Vakhtangov "gradually approached the realm of the subconscious, at times kind, at times dark, at times contradictory, often tumultuous and passionate—the kind he knew how to awaken in an actor." In *The Deluge*, however, the inner concentration began to find itself an external form.

The tumultuous nature of Vakhtangov's new theatre found its expression both in the inner life and in the shapes, images and rhythms of *The Deluge*. As evident from Markov's (1925: 131) study, "the

Figure 15.1 Michael Chekhov as Frazer in *The Deluge*, 1920.

American shape of the play prompted Vakhtangov to seek edgy artistic means: the play developed in the dichotomy of rhythms; its flights were followed by catastrophic falls."

Vakhtangov's descriptions of *The Deluge* characters (*Sourcebook* 2011: 203–5) and photographs from the performance, reveal that no mundane physical elaboration was present in this performance. Every single character, and every composition of characters on the stage, was as if dedicated to one single spiritual dynamic. In *The Deluge* composition, characters, individually drawn by actors, are merging into a clear and definite whole. Their reactions to larger-than-life events are precise and distinct in their individuality. Actors' bodies and souls, in Vakhtangov's rendition, appear as if chiseled from stone (see Figure 15.2).

No physiological split, characteristic of the MAT naturalism, is found in *The Deluge*. The life of *The Deluge* character, at any given moment, is focused, dedicated to one particular spiritual movement and simultaneously harmonized with the life of the overall ensemble. Where Chekhovian characters at the MAT were enveloped by common atmospheres, the characters of *The Deluge* remained apart. They each lived with their own distinct emotions, contrasting to the rest of the ensemble. A jarring dissonance of the individual lives, nevertheless, merged into a powerful and dynamic harmony.

The texture of *The Deluge*'s harmony did not tolerate unisons; it was built on discord, resolved or unresolved. This harmony, as well as the syncopated rhythm of Vakhtangov's composition, resembled jazz. Vakhtangov's actors, nevertheless, possessed a full sense of the harmony. This feeling of the whole allowed them to distort the harmony in their individual way—without sacrificing the *overall* unity of the scene. Vakhtangov's communal living was antithetic to Sulerzhitsky's, as it was built out of distinct individual impulses, positive and negative, and not united by common goodness.

Vakhtangov's actors were leading the audiences on a journey. Each act, and each moment of *The Deluge* had a clear psycho-physical definition. For example, when the characters learned that the water is about to burst into the bar, they instinctively lifted their feet off the floor, onto their barstools. According to some accounts, this moment in the production was so convincing that the audiences unconsciously mimicked the actors' behavior (Smirnov-Nesvitsky 1987: 91). The actors focused their spectators' attention, and their emotions, as if by a powerful lens. The unison, the common feelings and atmosphere were finally there. It was the atmosphere of the cataclysm, of the shock.

Equally concentrated and powerful was Vakhtangov's image of the "chain of union" from the second act. As the disaster drew near, Frazer connected the hands of every inhabitant of the bar, initiating the chant of complicity—it was picked up by the entire company. The characters, in the face of the fear of death, were seeking (and finding) support in one another. In flickering candle light, they moved in a mysterious round dance, their shadows bouncing off the white walls of the bar. This moment always produced a strong psychological effect upon the audiences, and the strange melody chanted by the group went to the heart of the audience (Markov 1925: 131). This melody,

Figure 15.2 Scene from Act 1 of *The Deluge*, 1915. Courtesy of Vakhtangov Theatre Museum.

identified by most critics as an African-American march, was apparently based on an Armenian folk tune.

However definite the form of *The Deluge* may have been, Vakhtangov demanded that actors must rediscover it anew, relive it at every performance. The essence of the characters, and of their behavior, had to remain. Psychological nuances had to be different every night. Vakhtangov's demand was justified, as the form of *The Deluge* was born intuitively, improvisationally. Even the image of the chain of union, and the famous song from *The Deluge*, were improvised in rehearsals. According to Boris Schukin's memoirs, the scene of union initially presented a problem to the actors:

> Things came to a halt in rehearsals; in fact, things were so bad that day after day actors had to stop their work at that very moment— they could not proceed. Actors became angry with themselves. Once, after another fiasco, everybody was so nervous they could not face each other and each withdrew into their own corner. Vakhtangov approached a piano and, quite mechanically, started to play. He did not have a conscious account of what he was playing . . . he just played something that suited his mood. He improvised. Then he began to listen intently. The music became louder. Then he yelled: "Go ahead, let's do it!"—and he led the scene. In music, in this tune, he discovered the expression of the inner state he could not otherwise discover and naturally express during the rehearsal. The only correct solution was discovered in the "subconscious" revelation of the bit, and it was discovered intuitively.
>
> (Schukin interviewed in Khersonsky 1940b: 112–13)

It is in connection with *The Deluge* that Vakhtangov developed his formula: "Every performance is a new performance" (*Sourcebook* 2011: 207). Improvisation, subconscious creativity—in training, in rehearsal, and in performance—became Vakhtangov's motto, and the essence of his approach. The contrast between the improvisational approach and Vakhtangov's demand for clear, precise form is a seeming contradiction. In practice, it was resolved by Vakhtangov through trust in creative intuition and the subconscious. The director knew that those actors who surrender to their intuition in every performance, subconsciously fill the precise form with new psychological life. Vakhtangov insisted that the most elaborate characterization will come on its own to an actor who dares step onto the stage psychologically "naked" (Leonid Volkov, interviewed in Khersonsky 1940b: 62).

Goodness or honesty?

Once again, in *The Deluge*, Vakhtangov entered into a philosophical disagreement with his teachers Sulerzhitsky and Stanislavsky. Sulerzhitsky insisted that the approaching deluge brings out the inner goodness in characters. The central event of *The Deluge*, according to Sulerzhitsky, proved that human beings are essentially good—they come together in the face of disaster, united by the spirit of complicity.

Sulerzhitsky suggested that the union of the second act throws an overall positive light onto *The Deluge* characters. He wanted to see the characters in this light throughout the entire play. Having watched the first run, as directed by Vakhtangov, Sulerzhitsky exclaimed:

> Oh, what funny people! [. . .] They are all so warm-hearted and nice; they each have a perfect chance to be good, but they have been corrupted by this rat race, by the dollar, and by the stock market. Discover their kind heart, and let them reach ecstasy as they revel in their newly revealed feelings.
>
> (*Sourcebook* 2011: 238)

Vakhtangov, while honoring the second act, was interested in the entire spectrum of *The Deluge* composition. The director firmly stated his views on the play at the first discussion of the play on October 1, 1914:

> To show the street, heartless and practical, a group of people, a group from this street accidently comes together at a restaurant; the forces of nature put this group into a situation remote from everyday life—and they reveal the most important aspect of their selves—their souls. Such is act one.
>
> The second act must move everyone—look how good a Man is.
>
> Third act. Delivery from natural calamity. Life, vulgar and practical, gets back into its routine. It floods everyone, once again, with its waves ("*The Deluge*"), and men, once again, harden and go back into their shells. "*The Deluge*" must be understood allegorically—as a moral deluge.
>
> In order to move the audience, we must ourselves become better; we must approach this play with a positive feeling.
>
> (Ivanov 2011 vol. I: 381)

Vakhtangov's speech appears to be in harmony with Sulerzhitsky's philosophy; however, there is a distinction. Vakhtangov agrees that the *actors* must strive to become better, but he denies this striving to the *characters*. Like Sulerzhitsky, he considers the second act of *The Deluge* its central, pivotal part. At the same time, Vakhtangov sees it as pivotal for different reasons. He clearly plans to "trick" his audiences in the second act—"Look how good a Man is!"—only to flood them in the third with the "moral deluge."

The directorial plan of *The Deluge* changed in practical work. The apocalyptic notes, originally reserved by Vakhtangov for the third act, appeared already in the second. They were clearly heard both by Vakhtangov's contemporaries, and by the future generations. Vakhtangov's biographer Smirnov-Nesvitsky (1987: 92) wrote:

> The naturalistic bar turned out to be a Noah's Ark. The performance no longer spoke of a group of people in trouble, but of humanity standing on the verge of global catastrophe. There was a certain bitter, prophetic meaning to the fact that the people awoke and united only on the threshold of death.

At the time of *The Deluge* premiere, Russia was involved in World War I. Although Vakhtangov's production never mentioned the war, both the audiences and the critics felt that it spoke of the time (Efros 1984: 146). Vakhtangov's nightmarish dance of union—this "feast in the time of plague"—was not the only instance where the director widened the boundaries of Berger's play. Vakhtangov connected far-reaching hopes with the second act of *The Deluge*.

Leonid Volkov, one of Vakhtangov's favorite students, left us a priceless witnessing of Vakhtangov's thoughts behind *The Deluge*. Volkov, who was often allowed inside the director's laboratory, explained what Vakhtangov sought in the second act of the play:

> When he [Vakhtangov] staged *The Deluge* [. . .] at the First Studio, he used to say that theatre must present people and the essential in them, and in doing so, it must reach the ultimate revelation. He said that at the MAT this is missing, that there *an actor* prevails; in the meanwhile, everything actor-like must be removed, and only everything human and naked must be left, as it is. He was keen on *The Deluge*, because its characters, doomed to die, finally stop acting the way they always do in life and therefore, become their true selves—*with all their positive and negative qualities*.

I remember he used to say that actors must find themselves in their roles as they are when they remain alone, at their home—when no one sees them. Imagine that you are preparing to go to bed, undressing. You know that nobody can see you, and you are too exhausted at the end of the day to pretend. Then you become yourself. Perhaps, Vakhtangov took this image of undressing on purpose—he wanted to say that when people take off everything extraneous, they naturally reveal what is real in them.

(Leonid Volkov, interviewed in Khersonsky 1940b: 68)

Where Sulerzhitsky considered it essential to reveal the characters' inner goodness, Vakhtangov tried to arrive at a more complex revelation. He strove to achieve the kind of honesty, unprecedented in theatre. In the circumstances of the play, he sought external motivations, which would allow his actors to rise to a new level of sincerity. To sum up, Vakhtangov was after a new kind of acting altogether. He pursued new, confessional theatre, in which human beings (actors) would reveal themselves to their very depths.

Vakhtangov and Michael Chekhov as Frazer

Vakhtangov was dissatisfied with the final results of *The Deluge*. According to the First Studio's custom, the young director started rehearsing the production, and then passed the director's wand to the studio head Sulerzhitsky. After Sulerzhitsky had rehearsed *The Deluge* for some time, Vakhtangov regained control of the rehearsal room, only to have to pass the production over to Stanislavsky, who put his "final touches" on Vakhtangov's work (Ivanov 2011 vol. I: 393). As a result, on the eve of the opening (December 13, 1915), Vakhtangov wrote in his diary:

Tomorrow is the first performance of *The Deluge*. The play I took close to heart, the play I loved, the play that burned in me, the play I felt, and, most importantly, the play I knew how to convey to the audience.

And then came other people: Sulerzhitsky and Stanislavsky; they came, crudely forced themselves onto the play, insensitively trampled upon everything mine, bossed around, without asking me, cut it and axed it.

(*Sourcebook* 2011: 206)

Vakhtangov did not give up. He continued his work on *The Deluge* from backstage—giving feedback to the actors. Moreover, Vakhtangov found a way of directing *The Deluge* from inside: shortly after the opening of *The Deluge*, he began to share the role of the failed stock broker Frazer with Michael Chekhov (see Figure 15.3). A First Studio stage manager Sergei Barakcheyev remembered that after the opening of *The Deluge*, Vakhtangov proceeded to make the production "edgier, especially when he personally performed"; he did so by "introducing dynamism" (Ivanov 2011 vol. I: 393). Besides Frazer, Vakhtangov picked up three more roles in *The Deluge*, thus becoming a kind of a field coach to his actors.

Figure 15.3 Vakhtangov as Frazer in *The Deluge*, 1915. Courtesy of Moscow Art Theatre Museum.

Unlike Chekhov's Frazer, who appeared degraded and defeated, Vakhtangov's Frazer "wants to live more than anyone else" (*Sourcebook* 2011: 204). According to some accounts (Smirnova 1982: 13), in Vakhtangov's interpretation, Frazer was also the only character in *The Deluge* who did not go back to the old ways at the end of the play. This downtrodden man, who formed the nighttime circle of union, remained deeply affected by the events of the night. His spiritual change was not superficial, but rather long lasting and profound. Not unlike Vakhtangov's Tackleton, his Frazer truly transformed, and remained transformed through to the end. This transformation was profound and truthful by the fact that the transformed Frazer, like Tackleton, never stopped being himself.

The apocalyptic analogy in the second act of *The Deluge* was mentioned before, as well as Vakhtangov's thought of the moral Apocalypse (Ivanov 2011 vol. I: 381). It is equally significant, however, that Vakhtangov interpreted the first and the third acts of *The Deluge* as a sinister ritual of hunt, where all participants faced the choice of destroying their rivals, or themselves being destroyed. This life on the threshold of death, according to Vakhtangov, was the permanent state of *The Deluge* characters:

> They are all wolves to one another.
> Not a drop of compassion. Not a drop of attention. Everyone looks after their own profit. They snatch [it] out of each other's hands. Disconnected. Drowning in business.
> (*Sourcebook* 2011: 203)

Only Frazer, the bankrupt businessman, himself a predator, who got eaten, appeared to have occupied a special "space" in Vakhtangov's production. Anyone else in the play was protected against the ultimate struggle of good and evil by the impenetrable armor of their class's morale. By belonging to one of the camps (the strong or the weak, victors or victims, exploiters or the exploited) most of the inhabitants of the bar were exempt from the battle. Only Frazer, who stood between the social camps and, therefore, was not protected by either of its respective morals, could gain a special understanding of the truth that exists on "the other side."

When forming the joyful chain of union in the second act, *The Deluge* characters simply followed Frazer with his divine intuition. They went along with this improbable leader, as the threat of death paralyzed their will. As insightful Michael Chekhov put it in one of the rehearsals, they "sunk into purity" (Ivanov 2011 vol. I: 389). As soon as the false threat dissipated, however, these characters (essentially unchanged) regained their will and resumed following their true idol—the golden calf. Philistines remained Philistines, while the prophet Frazer remained distinctly separate from them in the play's finale (just as he remained essentially an outsider at the top of the play).

The title of the play, *The Deluge*, was one of its many biblical references. One of Vakhtangov's disciples shared in his book (Zakhava 1930: 106) that Vakhtangov dreamed of playing the biblical Moses. Vakhtangov, who, on one occasion, advised Michael Chekhov to play Frazer as a Jew, did play Moses in Frazer, as evident from his famous photo in this part. Vakhtangov's Frazer, who substituted sermon for a song, was the most improbable of all prophets, yearning with a longing for life, and unable to clearly communicate the true meaning of life to those around him. According to another disciple, Gorchakov, Vakhtangov considered *The Deluge* a tragic comedy, while Frazer was dearer to him than "many 'profound' classical characters" (Gorchakov 1957: 99).

16 The end of Leopold Sulerzhitsky

Vakhtangov as the new leader of the First Studio

The *Book of Records of the First Studio of the Moscow Art Theatre* provides a unique glimpse into the atmosphere of this theatrical collective. Established by Stanislavsky and Sulerzhitsky, this book was meant to encourage studio members to share their thoughts. They were invited to write on the given performance, on the life of the studio, or perhaps on the art at large.

One of the very few serious entries in the book belongs to the Studio director, Sulerzhitsky himself. In these entries, Sulerzhitsky called on studio members to be complicit with those less fortunate. For example, he asked his students to develop a habit of noticing the hard life of the simple folk employed in the positions of service at the Studio—for example, the Studio custodian, who also doubled as the boiler man and stagehand. Sulerzhitsky insisted that Studio members not take service people's labor for granted, or treat them as hired help. He asked the actors to take the trouble to investigate the hard conditions of the service people and their families' lives.

On a different occasion, the First Studio actor Geirot, who had recently made a failed attempt to "defect" to Tairov's Chamber Theatre, came back to the Studio. In a somewhat long-winded and sentimental entry, Geirot wondered how the Studio could "reflect the great epoch—in our theatre, in our creative work" (*Sourcebook* 2011: 233). Clearly, many Russian artists were occupied with such a question while in the midst of a bloody world war. Vakhtangov, who believed that the less directly art reflects time, the better the outcome, answered Geirot with a caustic remark:

> Firstly, prodigal son, do not write on the left side of the ledger—leave it to the leisurely and witty commentators—and, secondly, my dove, if you want my opinion on what you wrote, be so kind

as to clarify what it means "to reflect the great era—in our theatre and in our creative work."

Does it mean that we need to perform a play that reflects our era?

In this case, either indicate such a play or, be so kind, if time permits, do write one.

Does it mean that the nature of our productions should reflect our era?

As far as I am aware, principles of theatrical productions never depended on war.

Does it mean that our creative work must have some kind of a great goal in such an era as ours?

The Cricket on the Hearth, The Deluge . . .

Let us suppose that it is characteristic of some era that the art comes to meet the worn-out soul of a man. In such a case, our era would be reflected in the very fact of the production, and in the choice of plays.

(*Sourcebook* 2011: 233)

On another occasion, Vakhtangov addressed the cast of his *The Deluge* with a detailed entry that spoke of theatrical festivity, as an essence of the creative state. The same entry also featured concrete notes on the latest *Deluge* performance (*Sourcebook* 2011: 108–9, 205–6).

Meaningful entries, however, were rare—the irreverent jester that lives inside every actor ruled on the pages of the *Book of Records*. Sulerzhitsky's entries on complicity drowned in the Studio members' mocking remarks. Occasional attempts to defend Sulerzhitsky from his offenders were contributed by the female Studio members—these entries, however, sounded sentimental and somewhat subservient. The *Book of Records* gives an impression that Sulerzhitsky's voice, speaking of complicity with the world, remained "the voice of one crying in the wilderness."

Was it this irreverent and selfish atmosphere that made Sulerzhitsky, in December 1915, draft his letter of resignation to Stanislavsky (Polyakova 1970: 379–83)? In this letter, apparently never mailed, Sulerzhitsky was asking to be relieved of his duties as the First Studio director. This man, who subscribed to Tolstoy's ideas of non-resistance to evil, was dying—literally destroyed by the sight of human suffering surrounding him, and of people's indifference toward their neighbors' suffering. In yet another letter to Stanislavsky, written shortly before Sulerzhitsky's death, we find the following lines:

Oh, my God, how bitterly, how ardently and warmly I cried this entire morning. I cried so, my pillow, and my hands got wet. Why did I cry? Because, there are children. Many children in the streets with hands, thin as sticks. [. . .] Because there is such an endless number of the newly born in the orphanage with thin, withered, old faces and with pale, hardly moving fingers; they lay in rows, lonely, on tables, with numbers sewn onto them, hungrily gasping for air; they scream, hungry, to exhaustion; they quiet down and wither, and die, looking into the empty space, their dying eyes trying to find love in this emptiness; yearning for love, they die lonely in their wet, cold diapers.

(Polyakova 2006: 274–75)

An ardent follower of Tolstoy, Sulerzhitsky, on the verge of his death, let out a purely Dostoyevskian cry. His letter, unintentionally, is almost a direct quotation from Dmitry Karamazov's dream on the fateful night of his arrest. In the dream Dmitry sees a group of hungry, frozen peasant women, their skin dark, standing by the side of the road, next to a burnt-down village. In the hands of one of the women is a babe—crying, hungry, his clothes frozen. Overwhelmed by the spectacle, Dmitry exclaims:

Tell me, why it is those mothers stand there? Why are people poor? Why is the babe poor? Why is the steppe barren? Why don't they hug each other and kiss? Why don't they sing the songs of joy? Why are they so dark from black misery? Why don't they feed the babe?

(Dostoyevsky 1922: 547)

When Sulerzhitsky, defeated morally and physically, passed away in December 1916, Vakhtangov was the one to summarize his lessons, to rightly name Sulerzhitsky's credo, and to call on the Studio to carry it into the future.[1] He did, in fact, carry it into the future in his Studio works created after Sulerzhitsky's death. Six years later, Vakhtangov himself was dying, surrounded by his students. Vakhtangov was dying in excruciating pain, and the times were, perhaps, even more bloody and unjust than the one in which his teacher had died. Despite all that, and despite the injustice of dying at the height of his creative powers, Vakhtangov was dying as a victor.

---

1 See *Sourcebook* (2011: 235–40).

No less sensitive to the worldly evil, and to the human suffering, than his teacher, Vakhtangov was, nevertheless, leaving this world as someone who possessed a secret ultimate knowing (see Plate 20). Vakhtangov, whose artistic style and philosophy can be compared with Dostoyevsky's more than with Tolstoy's, nevertheless acquired a truly Tolstovian wisdom and objectivity. In the summer of 1915 he wrote to one of his students from the Sulerzhitskys' Crimean retreat:

> I no more think about the war, or rather I no more think of it with fear. [. . .] It was inevitable, and therefore it was necessary. It will serve the betterment of the humanity: as a result of it, fewer wars will follow—2–3.
>
> And then peace will come to earth.
>
> Prior to the war, people became bad, egotistical and cheerless. If the course of history requires that we be killed by people—so be it. I was afraid of it before—and now I calmed down. This was aided by my careful reading of *War and Peace*; I only now truly understood this remarkable book.
>
> (Ivanov 2011 vol. II: 108)

As every great student, Vakhtangov tried to absorb his teacher Sulerzhitsky's strength, while learning from his mistakes. Nevertheless, Vakhtangov's independent path as the leader of his own Studio resembled Sulerzhitsky's—both in its strengths, and in its weaknesses. In many ways, Vakhtangov-the-Studio-leader mimicked his teacher Sulerzhitsky, and yet in many ways, he remained original. At the First Studio, he picked up the reins from Sulerzhitsky at the time of the deepest crisis in Russian society and at the studio itself. Vakhtangov tried to resolve this crisis, connected with the Bolshevik Revolution, while working on the First Studio production of Ibsen's *Rosmersholm*.

17 Ibsen's *Rosmersholm*

The inception: directorial plan of *Rosmersholm*

On the surface, the plot of Ibsen's *Rosmersholm* fits a typical Vakhtangov "scenario." "The last, childless leaf of a once powerful family branch" (*Sourcebook* 2011: 217)—Johannes Rosmer (see Figure 17.1)—reverses on his conservative ideas. By doing so, he challenges the very order of life established by his ancestors. The stagnant world of the familial Rosmersholm estate is described in Vakhtangov's directorial plan as the classic kingdom of death. The very drapes of Rosmersholm are soaked in "silence and order, austerity and stableness, brutality and unbending will" (*Sourcebook* 2011: 214). Rosmersholm appears in Vakhtangov's directorial notes as a major force, and one of the main "characters" in the play:

> A single will and a single spirit has always reigned here. The only reason these heavy sofas, tables, and armchairs—massive, ancestral, and silent—keep their stillness and don't die of shame for the only black sheep in the Rosmer family, is that their body is wooden, and they cannot move.
>
> (*Sourcebook* 2011: 214–15)

Rebecca, a young American woman, a former companion for Rosmer's sickly wife, Beata, stayed in the house after Beata's suicide. By the start of the play, Rebecca has become Rosmer's ideological disciple. Inspired by his new friend, Rosmer decides to leave Rosmersholm and preach emancipation to the common people. Rebecca is ready to follow Rosmer on his missionary path.

At that very time, Rosmer's old teacher Ulrich Brendel, another source of inspiration behind Rosmer's revolutionary turnaround, appears on his student's doorstep. Brendel is down on his luck, and

Plate 1 Pavel Uzunov's preliminary set design for *The Deluge*, 1914. Courtesy of Vakhtangov Theatre Museum.

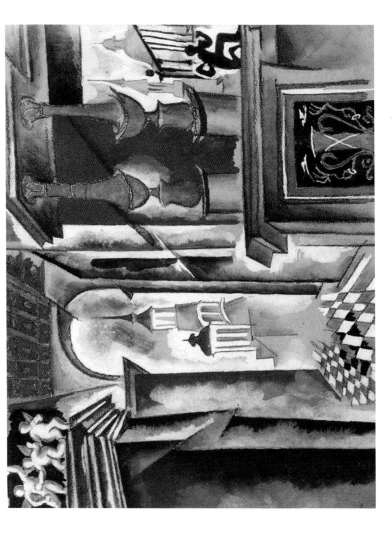

Plate 2 Ignaty Nivinsky's set design for Act 1 of *Erik XIV*, 1920. Courtesy of Vakhtangov Theatre Museum.

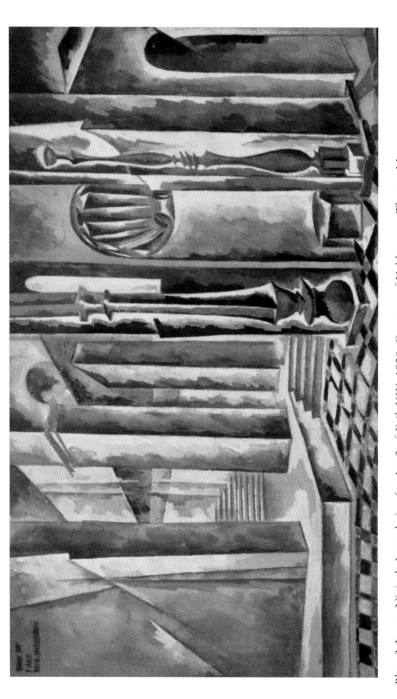

Plate 3 Ignaty Nivinsky's set design for Act 2 of *Erik XIV*, 1920. Courtesy of Vakhtangov Theatre Museum.

Plate 4 Ignaty Nivinsky's set design for Act 3 of *Erik XIV*, 1920. Courtesy of Vakhtangov Theatre Museum.

Plate 5 Ignaty Nivinsky's design of King Erik's costume for *Erik XIV*, 1920. Courtesy of Vakhtangov Theatre Museum.

Plate 6 Ignaty Nivinsky's design of Queen Mother's costume for *Erik XIV*, 1920. Courtesy of Vakhtangov Theatre Museum.

Plate 7 Ignaty Nivinsky's design of procurator Persson's costume for *Erik XIV*, 1920. Courtesy of Vakhtangov Theatre Museum.

Plate 8 Ignaty Nivinsky's design of Karin's costume for *Erik XIV*, 1920. Courtesy of Vakhtangov Theatre Museum.

Plate 9 Ignaty Nivinsky's design of warrant officer Max's costume for *Erik XIV*, 1920. Courtesy of Vakhtangov Theatre Museum.

Plate 10 Isaak Rabinovich's set design for *The Wedding*, 1921. Courtesy of Vakhtangov Theatre Museum.

Plate 11 Natan Altman's design of Third Batlan's costume for *The Dybbuk*, 1921. © The Israel Goor Theatre Archives and Museum (non-profit organization).

Plate 12
Natan Altman's design of
Wailing Woman's costume for
Act 1 of *The Dybbuk*, 1921.
© The Israel Goor Theatre
Archives and Museum
(non-profit organization).

Plate 13
Natan Altman's design of
Hannah Hendler's costume
(The Toad) for *The Dybbuk*,
1921. © The Israel Goor
Theatre Archives and Museum
(non-profit organization).

Plate 14 Natan Altman's design of In-Laws' costumes for *The Dybbuk*, 1921.
© The Israel Goor Theatre Archives and Museum (non-profit
organization).

Plate 15
Natan Altman's design of
Nechama Wiener's costume
(Beggar Woman) for *The
Dybbuk*, 1921. © The Israel
Goor Theatre Archives and
Museum (non-profit
organization).

Plate 16
Natan Altman's design of Ben
Ari Raikin's costume for *The
Dybbuk*, 1921. © The Israel
Goor Theatre Archives and
Museum (non-profit
organization).

Plate 17 Natan Altman's set design for Act 2 (Sender's House) of *The Dybbuk*, 1921. Courtesy Arsis Design.

Plate 18 Ignaty Nivinsky's stage platform for *Princess Turandot*, 1921. Courtesy of Arsis Design.

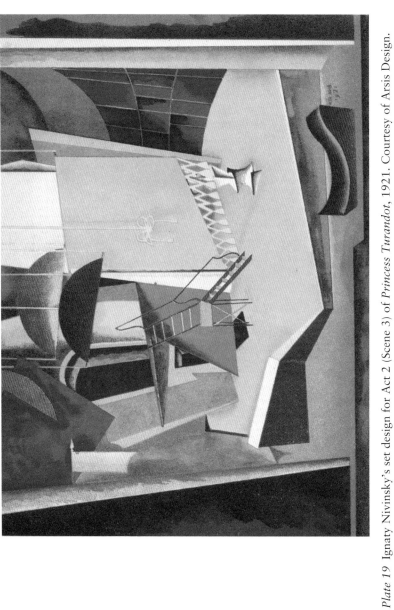

Plate 19 Ignaty Nivinsky's set design for Act 2 (Scene 3) of *Princess Turandot*, 1921. Courtesy of Arsis Design.

Plate 20 Konstantin Korovin's unfinished portrait of Yevgeny Vakhtangov, May 1922. Courtesy of Vakhtangov Theatre Museum.

Figure 17.1 Grigory Khmara as Rosmer in *Rosmersholm*, 1918. Courtesy of Vakhtangov Theatre Museum.

looks more like a homeless drunkard than an academic; nevertheless,
he is also determined to start his life anew. He will preach revolutionary ideas to the locals. Brendel's arrival strengthens Rosmer's
determination to follow his new path.

   The forces of death respond to the challenge. Rosmer's conservative
friends are appalled by his change. Their own political weight may be
diminished by the betrayal of a man as influential in the local circles as
Rosmer. The left-wing camp is also stirred by the prospects of Rosmer's
support. Rosmer's former brother-in-law, the arch conservative Kroll,
and the unscrupulous left-wing newspaper man Mortensgard, appear
at Rosmer's house. Coincidently, they both bring Rosmer to suspect

that his ideological companion, Rebecca, may be the cause of his wife's death.

Rosmer interrogates Rebecca and finds out that she was in love with him for some time, and that she, in fact, did indirectly encourage Beata's suicide. (Apparently, the sickly Beata learned of Rebecca's love for Rosmer and decided not to stand in the way of this love.) It is at this crucial moment of recognition that the old philosopher Brendel makes his second and final appearance in Rosmer's house. He abandoned all of his aspirations to transform and fully embraced his own downfall. This degraded and deeply disillusioned man now appears as a perfect caricature on Rosmer's naive idealism.

The specter of the white horses (a symbol of death in the play) has been seen in the sky. The dead Rosmersholm celebrates its victory—Rosmer is now disillusioned in his progressive ideas; he becomes convinced that he too is responsible for his wife's death, however indirectly. Rosmer concludes that he does not have the right to preach to the people when his own conscience is not clear. He reconciles with his conservative friends.

In the end, however, Rosmer discovers that he cannot let go of Rebecca. He has a talk with Rebecca and offers her the chance to become the mistress of Rosmersholm estate. Rebecca, who used to hold this as her fondest desire, can no longer settle for domestic bliss. Neither can Rebecca and Rosmer any longer embark upon their lofty mission. Their guilty conscience prevents them from facing the people. Unable to fulfill their dream, the couple agrees to end their lives together. Holding hands, Rosmer and Rebecca will plummet into the same waterfall where Beata met her end.

Vakhtangov, in his directorial plan, recorded the following fantastical vision of the *Rosmersholm* finale:

> The white horses darted past. There is no getting away now . . .
>
> Now the dead Rosmersholm is triumphant.
>
> The sofas, tables, and armchairs squeak—they can breathe freely now.
>
> The drape folds rustle viciously.
>
> The portraits' eyes gleam.
>
> Praise be to the gods of the past—we have been rid of the evil spirits.
>
> The white horses will take them right now.
>
> They have been crushed, those pathetic, tiny creatures that dared trespass against what is ours . . .
>
> But what's this?

Why do these people, condemned to death, look so bright and radiant?

Why is this woman so festively clad in her shroud, and why are the flowers in her hands so joyful?

Why does a triumphant Rosmer embrace her, and walk toward the dreadful footbridge so freely, resolutely, and radiantly?

(*Sourcebook* 2011: 216)

In Vakhtangov's interpretation, Rebecca and Rosmer's suicide was not the act of desperation, but their last challenge to death. By wiping out the very Rosmer dynasty, they clear the way for the new people to come. They go to their end joyfully, without fear, and they win in the end. Their joyful act ends the rule of the stagnant Rosmersholm, once and for all:

Remove the drapes, carry out the furniture, take down the portraits—for *they* have died, *they* are corpses now.

They could not withstand the daring flight.

The white horse had come for *them*.

(*Sourcebook* 2011: 216–17)

The "perfect" Theatre of the Mystery scenario, drawn by Vakhtangov for *Rosmersholm*, unexpectedly misfired. Upon the production's opening in 1918, it went almost unnoticed. Apparently the director and his cast, as well as their audiences, outlived the Sulerzhitskian Theatre of Mystery. Vakhtangov's *Rosmersholm*, premiered in 1918, broke the triad of harmony (Author—Time—Creative Collective) to be formulated by Vakhtangov in the years to come. While remaining true to the First Studio credo, as established by Sulerzhitsky, *Rosmersholm* did not absorb the spirit of the time.

In the history of the Moscow Art Theatre, however, Vakhtangov's production of *Rosmersholm* became an unprecedented event in, at least, three aspects. Firstly, in *Rosmersholm*, Vakhtangov, for the first time in MAT history, abandoned the art of physical characterization and introduced the art of internal grotesque. Secondly, in *Rosmersholm*, Vakhtangov entered the artistic sphere of Nemirovich-Danchenko. The detailed discussion between the two directors, following the *Rosmersholm* dress rehearsal, contributed to their understanding and appreciation of each other's talents.[1]

---

1 See *Sourcebook* (2011: 317, 326).

Finally, *Rosmersholm* marked the first (and, perhaps, only) occasion when two MAT elders, Olga Knipper-Chekhova (see Figure 17.2) and Leonid Leonidov (see Figure 17.4), acted in a major First Studio production; it also marked the first (and only) time Vakhtangov collaborated with the MAT elders, as a director. This was a mixed blessing as the eclectic cast made the individuality of the creative ensemble muddled, and difficult to define. The MAT old-timers, although significant artists in their own right, could not completely embrace the new artistic principles introduced by Vakhtangov.

The surviving detailed directorial plan of *Rosmersholm*, written by Vakhtangov, is the only document of that kind ever created by the director. It evidences how seriously Vakhtangov prepared for this

Figure 17.2 Viktor Simov's portrait of Olga Knipper-Chekhova as Rebecca in *Rosmersholm*, 1918. Courtesy of Moscow Art Theatre Museum.

work. In Vakhtangov's mind, this production was meant to summarize his experience of several years, and open a new chapter in the First Studio's work. In his directorial plan, Vakhtangov carefully outlined the intentions of the author, Ibsen, and also strived to identify where he could employ Ibsen to fulfill the First Studio's credo, still identified by him as "The Theatre of Mystery."

In Vakhtangov's mind, the *Rosmersholm* actor was supposed to enter their work as one enters a temple—spiritually honest and unpretentious, cleansed from anything superficial, inessential, or assumed. Therefore, the transformation to be achieved in *Rosmersholm* had to happen "by the power of the inner impulse" (*Sourcebook* 2011: 211). This means that the actor was supposed to remain their own creative self onstage and be transformed by the deep sense of their artistic mission—rather than by the given circumstances of the play. In *Rosmersholm*'s directorial plan, Vakhtangov formulated an entirely different type of transformation from the one taught by any other school.

Vakhtangov insisted that *Rosmersholm* actors should not hide behind the mask of the character, but rather offer their own soul as material that would create the character. As a result, the entire persona of the artist-creator should be present on the *Rosmersholm* stage; the *artistic* significance of this persona is supposed to stand behind the character, thus making it spiritually a more sizable human. Some inner aspects of the actor's persona may be utilized less than the others, as prescribed by the "character." At the same time, the unutilized sides of the actor's soul will remain as a hidden perspective, making the character appear "bottomless" to the audience.

The principles of acting outlined in *Rosmersholm* prescribed that actors must proceed from their own creative individuality, rather than from character and characterization. At the same time, Vakhtangov did not yet know what kind of transformation, and what kind of outcome, this device might lead to. He sensed, quite subconsciously, that such a principle of transformation might allow his actors to make a step into the realm of tragedy, harmonious with the turbulent revolutionary times. A hint of the kind of transformation Vakhtangov wished to accomplish is present in his directorial plan. When describing the two main characters, Rebecca and Rosmer, Vakhtangov writes of the anticipated effect of the new type of transformation—to be achieved "by the power of the inner impulse":

> The faces of Rosmer and Rebecca, thin and pale, reflect the subtlest curve of their spirit and thought. Their eyes are horrific and alive with overwhelming desires. They are horrific, because it

is terrifying to see such a transformation in an actor. These eyes are joyfully excited, as *they are not the eyes of those who lie, but of those who believe.*

(*Sourcebook* 2011: 215)

Vakhtangov speaks of the absolute actors' faith in the power of their mission. Anything less amounts to a lie in Vakhtangov's eyes. Some of the most insightful of Vakhtangov's contemporaries, such as Pavel Markov, recognized his formula of transformation. Markov wrote on this different approach to character in 1925:

Vakhtangov dove for the essence of the man-actor and suddenly discovered that no split [between actor and character] exists. He discovered that for the actor the truth of theatre consists of the following fact. While playing his character, and freely owning the character, the actor must speak through the mask of the character— his own truth, intrinsic to him alone. Where the character used to be predominant, he [Vakhtangov] gave the right of dominance to the actor's individuality. When Vakhtangov did that, all of the "system's" principles gained a new life—brilliant, bold and free.

(Markov 1925: 148)

In the end, Vakhtangov became the only *Rosmersholm* actor bold enough to make a breakthrough into the realm of the tragic grotesque. On the opening night, he had to step in for the sick Leonidov in the role of Brendel (see Figure 17.3). As a result, the smaller role of Brendel, as performed by Vakhtangov, suddenly stood at the center of the production. Vakhtangov's Brendel became paramount to the overall meaning of the piece.[2]

Nemirovich-Danchenko, who had first-hand experience of working on the Ibsen play, considered this character one of the play's main challenges:

Rosmersholm was previously staged at the First Studio's metropolis—at the Art Theater. It was a failure—my failure, as much as the actors'.[3] The role of Brendel presented the most problems.

2 Similarly, in Vakhtangov's *The Festival of Peace*, the episodic character of old servant Friebe, performed by Michael Chekhov, could be perceived as key to the main idea of the production.

3 Nemirovich's own production of *Rosmersholm* failed at the Moscow Art Theatre ten years prior to the opening of Vakhtangov's First Studio production.

Figure 17.3 Vakhtangov as Brendel in *Rosmersholm*, 1918. Courtesy of
Arsis Design.

Neither the actor who played the part, nor I could discover the
right synthesis of satire and drama. In the meantime, this synthesis
was necessary in order to perceive this liberal, who went broke
before he ever accomplished anything.

(Nemirovich-Danchenko interviewed in
Khersonsky 1940b: 11)

At the same time, Nemirovich-Danchenko (1984b: 454) claimed that
Vakhtangov, in his performance of Brendel, not only successfully
solved the riddle of this role, but also discovered new theatrical principles: "The amazing ease with which Vakhtangov played Brendel

[. . .] gave a distinct perception of the tragic forms he sketched for the new theatre."

It is not surprising that Vakhtangov's sympathies lay with the old philosopher Brendel. After all, Brendel had a lot in common with all of the focal characters of the previous Vakhtangov productions. Like Friebe from *The Festival of Peace*, Brendel, a political windbag, was perceived by the audience as a jester, the crooked mirror onto the world of the play. In *Rosmersholm*, Brendel's appearance satirized the incapacity, and absence of true principles, in the play's liberals. In addition to that, Brendel shed light onto the utopian nature of the noble Rosmer's intentions.

The character of Brendel also had a lot in common with the old Scholz of *The Festival of Peace*. Like Scholz, Brendel was a wanderer, and an alcoholic, who abandoned his bourgeois prosperity and became a declassed homeless man. Like Frazer of *The Deluge*, Brendel was bankrupt—both financially and ideologically. In Vakhtangov's interpretation, this jester, nevertheless, appeared as tragic, and as a man who possessed the ultimate knowledge. The photograph of Vakhtangov as Brendel resembles another wanderer—the mad King Lear. It is not by chance that Nemirovich heard tragic overtones in Vakhtangov's performance.

Pavel Markov echoed Nemirovich's thought on the key importance of the character of Brendel for Vakhtangov's production. When describing the style of acting achieved by Vakhtangov in *Rosmersholm*, Markov wrote:

> Deeply saturated characters and reserved passions, at some moments, burst out in a storm of agitated emotions—at such moments, actors' gestures became grand and wide, their eyes—sharp and fiery, their voices—mighty and expanded. At such moments, feelings and thought "yelled, roared with laughter, and screamed" on the stage— the intimacy gave way to the thematic depth opened up by Vakhtangov. These tendencies were especially clear in the character of Brendel. Vakhtanov wrote that "Brendel remembers an idea of Rosmer; he remembers him as one would remember an aroma".[4] Brendel walked through the stage as such a strange (defamiliarization) being. He appeared from the twilight, and he disappeared into the twilight. When he spoke to Rebecca [. . .], listeners felt connected with his mysterious and cold speech.
>
> (Markov 1925: 137)

4 *Sourcebook* (2011: 224).

Figure 17.4 Leonid Leonidov as Brendel in *Rosmersholm*, 1918. Courtesy of
Vakhtangov Theatre Museum.

One of Vakhtangov's close First Studio of MAT colleagues, director
and actor Boris Sushkevich, expressed an unorthodox idea that
Vakhtangov was an actor first and foremost (Sushkevich 1959: 370).
Sushkevich's voice, although not entirely unsupported, has not been
heard in the criticism on Vakhtangov. Clearly, Vakhtangov is better
known today as a director than an actor. At the same time, one might
notice that Vakhtangov's method of organizing a performance, in all
of his First Studio productions, is an actor's way. Whatever character
Vakhtangov identified himself with as an actor (and ultimately either
performed, or wanted to perform) became the key to both the ideological and artistic world of the performance.

Within the Moscow Art Theatre troupe, Vakhtangov had his artistic
alter-ego—the great Michael Chekhov. These two artists, who
appeared inseparable to all of their colleagues, shared some of the
same parts (Frazer, Master Pierre), or rivaled over a part (Erik XIV).[5]
When Vakhtangov directed Chekhov in a role, according to
Vakhtangov himself, he would give Chekhov "everything he himself

5 Although the role of Erik was made famous by Michael Chekhov, Vakhtangov
   dreamed of performing this part.

had for a role" (Deykun 1984: 355). Vakhtangov vicariously lived through Michael Chekhov, and that includes the parts Vakhtangov ultimately did not get to perform (Erik, Friebe). It is these parts, as performed by Michael Chekhov, or by Vakhtangov himself, or both, that ultimately *interpreted* Vakhtangov's First Studio production.

Vakhtangov's reliance on a single role to interpret, or mobilize, a production does not imply that the director did not achieve a harmonious ensemble in his works. The significance of the creative collective for Vakhtangov was paramount; in this collective, however, everyone fulfilled their own unique function. Vakhtangov's ensemble always had a distinct center. Ultimately, every actor in Vakhtangov's collective was interpreting the play by occupying a certain place in relation to a key production character.

As a result, the audience saw the reality of a Vakhtangov production as reflected in such a character's soul. Thus they saw *The Festival of Peace* as if reflected in the servant Friebe; *The Deluge*—as if reflected through Frazer; *Rosmersholm*—as if reflected through Brendel. In all three cases, the key character appeared to the audience as essentially tragic, despite the fact that a strong satirical element was also present in each of Vakhtangov's key characters. Perhaps it is this very combination of comedic and tragic, concentrated within the same character, that made it stand out from the ensemble. Such a play on contrasts constituted the secret of Vakhtangov's art—it was responsible for the inimitable lightness of Vakhtangov's tragedy.

Edward Gordon Craig's influence upon Vakhtangov

Vakhtangov's tendency to present the world of the play through the prism of one of its characters, on the surface, resembles Craig's concept of mono-drama.[6] At the same time, there is a substantial difference between Craig's device, as outlined in his directorial plan for the MAT's *Hamlet*, and Vakhtangov's methods. Craig did not intend for the world of Shakespeare's *Hamlet* to be seen through its main character's eyes; rather, Craig-the-director measured the world of the play, and its characters, by Hamlet's measure. As Craig considered Hamlet as an ideal man, such a measure inevitably downsized those characters surrounding Hamlet.

Vakhtangov, on the contrary, saw the world of his plays through the eyes of Friebe, Frazer, Brendel—these characters' point of view

6 See p. 56.

contributed to the inimitable style of the given production. The characters of *Rosmersholm*, for example, were seen not in relation to Brendel but rather through the prism of his *atmosphere*: tragically mysterious, crooked (defamiliarized) and unbearably light. This atmosphere existed in the play before Brendel's appearance, and it remained there after he was gone. When Brendel appeared, however, the atmosphere of the play materialized in him.

Nevertheless, Gordon Craig's influence can be traced in Vakhtangov's *Rosmersholm*. When thinking of an ideal designer for his future production of *Rosmersholm*, Vakhtangov wrote: "Out of all Moscow Art Theatre designers ([Alexandre] Benois [1870–1960], [Mstislav] Dobuzhinsky [1875–1958], and [Victor] Simov [1858–1935]), Gordon Craig comes the closest [to the ideal]" (*Sourcebook* 2011: 214). In Craig's design for the MAT's *Hamlet*, the courtiers' gilded costumes were set upon the background of 25 giant canvas-covered screens, and 30 similar cubes. Craig's design created the kind of *theatrical environment* that symbolized the royal palace of Elsinore, rather than literally representing it. In that regard, Craig's design was revolutionary for the MAT—it created a purely theatrical structure of the stage space. At the same time, the choice of the golden texture, and the gigantic size for the screens, did hint at the royal palace's grandeur, and at the predominance of the materialistic values, foreign to prince Hamlet. Craig's set was capable of evoking the *atmosphere* of the place of action and serving as an actual setting for the play, while also contributing to the artistic image of the production. The harmony of the symbolic and the illusory, created by Craig in his set for the MAT's *Hamlet*, was unique, and it clearly influenced Vakhtangov.

In his concept of *Rosmersholm*'s design, Vakhtangov tried to follow Craig's example. At the same time, in 1918 Vakhtangov was not prepared to step into the purely symbolic realm. His *Rosmersholm* theatrical environment only toyed with the idea of a symbolist set, while creating a realistic illusion of the actual place—the Rosmersholm estate (see Figure 17.5). In his directorial plan of the Ibsen play, Vakhtangov wrote:

> I imagine heavy, somber, dreadful drapes.
> These are not the drapes of the theatre school stage.
> Neither are these the abstract drapes.
> This is not a "directorial concept".
> These drapes are a fact.
> They actually exist.
> They are the drapes of the Rosmersholm estate.
>
> (*Sourcebook* 2011: 214)

Figure 17.5 Set design by Mikhail Libakov for Act 1 of *Rosmersholm*, 1918. Courtesy of Vakhtangov Theatre Museum.

Similarly, the lighting in *Rosmersholm*, as outlined by Vakhtangov, strove to create its own artistic image. At the same time, Vakhtangov's lighting was also carefully "justified" so that it would appear realistic:

> When the lamp is lit, it becomes even darker and gloomier in this room. Then the portraits' austere, unmoving eyes sharpen, as they pierce the darkness below the ceiling. They gaze persistently at the bright spot—the circle around the lamp, where only the faces of the new people, excited at something new, can be seen brightly and softly.
> [. . .]
> When the lamp is lit, the outline of the furniture and the drapes is barely visible. In the narrow field of light—people's faces appear, especially their eyes, and the faint outlines of their clothing; perhaps, the clothing is not even visible. Above them are the piercing eyes of the portraits.
>
> (*Sourcebook* 2011: 215)

It was noted by critics and Vakhtangov scholars that the lights seemed to have had an independent life in Vakhtangov's production:

> Vakhtangov used lights as one of his chief directorial devices—at times he immersed the stage in darkness, at other times he flooded it with blinding light, or threw glares onto the stage. Through these simple means, Vakhtangov symbolized Rosmer's house, where life is uneasy and somber, with ghosts walking all around it.
>
> (Markov 1925: 137)

The ghostly atmosphere of Vakhtangov's *Rosmersholm* anticipated two of his final masterpieces—*Erik XIV* and *The Dybbuk*. The immaterial realm of the mysterious permeated the space of the production; this sensation was further amplified by the strong sense of the larger mysterious realm that *surrounded* Rosmersholm. The atmosphere of the mysterious was created not only through the use of lighting; it was supported by the quality of acting Vakhtangov achieved in his production, especially in his own performance. Vakhtangov's treatment of the mysterious in *Rosmersholm* also echoed Craig's ideas, as outlined in his book collection *On the Art of the Theatre*. Craig's influence upon Vakhtangov is especially evident when it comes to the portrayal of the supernatural in tragedy as intangible and invisible matter.

While Vakhtangov's *Rosmersholm* was a definite step toward pure theatricality, it did not fully break with the First Studio's tradition of spiritual realism. On the contrary, Vakhtangov's expressive means amplified this tradition. The lighting score, featuring a series of flowing narrow spotlights, for example, was meant to govern the audience's attention, and concentrate it on the slightest movements of an actor's soul.

On the other hand, Vakhtangov's symbolic design, however half-hearted, contributed to the development of his future model of theatre. The draped environment foreshadowed the director's future concept of theatrical platform, inspired by Meyerhold. (This concept was fully developed by Vakhtangov in his production of *Princess Turandot*.) Despite his initial directorial plan, Vakhtangov treated Ibsen's *Rosmersholm* as a *pretext for a performance*, thus also anticipating his future masterpieces.

Part III
The Vakhtangov Studio

18 In the beginning, 1913–1915

The Lanin Estate

Vakhtangov's own studio originated in 1913—the same year the First Studio of MAT opened its doors for the audiences. Unlike the First Studio of MAT, Vakhtangov's studio was not founded by actors. Neither was it started by Vakhtangov himself. A group of Moscow university students, who were interested in serious theatre, formed a dramatic circle. The students invited Vakhtangov, already a popular teacher at the time, to head the circle. It soon received the fitting name of The Students' Studio.

Vakhtangov accepted the students' invitation with enthusiasm, even though his honorarium could hardly cover cab fare. The studio had no space of its own, so meetings and rehearsals were held at studio members' apartments. The studio members soon outstayed their parents', relatives', or roommates' hospitality—rehearsals had to be moved to restaurants' private rooms.

Vakhtangov yielded to his new students' wishes and started directing them in a contemporary play—Boris Zaitsev's *The Lanin Estate*. He did not particularly care for the play, but he used the rehearsal process to get to know his students. Once again, Vakhtangov provoked his students into performance by not separating between the character and the actor. He looked for the affinity between particular studio members and Zaitsev's characters. He used interpersonal dynamics within the studio to create the performance's life.

The Lanin Estate rehearsals[1] were an elaborate play where studio members engaged in a thrilling game with themselves, and with each other, while seemingly creating the tapestry of the piece. Vakhtangov

---

1 For the records of *The Lanin Estate* rehearsals see *Sourcebook* (2011: 245–56).

defined the "through line" of the performance as "intoxication with love" (*Sourcebook* 2011: 250). Young studio members indeed were intoxicated with love toward each other, the play, their studio, and the new leader. This atmosphere, sustained by Vakhtangov, allowed him to conduct "intimate, candid rehearsals, where actors were required to literally lay out their whole soul and reveal all their subtlest qualities and emotional experiences" (Leonid Volkov, interviewed in Khersonsky 1940b: 55–56).

Vakhtangov, who clearly saw the play's shortcomings, nevertheless capitalized on his students' connection with the material. He considered his job not to separate between the life of the studio and the life on the stage. As evident from Leonid Volkov's memoir, Vakhtangov even used this principle in the performance design:

> *The Lanin Estate* design was quite meager.
>
> Vakhtangov always introduced elements of improvisation in his work. Quite often—this is before we had a space of our own—he liked to use what was there at hand to create a costume, set, or an *etude*. This could be some rags, curtains—anything random.
>
> He always loved to organize a rehearsal mischievously—to put on what was at hand, to place something on the stage (to create a mood), and theatre was ready to go.
>
> The same improvisational approach was used in *The Lanin Estate* design.
>
> (Leonid Volkov, interviewed in Khersonsky 1940b: 56)

Vakhtangov treated *The Lanin Estate* rehearsal process as a "school on the go" (see Figure 18.1). While some aspects of the inner technique finally made their way into the rehearsal process, no part of the external technique was ever approached in *The Lanin Estate*. Vakhtangov was justified in his reluctance to demonstrate to his actors how they should move and speak—in order to convey their inner life. This would have killed the students' psychological connection with the play. The actors would have become mere imitators of the director's form. In the meantime, Vakhtangov considered his goal to instigate each of his students' creative individuality. It is for that reason that he did not want to focus on the external approach.

Vakhtangov's approach to *The Lanin Estate* utilized, among other things, an under-explored part of the actor's inner technique, such as *atmosphere*. Vakhtangov's concept of atmosphere differed from that of the MAT. As evident from the rehearsal records of *The Lanin Estate*, by 1914 Vakhtangov developed his own approach, where

Figure 18.1 Vakhtangov rehearsing *The Lanin Estate*, 1915. Vakhtangov seated at the table, right, with a script in his hand. Courtesy of Arsis Design.

atmosphere was achieved by shifting an ensemble's point of view on the environment. MAT's atmosphere was produced by the use of stage effects (lighting, sound, etc.). In addition to that, a common emotional mood uniting the majority of participants in a scene was often used to create atmosphere.

In contrast to MAT's approach, Vakhtangov's atmosphere was *perceived* by an actor from the theatrical space. This space, of course, had to creatively transform by the power of the actors' imagination. As Vakhtangov himself put it, atmosphere "is not taken from within, but from without, from the image [. . .], 'from out there' " (*Sourcebook* 2011: 248). By the time of his death in 1922, however, Vakhtangov arrived at the conclusion that Festivity (heightened and ecstatic existence on the threshold of life and death) constitutes both essence and atmosphere of every stage object and circumstance. He told his students:

> No atmospheres should exist in the theatre. Only joy should exist in the theatre, and no atmospheres.
>
> (*Sourcebook* 2011: 151)

Vakhtangov achieved his desired goal in *The Lanin Estate*—his actors "lived" onstage. At the same time, his actors' emotions (and even some of the lines!) forever remained a secret for the opening night's audiences. This misfortune can be partially blamed on the size of the Moscow Hunters' Club, where the performance premiered. Vakhtangov's studio rented this historic space for a short technical period, and for the one and only performance. The grand auditorium of the Hunters' Club literally swallowed the feeble life of Vakhtangov's performers. Vakhtangov's "improvised set" looked even poorer on the Club's stage than it did in rehearsals.

The Hunters' Club in Moscow, where *The Lanin Estate* premiered on March 26, 1914, was established in the second part of the nineteenth century. By the end of the century, the original meaning of the organization was lost, and the Hunters' Club, located at number 6, Vozdvizhenka Street, was transformed into a cultural center. Stanislavsky himself made his professional debut on the stage of the Club. In the 1890s, Stanislavsky's Society of Art and Letters productions were performed there. Ironically, Stanislavsky was furious when he found out that Vakhtangov affiliated his name with the group of young amateurs. His displeasure was also provoked by the fact that the press reviews on *The Lanin Estate* were extremely negative. After *The Lanin Estate* incident, all of Vakhtangov's engagements outside of the MAT circle had to be approved by Stanislavsky.

Despite Stanislavsky's "orders," Vakhtangov continued to head his new Studio in secret. The Studio rented a space on Mansurov Lane, while Vakhtangov and his family rented a flat in the same building. This way, no outsider could tell if Vakhtangov conducted classes and rehearsals at the Studio. Moreover, every Studio member took an oath of secrecy. The atmosphere of conspiracy united members of the Vakhtangov Studio even more than the ecstatic experience of *The Lanin Estate*. The Vakhtangov Studio of the period resembled a religious order; the Sulerzhitsky model of the Studio-monastery was actually implemented.

Vakhtangov announced that there would be no more performances in the Studio's near future, and held to that promise—much to his students' disappointment and to his own surprise. Formal exercises and scene study followed. No public productions were presented by the Vakhtangov Studio for the next four and a half years. The three performance evenings, presented respectively in 1915, 1916, and 1917, featured some of the scenes developed in classes. These three evenings did not pursue the goal of the formal productions; rather they served to provide studio members with the essential experience of a *public* creative act.

Actor cultivation and training

At the Students' Studio, Vakhtangov conducted the daily work of "cultivating" his actors. He did so in the hope of developing an exclusive theatrical group. In addition to lectures on the art of theatre, exercises, scene study, and character work,[2] Vakhtangov conducted frequent talks with his students on the theme of theatre ethics and discipline. Here is an example of one such talk held shortly after the celebration of the Studio's one-year anniversary on November 27, 1914:

> December 5, 1914
> [. . .]
> *Vakhtangov*: I noticed something unhealthy in all of you. After the November 27th celebration, I noticed: you are letting yourselves loose. You go to the stage unwillingly. Can it be because you are not performing a play? If the play alone excites you, if you need a play for the sake of a play, there is nothing for me to do

2 Samples of such sessions can be found in *Sourcebook* (2011: 87–123, 171–90).

amongst you. In this case, I would become your director, not your teacher. But I don't think that this is the case. What is the reason then? I see that you are cooling off, although you attend your classes.

Having listened to some answers—personal circumstances get in the way, the mood within the society, the war, etc., Yevgeny Bogrationovich continues:

So, I decided: I will not direct a play with you; this only corrupts you. May the etudes substitute as a play for you. We will improvise. We will present a performance-improvisation. This is an excellent exercise: the audience is invited, and you don't know *how* to act, but you do know *what* to act. We will compose our own play. Think about it.

The next stage in your work, if the improvisation succeeds, might be *The Green Cockatoo* by Schnitzler.

(Vakhtangova et al. 1939: 287)

The conversation started by Vakhtangov on December 5, continued during the next class (December 11). One of the Studio "elders," Boris Vershilov,[3] attempted to express the mood of the collective:

VERSHILOV: *(to Yevgeny Bogrationovich):* Instead of making the demands of the absolute art of us, you are making them relative. You are not strict with us. Perhaps, this is the cause of our confusion.

VAKHTANGOV: I am not at all intending to stir you up. I repeat what I said many times, how I look at our work: we are resting here. (No one can reproach me for the lack of strictness.) My job is to give you tasks—*etudes*, and then I could say nothing. I don't even need to be in your classroom. The teacher's notes are not even that important. You now know yourself if you were in the circle [of attention]. The very opportunity to be onstage is valuable. An actor's struggle that takes place in you and cultivates [an actor] in you is what's valuable. My role is not just the one of a teacher and director, but of a mentor. The duty that lies on me is to create an atmosphere. You placed upon my shoulders not just

---

3 Boris Vershilov (1893–1957), Russian director and teacher, one of the founding members of the Vakhtangov Studio. Vershilov left the Studio in 1919, and joined the MAT and its Second Studio.

the work of leading the Studio, but also the sole responsibility for the studio.

(Vakhtangova et al. 1939: 287–88)

At his Studio, Vakhtangov continued to act as an invited director. He did so, in part, to stimulate his students' initiative and their sense of studio ownership. On the organizational level, Vakhtangov established the Studio Council, a self-governing body that consisted of the oldest and most dedicated studio members. Vakhtangov himself, however, frequently addressed the Council, urging them to think through or reconsider their decisions.

Granting or rejecting studio membership was among the most important decisions made by the Council. Vakhtangov carefully examined the Council's motivations in these decisions, exhibiting an insight into his students' inner world and inmost thoughts—often teaching a lesson of complicity to his students.

Vakhtangov instilled in his students an understanding of the role art must play in their lives, and of the privileged status they enjoyed as Studio members. On one occasion, he wrote to his Studio:

> If only you knew how rich you are.
> If only you knew what happiness you possess in your life. If only you knew how wasteful you are. It is always so: you appreciate things when you lose them. If only you knew how sad I am at the thought that you too will have to discover this belated appreciation.
> What people strive to achieve for years, what they spend their entire lives for—you have it: you have your own corner.

(Vendrovskaya 1959: 60)

For two years—from 1914 to 1916—the Studio members worked on preparatory exercises and improvised *études*. Scenes and short plays were also worked. As mentioned before, once a year these scenes were presented at a so-called Performance Evening. Many of the scenes were dramatizations of non-dramatic works by authors, such as Chekhov (see Figure 18.2), Gogol, and Maupassant (see Figure 18.3). Vakhtangov's leaning toward dramatizations, rather than scenes from plays, was not accidental.

In a work of drama, a young actor is relying almost exclusively on the dialogue as a source of information on their character. A great deal of imagination is required from a young actor in order to recreate an entirety of the character's world. On the contrary, non-dramatic

Figure 18.2 Performance evening of 1917. Dramatization of Anton Chekhov's short story *Ivan Matveyevich*. Ivan Matveyevich—Georgy Serov, Professor—Alexander Chernov. Courtesy of Arsis Design.

Figure 18.3 Performance evening of 1917. Dramatization of Guy de Maupassant's short story *The Port (Le Port)*. Célestin Duclos—Leonid Volkov. Françoise—Kseniya Semyonova. Courtesy of Arsis Design.

fiction can include character description and biography, psychological motivations behind the character's actions, descriptions of settings with their unique atmospheres, etc. In other words, a scene from a non-dramatic work (short story, novel, etc.) provides a welcome set of "given circumstances" to a beginning actor, thus aiding their character work.

Among the Vakhtangov Studio training "repertoire," the so-called *vaudevilles*—light one-act comedies with short musical numbers— played an important role (see Figure 18.4). French vaudeville, and its Russian reincarnation, was extremely popular in Russia in the nineteenth and early twentieth centuries.[4] Vakhtangov believed that *vaudevilles* provided excellent training material for a beginning actor. Playing a vaudeville character requires beginners to master the kind of psychology that puts them in a creative state, similar to child's play. Vaudeville, therefore, stimulates inner and outer freedom in an actor.

Figure 18.4 Performance evening of 1917. A Russian version, by Dmitry Mansfield (1851–1909), of a French one-act vaudeville, by Livret d'Honoré (1793–1858), *A Match Between Two Fires* (*Une allumette entre deux feux*). Florette Duplessy—Kseniya Kotlubai, Bajazet Leriche—Georgy Serov, Georgine Esmériau—Vera Kurina. Courtesy of Vakhtangov Theatre Museum.

4 Eugene Labiche's *The Italian Straw Hat* is an example of a full-length vaudeville still performed today.

Vaudeville also teaches an actor how to find emotional honesty, and to make instantaneous psychological transitions from ecstasy to despair, and vice versa—at a meteoric vaudevillian tempo.

The vaudeville structure—charming, but rather superficial—would break at the introduction of any heaviness. As a consequence, vaudeville asks an actor to develop an important quality of lightness and ease, both physical and psychological. Plasticity of movement, and the ability to make an organic transition from the spoken word to song and dance—these skills are also exercised and refined in a vaudevillian. Finally, in a distinctly Russian tradition of moral justification, Vakhtangov insisted that every vaudeville should feature a heroic or sad note; such a note would create an emotional contrast and "shade" the otherwise lighthearted vaudeville content.

Vakhtangov and *commedia dell'arte*: The Vakhtangov studio improvisation project

In December 1914 and January 1915, Vakhtangov developed with his students an improvised scenario in the *commedia dell'arte* spirit.[5] Three classical commedia characters—Harlequin, Columbine, and Pierrot—were transplanted from Italy to Russia. Vakhtangov turned them into three provincial Russian actors—Fedya, Dima, and Natasha, who, on Christmas Night, dreamed of bringing joy to those unfortunates in the world.

Vakhtangov's improvisation elaborated on the idea Maxim Gorky shared with Stanislavsky in February 1911 (Vinogradskaya 1971 vol. II: 273–74). At the time, Gorky lived in Italy, on Capri, and studied popular Italian theatre, *commedia dell'arte*. According to Gorky's thought, a new type of play could be created through improvisations executed by the young MAT actors. The role of the author (Gorky) would be to supply the original theme, characters and plot, and to fulfill the final literary shaping of the material. The majority of the play, however, would be developed by the improvising actors.

At Stanislavsky's request, Sulerzhitsky worked on the improvisational project idea at the First Studio in 1913; two years later Vakhtangov independently tried to fulfill it at his Studio. Neither attempt came to fruition. At the same time, the echo of Vakhtangov's

5 By originating this work, Vakhtangov partially fulfilled the promise he made to his actors following the Studio's one-year celebration. See pp. 131–2.

commedia dell'arte improvisations was later heard in the director's final masterpiece—*Princess Turandot*.

The art of the *commedia* was extremely popular among the Russian theatre visionaries at the start of the twentieth century. Meyerhold experimented with the *commedia* in his productions, such as Blok's *The Puppet Show* (1907, 1908, 1914) and Schnitzler's *Columbine's Scarf* (1910, 1916). He researched the Italian *commedia*, and published a magazine entitled *Love for Three Oranges*, dedicated to *commedia*. Vakhtangov saw Meyerhold's productions in St. Petersburg in 1914 and 1916. In 1915, he carefully studied the accounts of Meyerhold Studio's *commedia* experiments, published in *Love for Three Oranges*. None of the methods outlined in Meyerhold's productions and publications, however, produced a visible effect on Vakhtangov until he began his independent study of the Popular Theatre in 1918.

In the meantime, Popular Theatre philosophy and technique permeated Vakhtangov's individuality. Despite the fact that Stanislavsky seemingly marked Popular Theatre as a taboo in his first talk to the MAT youth,[6] Vakhtangov practiced Popular Theatre's principles in his work. While implementing the idea of the Theatre of Mystery, Vakhtangov subconsciously continued merging it with the Popular Theatre content. The element of improvisation, representative of Vakhtangov's style of work, was deeply connected with the Popular Theatre tradition. His vision of the theatrical collective as a closely knit family of performers was grounded in the phenomenon of the *commedia* traveling troupe. Equally grounded in the *commedia* was Vakhtangov's tendency to mix the actual life of the collective with the reality of the play.

Also significant is Vakhtangov's inner dissatisfaction with the Stanislavskian principles, such as external characterization, public solitude, and the fourth wall. Vakhtangov's search for a different kind of actor's "creative state" was based in his striving for a more honest and open communion between the audience and the performer. The prototype of this kind of communion can be found in Popular Theatre. Finally, Vakhtangov's principle characters—social outcasts and tragic clowns—belonged as much to the Popular Theatre as they did to the Theatre of Mystery.

Popular Theatre, and specifically *commedia dell'arte*, permeated the theatrical landscape at the start of the twentieth century. Several

6 See p. 54.

influential Russian artists of the time, besides Meyerhold, found inspiration in this rich theatrical period. Among them were poet Alexander Blok, theatre directors and visionaries Alexander Tairov and Nikolai Evreinov, as well as a group of prominent artists belonging to the *Mir Iskusstva* association. In the West, theatrical innovators, such as Max Reinhardt, Edward Gordon Craig, and Jacques Copeau, also interpreted the Italian *commedia* in their works. Among these contemporary interpretations of the *commedia dell'arte*, Vakhtangov's approach stood out as unique.

From the start, Vakhtangov was more interested in the aspect of the traveling *commedia* troupe as a closely knit collective of artists, where actors live as one family—literally and figuratively. In other words, Vakhtangov's emphasis did not fall on the stock characters, or the *commedia* masks. Neither was he interested in the traditional *commedia* scenarios. The *commedia* actors' techniques and way of life, however, fascinated Vakhtangov. The *commedia* troupe served for him as a prototype of a theatrical collective, a closed organism, a kind of artistic commune, where a particular type of actor is cultivated. According to Vakhtangov, an actor's spirit was steeled through such an upbringing.

As for the *commedia* masks, instead of concentrating on their historic and national aspect, Vakhtangov concentrated on the *psychological and moral phenomenon of a mask*. A *commedia* performer, who wears the same mask throughout his or her entire career, often becomes inseparable from the mask. Relationships between the members of the *commedia* collective, their lives and destinies are closely interwoven with the plots and characters they perform onstage. As a result, the actors' *actual life* and their *stage life* often become indistinguishable. This was the theme that deeply interested Vakhtangov. In 1915, the same year Vakhtangov worked on the *commedia* project with his students, the director wrote two *Scenarios for Marionette Theatre*. The main theme of the scenarios—life and art can become one in a theatrical production—was foreshadowing Vakhtangov's *Princess Turandot*.

In 1915, Vakhtangov had already discovered that a high level of spiritual maturity is required from an actor who wants to work with a mask. If performers are weak at their spiritual core, a mask can permeate their psyche and even take it over. Therefore, an actor's creative individuality must be significant, so that a mask does not overtake it. Moreover, an actor should develop the kind of technique that can ensure the correct balance between the actor and the mask.

According to Vakhtangov, only actors with a rich inner world, who continued their spiritual cultivation as part of the collective, are ready to fulfill the actor's mission. However, Vakhtangov's concept of *actor cultivation* initially differed from Sulerzhitsky's Tolstovian ideal, with its faith in the inner goodness of every man. While working on the *commedia* project, Vakhtangov came closer to Anton Chekhov's philosophy and ethics than those of Tolstoy.

One of the actresses, cast in the improvisation, was creating an imaginary biography for her character—Natasha. Vakhtangov suddenly suggested that Natasha's personality was altered by a brief encounter with Chekhov. In a rehearsal session, Vakhtangov insisted that the actress playing Natasha should share with the entire collective the "intimate experience" of her imaginary meeting with Chekhov. The actress, who first insisted that the episode was too personal, did finally begin:

> *Natasha*: She spent a mere fifteen minutes at Chekhov's. Not a minute more. She felt, though, that it was very long. Chekhov was delicate and attentive, as always. He did not give her an answer, as she dreamed he would. (What to do next.) Only now she understood that he could not give her such an answer.
>
> She left Chekhov as a different person.
>
> Even though she did not express herself, she felt that she did, and also that she understood something. She became freer, or more cheerful, perhaps. Up till this point she was somewhat passive, but a visit with Chekhov excited her. It is most important that she came out of this meeting cheerful. She came in as a young girl, and left as an adult.
>
> *Vakhtangov*: Despair, anger, joy—these are all cheerful feelings—in that sense, she did leave energetic.
>
> (Vakhtangova et al. 1939: 290)

Vakhtangov, for whom human life's ideal was an inner battle between good and evil, was philosophically close to Chekhov. In Chekhov's works, there are no simple answers as to how one should live their life. Chekhov believed that everyone is responsible for answering their own questions, for making their own decisions and their own mistakes. Imposing one person's solution upon another person is counterproductive, as everyone is unique and so are their paths.

Moreover, with such an ideal, there is no right, or righteous, way of living one's life. Vakhtangov's student Anna Orochko (interviewed in

Khersonsky 1940b: 108) insisted that Vakhtangov could not tolerate people who were "spotless" and preferred those "imperfect" people, torn by inner dilemmas. A presence of a correct answer to deep inner questions was for Vakhtangov a sign of a person's inability to face their true self. As an actor's material, Vakhtangov far preferred the "imperfect" people—those open to constant cultivation.

19 The Vakhtangov Studio crisis, 1916–1919

The Vakhtangov Studio unfinished projects

The *commedia dell'arte* improvisation was one of the many unfinished projects conducted by Vakhtangov and his students between 1914 and 1919. Several full-blown productions were started and never finished, or finished but not shown to the audience, at the Vakhtangov Studio. Between 1915 and 1918, Vakhtangov worked at the Studio on Michael Chekhov's adaptation of Tolstoy's short story *The Tale of Ivan-the-Fool and his Brothers*. Discussions and rehearsals of this piece, based in Tolstovian Pacifist philosophy, continued, on and off, at a time when the country was in the midst of World War I, and then Civil War. Perhaps the topical nature of the tale prevented Vakhtangov from finishing this production; the director did not tolerate a superficial flirt with the time.

Vakhtangov's failing health was a contributing factor behind the number of unfinished projects. The director never finished rehearsing Pushkin's one-act verse play *The Feast During the Plague*.[1] At his Studio, Vakhtangov did not spare other director's productions if these works did not answer the Studio's creative needs, or its artistic credo. Alexander Blok's one-act verse play *The Strange Woman*, to be directed by the invited First Studio member Aleksey Popov in 1916, was never completed. Molière's *George Dandin, or the Abashed Husband*, directed by the MAT elder and Vakhtangov's former teacher Luzhsky in 1920, was never shown to the audience. Vakhtangov could not accept Luzhsky's exercise in abstract stylization.

Betrothal in a Dream, or Puss in Boots and *The Infanta's Doll*, two plays by one of the Vakhtangov Studio members, Pavel Antakol'sky,

---

1 Rehearsal records for this piece can be found in *Sourcebook* (2011: 282–86).

were directed by another studio member—Yuri Zavadsky. Rehearsed between 1917 and 1919, the two plays were never fully accepted by Vakhtangov. This event served as a contributing factor to the Vakhtangov Studio's split in 1919.

In connection with the production of *The Infanta's Doll*, Vakhtangov made some fascinating practical suggestions to the director and the cast. The theme of the living puppet, present in *The Infanta's Doll*, often appeared in Vakhtangov's own directorial and acting works. Vakhtangov suggested that *The Infanta's Doll* actors should play puppets that come to life. This meant that the actors, first and foremost, needed to discover the *psychology* of a puppet:

> If you proceed from the dolls, you will discover both the form and feelings. Feelings are utterly simple. Human feelings are very complex. This is especially true for contemporary humans, notable for their refined feelings. A toy, however, cannot experience complex, refined feelings.
>
> In your work, you did not proceed from an actual hand-made toy, but from the designer's sketch. You could have done much more, if you proceeded from a toy. You cannot discover the kernel of a role from a sketch. When it comes to your character's reaction to a given event—you can only *sense* it.
>
> (Vakhtangova et al. 1939: 319)

A similar suggestion was made by Vakhtangov to *The Infanta's Doll* director, Zavadsky:

> How should the director stage this play? He should imagine for himself a doll-director or, better yet, himself become a doll and sense how a doll would perceive what happens onstage, and what it would not understand. What would not be clear to a doll, must be cut.
>
> (Vakhtangova et al. 1939: 319)

From studio to theatre

In 1916, Vakhtangov started rehearsals for Maeterlinck's play *The Miracle of Saint Anthony*. Maeterlinck's comedy deals with a group of provincial French bourgeois, who are visited by a saint. The bourgeois prove to be incapable of believing in the saint's existence. Having witnessed a miracle, performed by the saint, they turn him over to the police.

Vakhtangov approached *The Miracle of Saint Anthony* as a production intended to move the Studio toward becoming a professional company. Vakhtangov, who carefully led the studio toward this step, made a speech at the start of the work on Maeterlinck's play. In his speech, Vakhtangov stressed to his students that the start of rehearsals was just a beginning, the first step in this new direction. He also reminded his Studio that the theatre to be built would not be a typical professional organization. It was supposed to be an exclusive, closed theatrical collective, united by a common artistic and spiritual goal:

> Remember that I do not mean theatre when I speak of a professional organization. Professional organizations feed—the art should not feed. One should study art at his leisure, as you have other duties except art. Everyone gives according to his possibilities. A truly aristocratic group can be developed this way, instead of a bourgeois professional group. As soon as the ruble makes its appearance, with it comes a deadline for the opening of the production.
>
> (Vakhtangova et al. 1939: 302)

Vakhtangov made a point of having no deadline for the opening of *The Miracle of Saint Anthony*. Rehearsals started on September 17, 1916, but the performance did not open until September 15, 1918 (see Figure 19.1). Throughout this period, the Studio remained closed to outside influences—a monastery where members developed and grew spiritually, as human beings, through theatre. Maeterlinck's play also interested Vakhtangov as a Mystery, aimed at making those watching it, and participating in it, better people. The satirical aspect of the play was downplayed by Vakhtangov, so that the audience could closer associate with Maeterlinck's non-believers. Vakhtangov told his actors:

> Upon watching this play, the audience should feel moved and embarrassed. The audience should be muttering under their breath: "We are no better . . .".
>
> (*Sourcebook* 2011: 258)

When the Russian Revolution of February 1917 took place, the outside world came knocking on the door of Vakhtangov's monastery. The inquisitive Vershilov was posing new questions—no doubt, on behalf of the Studio:

Figure 19.1 Vakhtangov rehearsing *The Miracle of Saint Anthony* (first variant), 1918. Vakhtangov seated on the right with a script in his hand. Courtesy of Vakhtangov Theatre Museum.

March 4, 1917

Vershilov asks what must be done so that politics do not inter-fere with the studio work. According to some studio members, political conversations inside the studio should be completely eliminated. This should be done, as the Studio is the only place for the members where they can rest from politics and other worldly concerns.

Vakhtangov: As an administrator, I cannot respond to your question with any administrative measure. I do know firmly, however, that if we begin training, we will forget all politics. It will happen on its own. If some significant event takes place, however, you will start talking about it no matter what. You cannot artificially stop this.

I only know that now is exactly the time to work as well and as much as possible. We must prepare a performance. We can use it better than before, as now arises a great necessity in theatres; we must not miss the moment. We represent a cultivated group. The stage material offered to you—everything we do here—all this affects your souls. Your artistic soul is being affected, as material for acting, but this is not all. I told you some time ago: we must become better humans. I feel it well, but I cannot be a preacher. I can only walk along this path with you. The realization that an actor must become purer, better, as a person, I inherited from Sulerzhitsky. We require the play we stage to serve good.

The demand that a play must have God in it, transformed into the same demand of an actor. There can be no God in one who does not live according to God. It is impossible to artificially create a monastery. Catharsis must first begin in a small group, in a caste; it will then spread further and further. Every actor must comply with certain requirements. These requirements, these norms can be formed gradually, having been first conceived even in dreams. A preacher must emerge [from within the group], who will carry the group along with him. Later certain commandments will be cast. These should develop gradually and organically.

(Vakhtangova et al. 1939: 317)

According to some of the Soviet criticism (Khersonsky 1940a: 178), on the verge of the Bolshevik Revolution Vakhtangov unexpectedly retreated to the Sulerzhitskian positions. The truth of the matter is—Vakhtangov never betrayed Sulerzhitsky's ideals. He embraced the universal battle of good and evil as inevitable and necessary. Vakhtangov was, nevertheless, never torn on the question of this battle's final outcome.

Vakhtangov and the Bolshevik Revolution

Less than a year later, in October 1917, the Russian Bolshevik Revolution came to Moscow. Vakhtangov belonged to the Russian Socialist Revolutionary Party that lost to the Bolsheviks during the October events. As with other members of the Russian intelligentsia, Vakhtangov was now forced to redefine his political views and sympathies. He did so, in an unorthodox way.

On the day of the declaration of peace, the director went for a walk. He decided to survey the extent of the damage made to his neighborhood during recent street fights. On his trip, Vakhtangov met a worker fixing a broken streetcar wire. Vakhtangov's political turnaround was instant:

> The worker's hands revealed it to me. *The very way* these hands worked—*the very way* they picked up and replaced the tools, and how calmly, confidently and earnestly they moved—this caused me to see and understand that the worker was fixing *his own* wire, and that he was fixing it *for himself*. Only *master's* hands can work like this. This is the meaning of the revolution. I am convinced, I know, that the worker who now owns the state, and who is now a *master* in it, will be able to fix everything that was destroyed. He will do more than "fixing"; he will also *build*. He will now be building for himself.
>
> (Zakhava 1930: 76)

In the worker's hands, Vakhtangov foresaw *the creative aspect of the Revolution*. He became convinced that it opened an opportunity, to create new—free, exquisite, and beautiful—forms of life. On the same day, Vakhtangov announced his new political sympathies in front of his astonished students, who gathered at his apartment. The monastery wall of the Vakhtangov Studio was suddenly broken, and its members invited to take a good look at the outside world. According to Boris Zakhava (1930: 77), Vakhtangov, who was yet to realize what exactly he was preaching, told his students: "We cannot work as before. One cannot make art for one's own pleasure. Your place is too stuffy. Open the windows—let the fresh air in. Let the life in."

On the surface, Vakhtangov's new politics caused him to abolish the Sulerzhitskian concept of the Studio-monastery. This turnaround is treated in literature about Vakhtangov as a significant ideological, artistic, and pedagogical shift. In actuality, Vakhtangov's convictions, as well as his world outlook, did not change. And neither did his pedagogical tactics. What did change significantly was the atmosphere outside of the Vakhtangov Studio windows.

The atmosphere of depression and decay was characteristic of pre-revolutionary Russia. This was a country involved in a senseless war, and standing on the verge of a social cataclysm. Until the time of the Revolution, Vakhtangov kept his Studio's windows tightly shut, so as to keep this stagnant atmosphere out. He had to do it, in order to preserve "the holy" atmosphere inside the Studio. This was an atmosphere, based in self-discipline, in the sense of great artistic purpose and inner freedom.

The moment Vakhtangov felt that the atmosphere in the street encompassed the same sense of greater purpose and freedom he strived to develop inside, he ordered the Studio windows opened. The kindred spirit had to be let in. Similar to the Russian symbolist poet Alexander Blok, whose lyrics and plays Vakhtangov praised, he called his fellow artists to "listen to the Revolution" (Blok 1960–63 vol. VI: 20).

Vakhtangov had held democratic and populist beliefs since his early youth, but he also was a great believer in the purposeful course of history. Vakhtangov grew to see the Bolshevik Revolution as an event of a cosmic order (Leonid Volkov, interviewed in Khersonsky 1940b: 67). The question of accepting or rejecting it finally seemed super-fluous to him. Vakhtangov believed that the period of the "proletarian dictatorship" would last a relatively short time. He looked past this period, trying to foresee the future forms of a democratic society.

In 1918, Vakhtangov began to study and practically implement the theory of the Popular Theatre. Vakhtangov read Richard Wagner's 1849 essay *Art and Revolution* (*Die Kunst und die Revolution*) and Romain Rolland's *The People's Theatre* (*Le Théâtre du peuple*, 1902). Vakhtangov's study of Popular Theatre resulted in an article titled *An Artist Shall Have to Answer*.[2] This article summarized the direc-tor's own ideas of the Popular Theatre—of its creative mechanism and imagery. The implementation of these ideas can be seen in Vakhtangov's productions of 1919–22.[3]

In 1918 Vakhtangov answered the call to head the newly estab-lished Directors' Section of the Theatre Division of the Commissariat of Education, headed by the Soviet statesman Anatoly Lunacharsky. Vakhtangov's illness prevented him from being able to execute his

2 Vakhtangov's article can be found in *Sourcebook* (2011: 165–67).
3 On Vakhtangov's concept of Popular Theatre see *Sourcebook* (2011: 66–70).

duties. Also in 1918, Vakhtangov was commissioned by the Theatre Division to supply the repertoire for the newly established Popular Theatre by the Bolshoi Kamennyi Bridge in Moscow. While the Popular Theatre existed for only one season, Vakhtangov and his Studio mounted several original productions on its stage, including those of Octave Mirbeau's *Thief* (based on the French author's 1902 play *Scrupules*), Lady Gregory's *The Rising of the Moon*, as well as the dramatization of Maupassant's *Le Port*.

By 1919, Vakhtangov found himself Moscow's most popular acting teacher. In Revolutionary Moscow, theatre studios and enterprises were organized by the dozen. Every one of the new studios wanted Vakhtangov as its leader or, at the very least, teacher. Vakhtangov's diary of 1919 shows the following entries:

> Today, February 16, 1919, Nemirovich-Danchenko invited me to his place [. . .] and offered to organize an operetta studio.
>
> Today, February 17, 1919, K[onstantin] S[tanislavsky] invited me to the Bolshoi Theater and offered [. . .] to organize classes with this theater's singers.
>
> Yesterday, Lazarev enlisted me as a lecturer for the Cooperators' Studio.
>
> March 6, 1919
> Gzovskaya organizes a theater troupe in the South with the purpose of forming a new theater. She invited me and offered me to be the director.
> [. . .]
> Suren Khachaturov offered me to start teaching at the Armenian Studio, as of the summer.
> A group working at our Studio (Opera Studio) on *Yevgeny Onegin*, invited me to train them.
> Oh, My God, how did I deserve this?
> (Vendrovskaya and Kaptereva 1984: 296–97)

Throughout the late 1910s and early 1920s, Vakhtangov continuously taught at nine theatrical institutions. At most of these studios, Vakhtangov was seen by the students as a mentor and spiritual guru.

The Vakhtangov Studio breakdown

Vakhtangov was highly sought after by every theatrical enterprise in Moscow and beyond, but "something was rotten" at his own artistic home. By the time *The Miracle of Saint Anthony* opened at the start of the 1918–19 theatre season, an obvious split was developing at the Vakhtangov Studio. His students divided into two camps. One group included the eldest and most dedicated members of the Studio who, nevertheless, could not serve as a solid basis for a theatre troupe. The second group included several studio members who developed into fine actors and, therefore, could serve as a foundation of the future Vakhtangov Theatre ensemble. At the same time, these people appeared to be less dedicated to the studio. Dissatisfied with the lack of performance work, they were developing their own independent projects. Several of them formed the so-called New Council that opposed the Studio's "legal" government.

The formation of the "New Council" was inconsistent with the Studio's moral code. Vakhtangov, nevertheless, approached the conflict within his Studio in the spirit of the Sulerzhitsky-Tolstoy ethics. After a series of lengthy conciliatory letters addressed to the Old Council, to the New Council, and to the entire Studio body, Vakhtangov found himself personally addressing the leaders of the two groups.

Alarmed by the events at the Studio, Vakhtangov prematurely left the hospital on the verge of a major surgery. In the middle of the night, he held a meeting at his apartment with two groups of five—the most active, irreconcilable representatives from the two councils. That night, according to Zakhava's account, Vakhtangov spoke to the two groups "like a prophet. He resembled ancient Moses, whose legendary character he wanted to create onstage so badly" (Zakhava 1930: 106). The following day, Vakhtangov attended the meeting of the entire Studio body:

> When Vakhtangov arrived at the meeting, he sat in the corner of a small room, while both hostile groups of five, by a strange coincidence, sat along the walls on the opposite sides of their teacher. Vakhtangov thus found himself between the two hostile camps. "This is not coincidental," said Vakhtangov, as he placed his hands on the shoulders of those closest to him on both sides. "*This is the only way the Studio can exist,*" he said, as he embraced the members of the hostile groups. "Both groups—are the two halves of my heart," Vakhtangov continued,—"I dissolved myself in you, and the very tendencies living in me now manifested themselves in the Studio. The struggle that began within the Studio is the reflection of the very struggle that constantly lives within my heart. If my heart is cut in half, I will cease to exist. Deprive the

Studio of one of these groups—and there no longer will be a Studio. One group is the aimless artistic striving, and a vague flight of the creative imagination, while the other group is ethics that makes artistic flights meaningful, and gives answers to the incessant question: 'what for.' If you keep this first group, the Studio will turn into a banal and vulgar theater, if you keep the other group—there will be a mere prayer, and no theater. Both groups, both halves of my heart, are needed for the continuation of the Studio's existence, and for the creation of a true theater."

(Zakhava 1930: 106–7)

At the time of these events, Vakhtangov was preparing to stage Byron's *Cain* at the First Studio. "God and Lucifer, Good and Evil, Abel and Cain—those were the problems Vakhtangov struggled to solve" (Zakhava 1930: 105). In Vakhtangov's speech, one can hear the echo of another eternal dilemma—how to reconcile the holy Theatre of Mystery with the irreverent Popular Theatre? This riddle, constantly tackled by Vakhtangov, also materialized itself in the walls of his own Studio (see Figure 19.2).

Vakhtangov always managed to reconcile the two theatres in practice—by introducing the holy, moral aspect to the lighthearted irreverence of the creative play. But now Vakhtangov was at a loss. His moving words produced an effect, and yet it was not lasting. Before the end of the 1918–19 theatre season, a group of 12 fully-fledged actors, prepared by Vakhtangov, left his studio. Vakhtangov remained with five of his eldest studio members ("mere prayer, and no theatre"), and a green group of beginning students.

The 1918–19 season was a tragic time for Vakhtangov. His own studio collapsed. His First Studio of MAT production of Ibsen's *Rosmersholm* went virtually unnoticed. His attempts to organize the Popular Theatre failed. His plans to stage Byron's *Cain* at the First Studio were canceled by Stanislavsky's decision to direct the play personally at the Moscow Art Theatre.

On top of it all, Vakhtangov's health was failing, with one surgery following another. Although the doctors concealed from their patient that he had cancer, Vakhtangov suspected the truth.[4] On October 24, 1918, while at the Ignatyev Clinic, Vakhtangov wrote in his diary: "Why is my heart so heavy today? What an incessant feeling. It is like

---

4 In March 1919, Vakhtangov wrote to Stanislavsky: "I know that my earthly days are short. I know calmly that I won't live long [. . .]" (*Sourcebook* 2011: 318).

Figure 19.2 Five-year anniversary of the Vakhtangov Studio, 1918. Vakhtangov seated center with his son Sergei next to him. Courtesy of Arsis Design.

a premonition of something. It's vague, and that makes me uneasy" (*Sourcebook* 2011: 240). The same diary entry, however, was filled with the foreboding of great discoveries. Despite his failing health, Vakhtangov burst with creative powers. As if anticipating both his early death and his future breakthroughs, Vakhtangov wrote: "It is time to start thinking of daring to take wing" (*Sourcebook* 2011: 241).

20 The Vakhtangov Studio revival, 1919–1922[1]

After the Studio catastrophe of 1919, Vakhtangov seemingly lost interest in his creative child. He concentrated on working at other theatrical institutions, and only occasionally visited his Studio. In the meantime, the five faithful disciples continued their work with the remaining youth. Soon, as if by magic, young talented actors began to arrive at the Vakhtangov Studio. They came from all over Russia, as well as from other Moscow theatre schools and studios.

The sudden flow of talent into the Vakhtangov Studio was, of course, motivated by Vakhtangov's personality. The First Studio of MAT's stage manager Barakcheyev (1939: 478), a rather pragmatic fellow, claimed that the chief reason Vakhtangov agreed to teach in so many studios and schools was to "select the best material" for his own. Although this explanation is rather narrow, there is some truth to Barakcheyev's words.

With a few exceptions, the people who led the Vakhtangov Theatre and School after Vakhtangov's death came to his Studio in the last two to three years of the master's life.[2] Such was the case of Boris Schukin, one of the theatre's leading actors, for whom the Vakhtangov School in Moscow is currently named. He arrived at the Vakhtangov Studio in 1920. The same is true of Ruben Simonov, who later served as the theatre's artistic director for 30 years. The future Vakhtangov Theatre manager, the noted tragedian Osvald Glazunov, came in 1919. The leading lady of the Vakhtangov Theatre, Tsetsiliya Mansurova, the original Turandot, also arrived in 1919. Aleksandra Remizova (see Figure 20.1), who was to become one of the most talented Vakhtangov

---

1 For further information on this period of the Vakhtangov Studio history see Gorchakov (1959).
2 The exceptions included one of the Studio founders, Boris Zakhava, tragic actress Anna Orochko, and one of the oldest Vakhtangov School teachers, Vera L'vova.

Figure 20.1 Aleksandra Remizova as Zelima in Vakhtangov's production of *Princess Turandot*, 1922. Courtesy of Arsis Design.

Theatre directors, came in 1920. So did Mariya Sinel'nikova, one of the Vakhtangov Theatre's best character actresses.

Vakhtangov's recruitment tactics could be unorthodox. Such was the case with the two youngest Studio members, Remizova and Sinel'nikova. Both actresses attended the director Vladimir Vilner's Studio, affiliated with Nikolai Sinel'nikov's troupe in Kharkov, Ukraine. The First Studio performed in Kharkov in the summer of 1920. After the performance of *The Cricket of the Hearth*, where Vakhtangov played Tackleton, Vilner Studio members invited Vakhtangov to speak to the group. Vakhtangov's visit was so inspiring that, immediately after the talk, a group of studio members surrounded Vakhtangov. They wanted to know what it would take to get accepted into his Moscow Studio. Vakhtangov replied that, first and foremost, they needed to come to Moscow for an audition; the rest would depend on its results.

The early 1920s was a time of Civil War in Russia. Most of the railway communications were dedicated to military needs, and special permission was needed for travel. Moreover, traveling during the Civil War was extremely dangerous, as the trains were frequently shot at and bombed. Travelers could be detained, arrested and shot without a trial by any of the fighting parties. Despite eminent danger, 17-year-old Aleksandra Remizova made the trip to Moscow in the fall of the same year, riding, for most of her journey, on the roof of a train. Throughout her journey, the young actress faced death on more than one occasion.

When Remizova arrived in Moscow, she went straight to Vakhtangov's Studio. At the time of her arrival, the Studio had just been granted a new name and a new space on the centrally located Arbat Street. On September 13, 1920, the studio received the honorable title of the Third Studio of the Moscow Art Theatre. It started the new season in a mansion that used to belong to a wealthy industrialist (Sergei Berg). Vakhtangov was sick, recuperating at the Health Rehabilitation Resort of All Saints, and Remizova was received by some senior studio members. The next day, Remizova inquired about the audition, and she was told that Vakhtangov, who had been informed of her arrival, had accepted her to the Studio. She was to start attending classes immediately.

The trip from Kharkov to Moscow *was* Remizova's audition. As far as Vakhtangov was concerned, she passed the most important test. Vakhtangov believed that a person whose desire to study and create theatre was so great as to make them risk their life for it belonged to the field. He did not need to see them do a monologue, or an exercise, to know that they will find their place in theatre. He was seldom wrong. Aleksandra Remizova was responsible for the majority of Vakhtangov Theatre's classical repertoire, becoming a godmother to several generations of the theatre's leading actors over 40 years. Remizova also distinguished herself during World War II. She served as the principal director for the Vakhtangov Theatre's Affiliate Company, performing for the Russian soldiers at the battlefront. As part of this company, she entered Berlin with the Russian army in 1945.

The cultivation of the actors continued at the renewed Vakhtangov Studio. The strict discipline and the Studio moral code were preserved by Vakhtangov in the final years of his work. According to a large body of memoirs, Vakhtangov seemed to have taught each and every one of his new students a moral lesson they did not forget for as long as they lived. And in each individual case, the lesson was tailored to that student's individuality.

In the mid-1980s, Aleksandra Remizova told me a story that became one of the Vakhtangov Theatre's myths, and is retold by her colleagues in several books of memoirs. Around 1920, Remizova, the youngest member of the Vakhtangov Studio, committed a misstep that conflicted with the Studio code of ethics and discipline. The actress was summoned to Vakhtangov's office. When she entered the office, the room was dark. Vakhtangov sat at his desk, a single candle flickering before him. Silently, Vakhtangov invited the trembling actress to sit at the desk opposite him. For a period of time that did not last longer than a minute, but seemed like an eternity to Remizova, Vakhtangov's giant eyes glared at the young girl. Vakhtangov's eyes were often described by his students as hypnotic. In rehearsals, the power of his gaze often turned mediocre actors into talents.

Remizova was weeping. She told me that, during this minute, she went in her mind over *everything* she had done wrong in her entire life, as if cleansing herself of it all. Vakhtangov finally interrupted the silence.

— Did you get it?
— I did, Yevgeny Bogrationovich.
— You can go now.

No lecture, no cheap preaching, no blowing-up—just a silent glare. Whatever Remizova saw in Vakhtangov's eyes produced a stronger effect. With someone else, older and less impressionable, Vakhtangov would have used a completely different tactic. Remizova, who was an essentially moral person, could say more to herself during this minute of silence than he could ever say to her in an hour. All Vakhtangov needed to offer was the mirror of his eyes.

When speaking at Vakhtangov's funeral, Stanislavsky expressed a paradoxical thought: he said that Vakhtangov was great because he was cruel (Vendrovskaya 1959: 290). The thought can be interpreted in many ways. Already at the time of Vakhtangov's production of *The Festival of Peace* at the First Studio, the critics noticed the cruel side of Vakhtangov's talent. His Tackleton from *The Cricket on the Hearth* was cruel. His production of *The Deluge* openly contradicted Sulerzhitsky's philosophy of the inner goodness present in every man.

Figure 20.2 Tsetsiliya Mansurova in the title role in Vakhtangov's production of *Princess Turandot*, 1922. Courtesy of Arsis Design.

Vakhtangov could be an authoritative leader—at his own Studio even more so than at the First Studio of MAT. He could blow up at an actor, the entire cast, or even the entire studio. He could easily cancel a ready production. He could refuse a delinquent studio member his services as a teacher. He could exile an actor from his Studio—for a period of time, or forever. He could reduce an actress to tears, in order to help her discover emotions necessary for a tragic moment in her role. On one occasion, he slapped his *Turandot* leading lady, Mansurova's (see Figure 20.2) hand. On another occasion, he threw a heavy paperweight at the stage, during rehearsal.

Vakhtangov was human in every way, and nothing human was alien to him. On one occasion, he asked one of his students if he, Vakhtangov, followed the same rule of chastity he demanded from his students. The actress summoned up her courage and replied: "No, Yevgeny Bogrationovich." Vakhtangov remained satisfied with her answer: "Very good, he said, do what I say, not what I do." This was an honesty test, conducted by Vakhtangov.

Vakhtangov's heart was exposed to the same eternal battle of good and evil he saw go on in the heart of every "intelligent" person. The creative play Vakhtangov often performed in everyday life was equally cruel and even cynical. This play also featured the battle between good and evil. Both Michael Chekhov and Sulerzhitsky participated in Vakhtangov's play. Chekhov did it because Vakhtangov's harsh sense of humor was close to his own individuality. Sulerzhitsky, who is perceived today as a kindly Tolstovian, was in reality a complex man. On one occasion, Vakhtangov shared the following episode with one of his students:

> One time I violated discipline. Sulerzhitsky put me in a corner, on my knees, for several hours. I wept and begged him to take pity on me, but he paid no attention. When the time of the punishment passed, he explained: you will profit a great deal from this punishment. Those who prepare to become actors must experience the taste of suffering. Everyone who pursues easy paths in theatre, becomes disillusioned in the long run and leaves this holy place.
>
> (Ivanov 2011 vol. II: 403–4)

Vakhtangov's students, in their vast majority, accepted Vakhtangov's harshness as a measure aimed at their own spiritual and artistic development. They understood that their master's measures were never personal. Vakhtangov never hurt anyone's *human* pride; at the same time, he was extremely demanding in questions of art. Vakhtangov did not tolerate artistic negligence, nor laziness and cynicism exhibited in relation to art, or to a fellow artist. When it came to artistic pursuits, Vakhtangov did not spare himself, or his students.

Vakhtangov's explosions usually gave way to his irresistible smile, and the words: "I did it so that you better remember the lesson" (Gorchakov 1957: 165). On occasions, when Vakhtangov overstepped the boundary, as he did with Mansurova, he apologized. Actors, who were banned from the Studio, or left on their own accord, were accepted back at the first sign of remorse. All disciplinary measures employed by Vakhtangov at his Studio seemed to have pursued the same goal—the one described by his student Sinel'nikova (interviewed

in Khersonsky 1940b: 161) as the goal of "deepening [his actors']
human nature." Vakhtangov's students knew that what their teacher
was doing was ultimately based in deep and genuine love for them.
And yet, even the most experienced of them, such as Yuri Zavadsky
(1959: 290), could not help but wonder: "If he loves us, how can he
be at times so cruel?"

Vakhtangov's students never forgot their teacher. While working at
the Vakhtangov Theatre in the mid 1980s, I was fortunate to witness
three of Vakhtangov's original Studio members in action—director
Aleksandra Remizova and actresses Vera L'vova and Mariya
Sinel'nikova.[3] The spiritual force and inner significance radiated by
these three women, all in their mid to late eighties, was phenomenal.
Their energy and passion was unmatched by any of their illustrious
colleagues—all much younger than them. At times, I wondered if this
was their own inner spirit, or that of Vakhtangov's radiating through
them.

When Vakhtangov's students spoke of their teacher (and they could
speak of him tirelessly), their radiation increased—they were literally
beaming with inner light. This feeling of entering the sphere of an
inwardly significant being was shared by everyone who came into
their presence—be it a stage hand, or a fellow actor. As the director
Remizova—a tiny and feeble old woman, bent almost in half—passed
through the Vakhtangov Theatre's corridors, or climbed the steep
flights of the theatre's stairs, everyone on her way stopped and greeted
her, many literally rising to attention. Remizova greeted everyone with
a dreamy, wise smile, and continued through.

Another amazing quality Vakhtangov's students inherited from
their master—they continued to grow as artists as long as they lived.
For example, Vera L'vova (see Figure 20.3), a noted teacher, but not a
distinguished actress, reached an unprecedented level of artistic revelation in her final role. As a result, her partners, many of them far more
significant actors, next to L'vova, appeared deliberate.

Similarly, when seeing Sinel'nikova (see Figure 20.4) perform in a
contemporary play, I, for the first time, saw what it meant to be both
sincere and expressive onstage. Sinel'nikova's acting was huge, but, at
the same time, it was matched equally by an inner fire; no one could
ever reproach Sinel'nikova for not being believable. This lesson the
actress obviously learned from Vakhtangov. Apparently, it could only
be learned directly from the master, as very few of Sinel'nikova,

---

3 All three also served as the Vakhtangov Institute teachers for decades.

Figure 20.3 Vera L'vova as a *Zanni* in Vakhtangov's production of *Princess Turandot*, 1922. Courtesy of Arsis Design.

L'vova, or Remizova's famous students could be as theatrical and sincere onstage.

By 1920, the replenished collective of the Vakhtangov Studio managed to lure back their leader. (It is also quite possible that Vakhtangov's detachment was merely a tactic aimed at energizing the remaining Studio.) Even some of the "traitors," such as Vakhtangov's leading man, soon to be famous Russian director Yuri Zavadsky, asked to be taken back. So did the future noted Russian poet Pavel Antakol'sky. Vakhtangov magnanimously returned both of them.

With the renewed Studio, Vakhtangov undertook the most significant of his final experiments. One of them—namely the production

Figure 20.4 Mariya Sinel'nikova as Adelma in Vakhtangov's production of *Princess Turandot*, 1922. Courtesy of Arsis Design.

of *Princess Turandot*—deserves a separate chapter; it receives it at the end of this book. The less influential productions, such as the second versions of Maeterlinck's *The Miracle of Saint Anthony* and Chekhov's *The Wedding*, also deserve much attention.

Part IV

The Vakhtangov Studio productions

21 Maeterlinck's *The Miracle of Saint Anthony* circa 1921

Two variants of *The Miracle*

The Vakhtangov Studio's production of Maeterlinck's *The Miracle of Saint Anthony* opened in 1918, after a two-year rehearsal period. Conceived before the Revolution, *The Miracle* was premiered one year after the Bolsheviks took power. The essence of this production did not change much throughout the rehearsal period. In 1921, however, Vakhtangov seriously revised his production. This revision was prompted by Vakhtangov's new understanding of the revolutionary times and of the theatrical form those times required.

In the 1921 version of *The Miracle of Saint Anthony*, the conflict between life and death, typical of a Vakhtangov production, was significantly heightened. Like many of Vakhtangov's works, *The Miracle* was based in a ritual. Vakhtangov was interested in two opposing sides of the ritual—its holy and solemn, or festive nature, but also its mechanical and deadening aspect.

Maeterlinck's play is set in a French province, and it deals with the funeral of a rich old maid, Mademoiselle Hortense. The funeral is interrupted by the arrival of a saint, Saint Anthony, who comes to revive the old woman. He is brought to the house of the deceased by her servant Virginie's incessant prayer.

In Vakhtangov's interpretation of the play, the challenge to the deathly side of the ritual was issued when the good soul, Virginie, called on God to revive her mistress. Vakhtangov stressed that Virginie could not tolerate the deafness, the indifference of everything dead toward life. As the maid Virginie scrubbed the floor of the lobby, dirtied by the funeral guests, she was trying to restore the true essence of the ritual by creating *the solemn atmosphere*, appropriate for the occasion. Vakhtangov insisted that "Virginie needs solemnity so that 'she' [her mistress] would feel it. Moreover, Virginie cries because she knows that 'she' would not feel it" (*Sourcebook* 2011: 272).

Together with Saint Anthony, who arrived to answer Virginie's prayers, the old servant became a nuisance—a bothersome, but temporary interruption to the unstoppable funeral routine. Relatives and heirs of the deceased, headed by her nephews Gustave and Achille, remained as unfazed by the idea of their aunt's revival as they were by her death. They had to attend to the Saint, but inwardly they continued waiting for the partridges to be served at the funeral breakfast. The heirs needed the formality of the funeral to be over with, so that they could begin to profitably manage their inheritance.

Even the deceased woman herself did not seem to care about her revival, or death. When she was brought back to life by Saint Anthony, she did not understand, or appreciate the fact. Moreover, she continued to act pettily, as if she had never died. At that moment in the play, one could make an assumption that the rich old lady, perhaps, had never lived. One could not help but wonder if her life, just as the lives of those around her, was, in fact, a form of death. The dead state ultimately better agreed with Vakhtangov's bourgeois.

In the first, pre-revolutionary version of the production, Vakhtangov's sympathies were with the bourgeois. Moreover, the audiences were supposed to identify with them.[1] After all, the Russian intelligentsia of the pre-revolutionary period, as well as members of the Russian bourgeoisie, all had their religious doubts. While considering themselves God-fearing people, they were also morally weak, and often succumbed to the "convenient" materialistic mood of the age.

According to the Vakhtangov of 1916–18, the bourgeois' weakness was a subject of Maeterlinck's kindhearted smile (*Sourcebook* 2011: 269–70). Evoking this smile in the audience was Vakhtangov's actors' goal. In the second, 1921 version, however, the sympathies of Vakhtangov-the-director lie almost exclusively with the maid Virginie and with the Saint. The bourgeois were seen through the prism of Virginie's popular consciousness, as mechanical puppets, or soulless automatons (see Figure 21.1).

1 See p. 143.

Figure 21.1 Boris Zakhava as Doctor in *The Miracle of Saint Anthony*, second variant, 1921. Courtesy of Arsis Design.

Dynamics and immobility: new expressive means utilized in *The Miracle of Saint Anthony*

Seemingly, by 1921 Vakhtangov moved along with the time, and, therefore with the audience. After the Revolution, the Vakhtangov Studio's audiences were no longer restricted to the good old intelligentsia, and the new Soviet bourgeoisie—the so-called *nepmans*.[2]

2 The word *nepman* came from the abbreviation NEP that stands for New Economic Policy. During this short period in Soviet history (1921–28), some forms of private property were suddenly allowed, and the fooled bourgeois, new and old, hurried to open shops, restaurants, small businesses, etc. Needless to say, all of their money and property was soon expropriated by the Soviet regime.

Vakhtangov's audience now also included members of the proletariat. At first glance, Vakhtangov's examination of Maeterlinck's bourgeois was realigned with the proletarian point of view. In actuality, however, Vakhtangov's point of view was much more complex.

In his notes to the actors, Vakhtangov insisted that "Bourgeois, in general, are never surprised" (*Sourcebook* 2011: 277). After all, to become surprised means, at least for a second, to go out of the dead realm of the predictable. The very organ that can sense the unusual is atrophied in the spiritually dead bourgeois. When developing the bourgeois' point of view on the miracle, Vakhtangov, knowingly or unknowingly, echoed the words of Dostoyevsky:

> The genuine realist, if he is an unbeliever, will always find strength and ability to disbelieve in the miraculous, and if he is confronted with a miracle as an irrefutable fact he would rather disbelieve his own senses than admit the miraculous also.
>
> (Dostoyevsky 1922: 21)

Vakhtangov used an uncommon directorial palette to portray the stagnant funeral group of *The Miracle*. An obvious approach would have been to use static immobility for their portrayal. Meanwhile, the author (Maeterlinck), national psychology and plasticity, and the social origin of the group, prompted different means to Vakhtangov. Nikolai Volkov offered the following description of the director's artistic means:

> Vakhtangov resorted to dynamic means for the embodiment of the small world of the French bourgeois. The inwardly dead Gustave and Achille, their wives, aunts, doctor, priest and the guests were presented by Vakhtangov as extremely agitated. Vakhtangov amplified Maeterlinck's irony to the satirical dimension. He did so by unleashing the actors' movements, making a caricature out of their faces, and condensing the senseless and the mechanical nature of their movements. Vakhtangov spared individual performers from a necessity to possess individual souls— instead, he pushed to the foreground the common element in their psychology, determined by their class. By doing so, Vakhtanov achieved two things—he created the impression of a unified ensemble, and he extremely saturated the overall tone of the performance. In moments, the tone of the production rose to that of a tragic farce.
>
> (Volkov 1922: 18–19)

The device of static immobility was also used by Vakhtangov in *The Miracle*. It accentuated the overall dynamic of the bourgeois' plasticity, creating strong contrasts. The dynamic of the bourgeois' movements and gestures was animalistic in nature. It leaned toward the horizontal line, as if striving for the earth (see Figure 21.2). This horizontal dynamic was counterbalanced by the solemnly static "wondrous human verticality" (Volkov 1922: 19) of the Saint. In addition to that, Vakhtangov constantly interrupted the flow of the bourgeois' movements with full stops, or "freezes."

When faced with Saint Anthony and Virginie's will, the bourgeois often froze in mid-movement. These freezes, however, did not take the philistine bourgeois out of their ritual. At those moments when their dream-like, mechanical life was interrupted by Saint Anthony and Virginie, the frozen group would appear strained. At the same time, the bourgeois never lost their overall sense of direction—while waiting for the interruption to be over, the guests continued inwardly moving toward the outcome of the funeral ritual. Vakhtangov insisted that the inner static must be accompanied by the increased inner dynamic (Zakhava 1930: 129).

The moment of truth in *The Miracle*

The bourgeois did prevail—if not morally, then certainly physically. At the end of the production, the two who sought to defeat death—Saint Anthony and Virginie—left the stagnant world of the play. The saint was taken to the police station, with Virginie following him in the rain, holding an umbrella over his head. No sooner had the two good souls crossed Mademoiselle Hortense's threshold than the revived woman collapsed. The dead order of the ritual was restored; the funeral could now "safely" move to its logical conclusion.

At that very point, however, something did awaken in Vakhtangov's bourgeois—a notion that, while securing the funeral, they nevertheless lost some faintly perceptible moral ground. The final moment of stillness that followed Mademoiselle Hortense's "second death" differed from the previous "full stops." This is how Vakhtangov described the psychology of the final full stop to his actors:

> Everything drooped on everyone, it all became unnecessary. Ah? What? They are stunned. Auntie sinks down. Everyone looks, but no one understands anything. During this moment, you must sense your neckties coming undone, swelling colors, etc. You must

Figure 21.2. Scene from Act 2 of *The Miracle of Saint Anthony*, second variant, 1921. Courtesy of Arsis Design.

Figure 21.3 Ruben Simonov as Joseph, the valet, in *The Miracle of Saint Anthony*, second variant, 1921. Courtesy of Arsis Design.

loosen your muscles and wish to ask something, but your tongue does not obey you [see Figure 21.3].

(*Sourcebook* 2011: 281)

The sense of spiritual nakedness, of the revelation of true human self—this very sense Vakhtangov sought in *The Deluge*—manifested itself in *The Miracle* finale. The impenetrable mask of the bourgeois was lifted, if only for a second, and the characters' human faces were revealed. In the words of Vakhtangov, "The humanity in them floated up onto the surface. Crabs, and sea monsters stuck to the human being, got unstuck" (*Sourcebook* 2011: 204).

Aspects of popular consciousness in *The Miracle*: characters of the servant and the saint

In both versions of *The Miracle of Saint Anthony*, Vakhtangov insisted that the actor playing the title role of Anthony should not play an iconic saint. In Vakhtangov's interpretation, Anthony was a kindly old man, extremely wise and observant. As he looked at people, he could read their hidden thoughts and desires. At the same time, there was nothing apparently supernatural about this old man. He appeared to the audience as a real person—more real, in fact, than the bourgeois.

According to Nikolai Volkov (1922: 19), "the human anthill" of Maeterlinck's bourgeois was "treated with exaggeration." Vakhtangov counted on this treatment to "graphically set off the noble figure of Saint Anthony of Padua" (see Figure 21.4). This is how Volkov described Vakhtangov's take on the role of the saint:

> Vakhtangov stressed in the saint the wondrous plainness of the human verticality; the director endowed the saint's movements with the naïve angularity of the primitivism, and illumed his face with the luminance of one of Christ's paupers. Due to this austere and laconic acting, Anthony appeared as inwardly alive and spiritual. He served as a steady center to the entire production, balancing the sweeping dynamic of "the dead".
>
> (Volkov 1922: 19)

This concept of the role of the Saint alarmed Soviet critics (Zograf 1939: 110). The fact that a Saint turned out to be "the most alive" character in the performance was seen by these critics as a lack of "the atheist, destructive fire of the revolution" (Khersonsky 1940a: 227). Moreover, Vakhtangov's take on the role was far from a denial of the supernatural.

The entire production of *The Miracle* was staged by Vakhtangov from the perspective of the simple old woman Virginie. For Virginie, a true believer, the notion of a saint's existence did not require any allowance for the supernatural. Virginie's "primitive," pre-logical consciousness did not distinguish between things real and unreal. A saint for her was as real as, or perhaps even more real than, the people surrounding her.

As a virtuous person, Virginie (see Figure 21.5) did not have a reason to fear the saint. Therefore, she did not approach Anthony as her superior, who could hold her accountable, or punish her for her

Figure 21.4 Yuri Zavadsky as Saint Anthony in *The Miracle of Saint Anthony*, second variant, 1921. Courtesy of Vakhtangov Theatre Museum.

wrongdoings. Virginie approached St. Anthony with respect and reverence, and yet she treated him as her equal. There was even a good measure of nurturing in Virginie's attitude toward the kind old Anthony. She considered herself worldlier, and therefore stronger than the saint. At times she even bossed him around, acting as his protector.

Seemingly, in the second version of *The Miracle*, Vakhtangov assumed the point of view of this most progressive, revolutionary part of the audience. Some of the Soviet critics (Khersonsky 1940a: 224) proclaimed that Vakhtangov aligned himself with the working class—against the parasites—the bourgeois. Vakhtangov himself was

Figure 21.5 Mariya Nekrasova as Virginie in *The Miracle of Saint Anthony*, second variant, 1921. Courtesy of Arsis Design.

known to say that in his second version of *The Miracle* he "exposed bourgeois" (*Sourcebook* 2011: 153).

What the majority of the Soviet critics overlooked in Vakhtangov's production was the fact that Vakhtangov aligned himself (and the audience) with the two true believers in the play—against the materialistically minded philistines. In addition to that, neither of the two positive characters of *The Miracle*, Virginie nor Saint Anthony, represented the working class. In fact, both of these characters attracted Vakhtangov's sympathies exactly because they were declassed—or did not belong to any class.

Virginie overstepped the boundaries of her class on more than one occasion. On the one hand, she prayed for the revival of her mistress, her exploiter, thus crossing her class's barrier. On the other hand, Virginie turned down the significant inheritance left to her by the mistress, thus crossing that border back. Moreover, at the end of the play Virginie was leaving her masters and joining Saint Anthony in his wanderings, thus changing her social status yet again. As for Saint Anthony, he was portrayed, in both the play and Vakhtangov's production, as a homeless wanderer, and, possibly, a mental patient—someone who had lost any social identity, whatever it might originally have been.

Once again Vakhtangov suggested that only those people who shed their social masks, and thus refuse the protection of their class's morale, can gain the special knowing. This knowing is achieved at the final threshold by those who expose their hearts to the battle of life and death, or good and evil. In Vakhtangov's productions (Berger's *The Deluge*, Chekhov's *The Wedding*) the main character's final exit from the stage often symbolized this threshold.

Both Virginie and Saint Anthony tackled the eternal moral dilemmas throughout the play. They claimed their moral victory in the end exactly because they trod those dangerous waters. Virginie, who prayed for her petty and wicked mistress, and Saint Anthony, who answered her call, both exposed their hearts to the battle of good and evil. They did so by crossing into the most unlikely territory, a place they clearly did not belong. Back in 1915, when first approaching Maeterlinck's play, Vakhtangov already sensed the borderline situation inherent in the piece:

> If Christ were to come to a dungeon, or to an insane asylum, we would accept it at once. But suppose we were told that Christ came to an ordinary apartment where there is a private doctor, dinner jackets, cigars, partridges, wine—this we cannot accept . . .
> (*Sourcebook* 2011: 259)

Vakhtangov's popular consciousness and morals contradicted both the Marxist and religious dogmas. His were based in the Popular Theatre, and they embraced the Theatre of Mystery—to the degree that these two theatres share some aspects in common. Historically, the Popular Theatre often used the religious myth. At the same time, the Theatre of Mystery made use of the Popular Theatre devices—these were essential to the religious "education" of the illiterate masses. Moreover, the pre-logical, popular consciousness is mystical in its very nature, while many religious faiths consider common moral and condition as pure.

Vakhtangov's synthesis of the two theatres (Theatre of the Mystery and the Popular), as realized in his final production of *Princess Turandot*, incorporated these historic realities. At the same time, Vakhtangov's new model of theatre revealed unexpected correlations between the two seemingly opposing theatrical aesthetics—the Popular and the Mysterious.

22 Chekhov's *The Wedding*

The formula of an Anton Chekhov play has been outlined by the playwright himself: "People are sitting at a table having dinner, that's all, but at the same time their happiness is being created, or their lives are being torn apart" (Gurlyand 1904: 521). The challenge in such a play consists of hitting both parts of the formula—the one where people "just have dinner," but also the one where "their lives are being broken up" in the meantime. Vakhtangov managed to achieve such a balance in his production of Anton Chekhov's *The Wedding*.

Chekhov's major plays revolve around mundane rituals—lunches and teas, arrivals and departures, lazy summer afternoons and evening games of lotto. Most people perform these routines without fully engaging, as if in their sleep. Behind them, Chekhov sees a chasm—the horror of human existence where an entire life, with its happiness and tragedies, can go by unnoticed.

When Chekhovian individuals do wake up from their ritualistic dream, they become horrified by the realization of their own non-existence, and of the life they have missed. Having made such a realization, a Chekhov character might hurry to go back to their sleep, or they might enter a phase of cataclysm. In this state of shock, or catastrophe, the Chekhov characters might hit the bottle, try to shoot themselves, shoot their "enemies," or declare love—however hopeless and inappropriate it may be. In other words, Chekhovian characters, at the phase of cataclysm, desperately try to catch up on the life they missed.

This desperate act of "catching up" with one's life can be interpreted as being just as petty, and just as absurd, as the preceding dream. Alternatively, it can be treated as an act of courage, a heroic fit, and an attempt to take one's destiny in one's own hands. Chekhov never clearly tells us which of the two points of view on his characters' "awakening" he wants us to take. Vakhtangov reflected on this phenomenon in his diary entries, while actively arguing with the

Moscow Art Theatre's interpretation of Chekhov plays as "lyrical."[1]
As part of this argument, Vakhtangov drew a bold parallel between
Chekhov's plays and Pushkin's *Little Tragedies*:

> I want to stage *The Seagull*. Theatrically. The way Chekhov has it.
>   I want to stage [Pushkin's] *The Feast During the Plague* and
> Chekhov's *Wedding* in one evening. *Wedding* has *The Feast
> During the Plague* in it. ~~These plagued people do not know that
> the plague has passed, that humanity was emancipated, that one
> does not need [to invite] generals to their weddings.~~
>
> (*Sourcebook* 2011: 133)

One line in this passage was crossed out by Vakhtangov. The director
realized that the similarities between the two one-act plays—Pushkin's
The Feast During the Plague and Chekhov's *The Wedding*—are not
exhausted by his brilliant, yet topical thought on humanity's
emancipation.

Both *The Feast* and *The Wedding* are one-act plays, based in the
condensed reality of non-mundane rituals. In Pushkin's play, set in the
Middle Ages, a group of aristocratic youth defies the plague by
throwing a feast in the streets of a diseased city. In Vakhtangov's interpretation of Pushkin's play, the feast meant to celebrate the plague
turns into yet another ritual—a death watch, or a kind of wake by a
common death-bed. According to Vakhtangov, all participants of the
feast are waiting for their own, as well as their neighbors', inevitable
death. The reader might have noticed that the same kind of ritual
stands at the heart of many of Vakhtangov's productions—be it *The
Festival of Peace, The Deluge*, or even *Rosmersholm*.

In Vakhtangov's production of Chekhov's *The Wedding*, the
seemingly joyful ritual also turns into a nightmarish wake. According
to Vakhtangov's student, Nikolai Gorchakov, before approaching
Chekhov's play, Vakhtangov asked him a question:

- So, you think that, in life, a wedding is a joyous event?
- One would think so . . .
- And according to Chekhov?
- Not quite!
- Who is right then—Chekhov?
    [. . .]

---

1 See pp. 75–6.

Perhaps, this is not life at all—[. . .]—living as they live in Chekhov's stories. Here they are dancing, and seemingly enjoying themselves, celebrating the wedding. Everything is as it should be; they even "bought" themselves a general, and yet this is not life! They only think that they live, while, in reality, someone pulls their strings and tells them: "That's the way." So, they dance, and they quarrel, and they reconcile, they eat, drink, love, hate, bribe, betray . . . [See Plate 10.]

(Gorchakov 1957: 30)

The dead kingdom of Vakhtangov's *The Wedding* was reminiscent of the funeral in *The Miracle of Saint Anthony*. Just as none of the funeral participants in *The Miracle* cared about Mademoiselle Hortense's death, in *The Wedding*, no one cared about the wedding as an act of holy matrimony. *The Miracle* funeral guests were waiting for their partridges and a wealthy inheritance, while *The Wedding* guests were waiting for the arrival of the general—a traditional guest of honor at a nineteenth-century Russian philistine's wedding. The presence of a general, in the eyes of the "petty bourgeois," was supposed to make the wedding "prestigious."

In *The Miracle,* Saint Anthony's answer to Virginie's prayer challenged the ritual of the funeral. In *The Wedding*, the deadly essence of the wedding was challenged by the arrival of a sea captain, a good-natured old man, initially mistaken for a general. (One of the bride's relatives, a young man in charge of "hiring" a general, brought the unsuspecting sea captain to the wedding. Needless to say, the young man "kept" the money given to him for the hire of the general.)

The "would-be general," unaware of his important role, carried himself naturally, as if among friends. A lack of "solemnity" in the general's behavior alarmed the bride's mother. When "the general's" actual rank was revealed, the wedding guests felt bitterly deceived in their expectations. They confronted the captain; the humiliated old man left the ceremony, "shaking the dust off of his sandals," just as Saint Anthony and Virginie did at the end of *The Miracle*.

Vakhtangov's approach to *The Wedding* was unorthodox. He turned an anecdote into tragic comedy. In *The Wedding*, Vakhtangov entered the inferno of a philistine's non-life—the kind of existence where a man does not actually live, but just goes through the motions.

While waiting for the captain, the wedding guests passed the time dancing a quadrille. Suddenly, in the middle of a dance, the music would stop (the pianist's fingers grew numb from the intense tempo) and the wedding guests found themselves facing each other in a moment of awkward silence.

The full stops, or freezes, used by Vakhtangov in this dance scene, appeared realistically motivated—just as they were in *The Miracle*. The wedding pianist had to rest his fingers, stiff from non-stop playing. Philosophically speaking, however, these full stops signified moments when Chekhov's characters "come to from the senseless, but 'most necessary' wedding ritual" (Gorchakov 1957: 40). These freezes represented instances of realization, by the characters, that their life is not real, that they are only lulled into believing that they exist. A moment of truth could not last longer than a few seconds, though. The "wound up" wedding guests eventually said to themselves: "This is how it must be! This is a custom! This is how one behaves at a wedding! Why waste time thinking! Let's dance!" (Gorchakov 1957: 38). And the dance would resume.

Deep within, however, Chekhov's petty bourgeois felt that the only thing that could save them from their empty existence was the miraculous arrival of a "messiah." Some kind of a higher being must arrive and, by its presence, breathe meaning into their senseless lives. A yearning for a better life—the classic through-action of a Chekhovian play—was represented in *The Wedding* by the anticipated arrival of a general. By gracing the wedding with his presence, the general was supposed to bring the missing "beauty" into the otherwise ugly and vulgar existence of wound-up puppets—philistines.

The theme of the living puppet—Vakhtangov's artistic leitmotif—received a new rendition in *The Wedding*. Boris Zakhava saw in *The Wedding* a variation on the device Vakhtangov suggested to his students, as they worked on Antakol'sky's play *The Infanta's Doll*:[2]

In *Infanta's Doll*, Vakhtangov wanted to portray a live toy, while in this production [*The Wedding*], he wants to reveal a dead essence in a living human being. In *The Infanta's Doll*, a marionette acted as a person, while in *The Wedding*, the person acted as a marionette.

As a result, Chekhov's comedy [. . .] gained some strange and unusual overtones—an amusing anecdote turned with its reverse side to the audience and revealed its senseless, ugly, and therefore, tragic essence—the audience laughed, but eventually they felt terrified of their own laughter. In fact, laughter froze in their throats—the comic incident transformed into tragedy; what was once funny became scary. If one were to bring a marionette to life,

2 See p. 142.

it would not seem scary, but merely amusing and funny; it would move the audience, and the audience would love it. When, however, in a live person, the audience senses a wound-up mechanism instead of a heart—they become horrified. Instead of showing the living in the dead, Vakhtangov showed the dead in the living— such was the world as portrayed in Vakhtangov's *The Wedding*.
(Zakhava 1930: 135)

Natalia Smirnova (1982: 41) rightly observed that the absence of a general constituted the first event in Vakhtangov's production, while the false general's arrival (closer toward the end of the play) constituted its second event. The third event occurred when the wedding participants discovered that that their guest of honor was in fact not a general—just a sea captain.

The meaning and beauty were, again, gone from the wedding participants' lives. The last hope of bringing some purpose into the ritual vanished. Having found themselves back in the tedium of their usual non-existence, the wedding guests angrily confronted the captain. The captain, in turn, realized *where he was*. He understood that he was tricked into posing as a "wedding general."

The tragic undercurrents of *The Wedding* surfaced in the last scene. As the old captain stumbled toward the exit, he yelled "Waiter!," apparently asking a waiter to help him find his way. In the Russian vocabulary of the time, a waiter was often referred to as "*chelovek*," which also means "human being." Vakhtangov's captain's yell had such a tragic subtext that the audience immediately perceived its double meaning—the old captain appeared to be striving to find a single human being, at least one living soul, among the marionettes, inhabiting the wedding hell. When the playwright's nephew, Michael Chekhov, came to see Vakhtangov's *The Wedding*, he reportedly told the director: "Zhenya, it is scary, what you have created" (Smirnov-Nesvitsky 1987: 179).

Part V

Three final masterpieces

23 *Erik XIV*

Vakhtangov and Michael Chekhov

Vakhtangov directed Strindberg's *Erik XIV* at the First Studio of the MAT in 1921. In this production, Vakhtangov, for the first time, introduced the new principles of expressivity to the First Studio troupe. The opposition of the ensemble was almost unanimous. The actors openly ridiculed the futuristic sets, costumes, and makeup, designed by Vakhtangov's new collaborator—Ignaty Nivinsky. One of the actors, Boris Sushkevich,[1] for whom Nivinsky designed a green wig, exclaimed: "If during rehearsals, my hair will, at the very least, turn yellow, then all right, I will wear this wig. If not—never!" (Sushkevich 1959: 369). Michael Chekhov, who played the title role of Erik, was the only member of the First Studio to accept Vakhtangov's new ideas from the start.

It is commonly believed, however, that Michael Chekhov and Vakhtangov were involved in a different artistic dispute during the rehearsals for *Erik XIV*. As the legend goes (Dikiy 1957: 311–15; Giatsintova 1989: 206), Vakhtangov intended to stage *Erik* as a piece pronouncing the doom of monarchy, while Chekhov wanted to play King Erik's tormented soul, lost in the labyrinth of a historic cataclysm (the Revolution).

Even if a conflict between the two artists existed originally, Vakhtangov was too sensitive a director not to incorporate Chekhov's artistic desires into his production. Moreover, proclaiming the doom of monarchy seems too topical a task for Vakhtangov, who used to warn his peers: "Don't do it, for God's sake! Do not reflect the era!"

---

1 Sushkevich was also responsible, as an assistant director, for the preliminary rehearsal period of *Erik XIV*.

(*Sourcebook* 2011: 234). Finally, a deeply moral soul of King Erik, exposed to the battle of good and evil, was a fitting theme for a Vakhtangov production.

The parable of the King from the New Testament

The plot of *Erik XIV* does deal with absolute power; however, in his play, Strindberg described a popular monarchy, or rather popular tyranny—a dictatorship, carried out by the people, on behalf of the people. In his mad fancy, King Erik alienated the nobility and relied on the alliance with the commoners. He takes up a common wife, Karin (see Plate 8), who is a daughter to a common soldier—Mons.

Before Erik claimed Karin, she was engaged to warrant officer Max (see Plate 9); she leaves Max for Eric, not so much because she prefers a king to a lowly officer, but rather out of pity for Erik. Karin is kind and noble at heart and, for that reason, Erik does not fully trust his bride's council. So, he appoints another commoner, Persson (see Plate 7), as his procurator.[2] Persson is ready to cut the throat of Erik's enemies—the aristocrats—and so he does. Erik goes along with Persson, but his inborn humanity (Erik is woven of contradictions) does not allow him to fully accept Persson's methods.

In Vakhtangov's production, just as in Strindberg's play, Erik's association with the people caused his demise. This fact was always overlooked by Vakhtangov's Soviet critics, as it shed a potentially dangerous light on the meaning of Vakhtangov's masterpiece. Vakhtangov's *Erik XIV* proclaimed that a power determined to establish the Kingdom of God on earth, and make "the last first, and the first last" (Matthew 20:16), can only function as a *tyranny*. Like every tyranny, it is doomed. When one looks at Vakhtangov's *Erik* from this standpoint, it stops being a moral justification of the Revolution, or a proof of its inevitability, but rather a sentence on the revolutionary utopia, and its bloody methods.

At the heart of Vakhtangov's production stood the allusion to the parable of the wedding feast from the New Testament. In the Biblical parable, the nobles refuse to attend the wedding of the King's son. The offended King orders his servants: "Go ye therefore into the highways, and as many as ye shall find, bid to the marriage." Strindberg's play features a variation on this theme.

---

2 Public prosecutor.

In the final act of Strindberg's play, King Erik himself marries a soldier's daughter and invites his bride's family, and their like, to his wedding feast. Erik's courtiers, unwilling to share the table with the commoners, do not show up at the feast. (This signals the coup against Erik.) When the aristocrats refuse to attend, Erik "orders to assemble the beggars from the gutter and the street harlots from the tavern" (*Sourcebook* 2011: 139) at the royal table. "Just like the King from the New Testament"—clarifies Vakhtangov in his article on *Erik XIV* (*Sourcebook* 2011: 139–42). The synergy of the popular and the mysterious was the main factor that attracted Vakhtangov to Strindberg.

The two worlds of *Erik XIV*

Among the formal innovations of *Erik XIV*, one in particular struck the viewer. Various groups of characters in Strindberg's play were defined by Vakhtangov through the use of different theatrical textures. In his article on *Erik XIV*, Vakhtangov enumerated three such textures: the dead world of the "pale-faced and bloodless courtiers," "the live world of simple people," and Erik, whose soul is torn between the two worlds.

Vakhtangov's article, written after the opening of *Erik XIV*, reflected the actual allocation of forces in the performance. The group of actors playing courtiers introduced the style of the monumental grotesque; their statuesque appearance read to the audience as immobility, as death (see Figure 23.1 and Plate 6). The group of actors playing commoners stayed more or less within the usual Moscow Art Theatre's realm: the texture of their acting allowed for realistic details.

The most complex texture in the production was assigned to Chekhov's Erik. His borderline existence placed him in a special space within the world of the production—not to mention that the dimension of Michael Chekhov's creative individuality equally justified Vakhtangov's bold experiment.

Michael Chekhov's acting as Erik could be described as "psychophysical grotesque." His life onstage was psychologically transparent—audiences were mesmerized by complete harmony between the movements of the actor's body and the impulses of his soul. This achievement of Chekhov's is well described by the Czech poet Karel Čapek:

> If I was an actor, I would drown myself having watched *Erik XIV*.
> If I was German, I would write some abstract tractate about an

Figure 23.1 Serafima Birman as Queen Mother in *Erik XIV*, 1921. Courtesy of Vakhtangov Theatre Museum.

actor's craft. If I was Russian, I would tell myself that one must never despair in life, that there must be some kind of redemption in this world where there is so much art, so much beauty of body and soul. These very two words—body and soul—contain the mystery of this amazing artistic achievement . . . For "body" can "dress" the soul, it can "symbolize" it, it can "express" it. But here comes this Chekhov and demonstrates that body (in a simple and yet mysterious way)—is the soul. The very soul, a despairing, passionate, vibrant, trembling soul.

I saw many truly inspired actors. Their loftiest art was the skill of convincing you that behind the shell of their character's body, somewhere inside them, there hid an intense life of the soul. Chekhov does not have this "inside"; everything is bared, nothing is hidden, everything is impulsive and sharp; with great intensity it flows into the play of his entire body—this delicate and tremulous tangle of nerves. At the same time, his acting is so inwardly pure, soulful, and so deep, as no other. Do tell me, how is it possible? I know nothing. But I am convinced that here, for the first time, I saw something truly novel and serious, a truly contemporary actor's art.

(Smirnov-Nesvitsky 1987: 160)

The rhythmic patterns Chekhov created in space and time were expressive, complex, and often contradictory. In his acting, the audiences observed not just the unison of the inner and outer, but also a certain dichotomy. At times, Erik's physical gestures ran ahead of his inner impulse, and at other times they dragged behind. At some moments, Erik's movements "got stuck," creating the effect of a living doll, or a puppet, whose mechanism jammed. This psycho-physical phenomenon would manifest itself in a repetitive gestural pattern, or even in a sudden "freeze."

Erik's wife Karin compared her husband with her childhood doll. This image was elaborated by Vakhtangov, who had been consistently exploring the phenomenon of a puppet come to life, or a human being turn into a puppet. Just as the image of a puppet is essentially archetypal, Chekhov's spiritual and physical life in Erik was also archetypal.

On the day Stanislavsky watched *Erik XIV*, Vakhtangov fled the theatre. Considering the poor state of Vakhtangov's health, he could easily claim illness. In the meantime, Stanislavsky accepted the production wholeheartedly. He first labeled it "futurism"[3] but then suddenly added: "This kind of futurism I understand" (Deykun 1984: 355–56).

Obviously, Vakhtangov's "justification" of the performance's style satisfied Stanislavsky. How did Vakhtangov manage to reconcile three different acting textures within one production?

The justification was supplied by the point of view Vakhtangov offered to his spectators. In the director's interpretation, the audience saw the production of Strindberg's *Erik XIV* as if through the eyes of mad King Erik (see Figure 23.2). The different textures of the performance were nothing but Erik's view on the different people

---

3 This word sounded like a swear word coming from Stanislavsky's lips.

Figure 23.2 Michael Chekhov in the title role in *Erik XIV*, 1921. Courtesy of Vakhtangov Theatre Museum.

surrounding him (Smirnova 1982: 24). Similarly, Ignaty Nivinsky's set
showed the world according to Erik—cluttered, chaotic, and askew.
(See Plates 2, 3, and 4.)

Vakhtangov's portrayal of the common folk using the device of
ethnographic detail (see Plate 8) was well-suited to convey Erik's
naive view of the people. This was not the theatre's or the director's
point of view. This was the portrayal of the common people, as seen
through Erik's lens. It must be noted, however, that Vakhtangov's
use of the Moscow Art Theatre's traditional techniques, in the overall
futuristic production of *Erik XIV*, looked somewhat ironic. By the
time *Erik XIV* premiered, Vakhtangov had outgrown the traditional

MAT devices, such as true-to-life external characterization, spiritual naturalism, and ethnographic accuracy of customs and period costume.

The same, however, can be said of the dead, statuary-like, and immobile courtiers. The stylized, futuristic portrayal of the court might have looked a direct quote from Meyerhold and Tairov—except that the quote was deliberate and, most importantly, artistically justified. What appeared as a formal experiment in Meyerhold and Chamber Theatre's productions, in Vakhtangov's production became organic to the world of Strindberg.

Vakhtangov's irony shed light on the true meaning of *Erik*'s two worlds—the dead and the living. The world of the common people, portrayed through the use of spiritual and physical naturalism, was *no* more alive in Vakhtangov's production than the monumentally dead world of the courtiers. This was not just a philosophical or political statement—this was equally an aesthetic sentence on the Moscow Art Theatre's style. *Erik XIV* signifies the last time that physical characterization was featured in Vakhtangov's production. Shortly after the opening of *Erik XIV*, Vakhtangov made the following entry in his diary:

> The theatre of everyday life must die. "Character" actors are no longer needed. All who have capacity for playing character roles must feel the tragedy (even the comedians) in every character part; they must learn to express themselves through the grotesque.
>
> Grotesque—tragic and comedic.
>
> (*Sourcebook* 2011: 109)

In *Erik XIV, the* tragic grotesque belonged to the creative palette of Michael Chekhov. Both physical naturalism (characterization) and statuesque immobility (stylization) represented the dead shells of social identity. In a Vakhtangov production, any social identity constituted a shell that protected an individual from the ultimate battle of Good and Evil. Vakhtangov believed that such a battle can only take place in an exposed human heart.

In the case of *Erik XIV*, the "popular" King Erik was the only character who forever remained torn, on the threshold. Consequently, he was also the only one to find his liberation in death at the end of the play. The finale of Vakhtangov's *Erik XIV* differed from Strindberg's. In the play, Strindberg makes it clear that Erik falls victim to the aristocrats' coup. In Vakhtangov's production Chekhov's Erik took his own life. Like a philosopher of antiquity, he drank of the poisoned cup.

Vakhtangov portrayed Erik's death as a liberation from his cursed earthly form of half-monarch/half-commoner. As his character "died," Chekhov stepped out of the puppet-like shell of his royal mantle, split by arrows (see Plate 5), and remained "spiritually naked." Motionless he stood, clad in a tight garment resembling a monk's robe. The audience finally saw the liberated soul of Erik.

A true liberation, Vakhtangov seemed to be saying, cannot be achieved on this earth. Last will never become first in this life. But those first who challenged the earthly order, and became last through their suffering, can find their liberation in their next life. The motive of liberation through death is present in all of Vakhtangov's tragedies. It is also heard in his swan song—the joyful and optimistic *Princess Turandot*.

The meaning of Vakhtangov's *Erik XIV* was universal. One could experience Erik's soul as the soul of a revolutionary, drowning in the very blood he shed. One could see Erik's soul as the soul of an artist, an intelligent member, torn apart by the contradiction of the Revolution. In truth, Chekhov's performance of Erik rose to the heights of the true inner grotesque; it gained a universal meaning in Vakhtangov's production.

Erik XIV and the Bolshevik Revolution

Several critics and artists, members of the Russian intelligentsia, noted the similarity between the image of the Time, as created in *Erik*, and the murky period of the Revolution. The atmosphere, the physical space, and rhythms of movement and speech in *Erik* were filled with anxiety. The anxiety reached its climax in the final act, in the scene of alarm in Erik's palace.

The king's enemies approach; their army is ready to capture the palace, and poor Erik is doomed. Pavel Markov offered the following description of this moment:

> Buzzing voices, mournful or sinister, are [. . .] heard from afar. [. . .] In the center of the stage stands Erik with his procurator. [. . .] And now, silently appears a courtier; he creeps in, as if rolling. He does not stop at the king's call. This is unprecedented. This is unheard of. This alone is a revolt. The second courtier comes in, alarmed, from the opposite stage wing. Due to the system of platforms—small sections of steps, like church porches on the stage, the impression is created of flowing movements, ascents and descents, exits and turns. Just with the use of three courtiers, secretively whispering upon the central platform (as the fourth courtier walks through the entire stage, as though he made

up his mind about something, and is now in a hurry to get some-where), the impression of the alarm is created. After a second, they break up, exiting diagonally, into four different stage wings. The palace *immediately* becomes empty. Through the use of four stage wings, four courtiers and the system of creeping, decisive movements, Vakhtangov populated the palace with [the atmo-sphere of] alarm, crossed it with transposing lines of people bustling about. Through the use of the cluster ("they are whis-pering secretly!") and one courtier moving past this cluster ("every man for himself!"), and by blocking all of them to exit diagonally into different corners ("rats ran away"), in half a minute he created an impression of the *deserted* palace.

(Markov 1925: 142)

In this passage, the critic stresses the simplicity of the means used by Vakhtangov to create the rhythm and imagery of the palace scene. The rhythmical pattern created by Vakhtangov picks up on the structure of Ignaty Nivinsky's set—"the system of platforms—small sections of steps, like church porches on the stage" (Markov 1925: 142) (see Plates 3 and 4). Moreover, Vakhtangov continues the rhythms of the set in movement, materializing what Michael Chekhov would later call Fantastic Psychological Gesture (Chekhov 2002: 184–86, 215).[4]

The birth of the Psychological Gesture

Vakhtangov and Chekhov's colleagues, who observed the two artists at work, noticed that it was impossible to perceive where Chekhov ended and where Vakhtangov began. The director and his actor complemented and, most importantly, continued each other's work. During their collaboration on *Erik XIV*, Vakhtangov and Chekhov developed a new rehearsal language—the language of the gesture. They no longer needed words to communicate with each other.

It would not be an exaggeration to say that some aspects of the future Michael Chekhov method, such as Psychological Gesture, came out of Chekhov's rehearsal work with Vakhtangov on the role of Erik.[5] Was it Chekhov who gave Vakhtangov the idea of the Psychological

4 In his Dartington Hall master classes Chekhov says that the Psychological Gesture is "rhythm and movement," thus connecting his search with Vakhtangov's.
5 Chekhov's techniques were also inspired by his observations of Vakhtangov's work at The Habima and the Vakhtangov Studios.

Gesture? Was it Vakhtangov who, having received this subconscious idea from Chekhov, gave it back to him in a concrete form? Did Vakhtangov simply help Chekhov make the idea of the Psychological Gesture conscious? Michael Chekhov had this to say on the subject:

> Vakhtangov possessed . . . [an] indispensable ability for a director: he could *demonstrate* to an actor what constituted the main pattern of his role. He did not demonstrate the character as a whole; he did not perform a role for the actor, but he *demonstrated,* or *acted out* a scheme, an outline, a pattern of the role. While directing *Erik XIV,* he demonstrated to me . . . the pattern of the role of Erik throughout an entire act, having spent no more than two minutes on this. After his demonstration the entire act in all its details became clear to me, even though Vakhtangov did not touch these details. He gave me the major will-power framework; later I could distribute the details and particulars of the role.
>
> (Chekhov 1995: 75)

In the preceding passage, Chekhov describes Vakhtangov's demonstration to him of a Psychological Gesture for a large unit of the play, or a Compository Psychological Gesture. On a different occasion, Vakhtangov demonstrated to Michael Chekhov the Psychological Gesture for the role of Erik as a whole:

> One night at a rehearsal he suddenly jumped up, exclaiming, "This is your Erik. Look! I am now inside a magic circle and cannot break out of it!" With his whole body he made one strong, painfully passionate movement, as if trying to break an invisible wall before him, or pierce a magic circle. The destiny, the endless suffering, the obstinacy, and the weakness of *Erik XIV* became clear to me. From that night I could act the part with all its innumerable nuances, though all four acts of the play.
>
> (Chekhov 1991: 89)

Chekhov in his technique mostly dealt with an internal (spiritual) gesture meant to stir the actors' psychology (this is why he called it Psychological); Vakhtangov boldly revealed his Archetypal Gestures on the stage. The degree of passion present in Vakhtangov's three final productions (*Erik XIV, The Dybbuk*, and *Princess Turandot*) was so high that it allowed for the Psychological, or rather Archetypical, Gesture to be openly manifested in the space.

24 *The Dybbuk* as the Theatre of Archetypal Gesture
Inventing Hebrew Theatre

Vakhtangov and The Habima

In his production of *The Dybbuk*, staged in 1922 at the Hebrew Habima Studio in Moscow, Vakhtangov created a working model for the contemporary Hebrew Theatre.[1] One can agree or disagree with this model, find it fitting or unfitting, accurate or inaccurate. At the same time, no one can argue that Vakhtangov's model determined the future of the Hebrew Theatre for generations to come.

The Habima Studio was organized by a group of Hebrew teachers, who came to Moscow in 1917—the year of the Russian Revolution—from Poland, Lithuania, and the outskirts of the Russian Empire. The young Hebrew teachers from Warsaw, Vilna, and Bialystok arrived in revolutionary Moscow to fulfill their dream of creating a National Jewish Theatre that would perform in Hebrew.

None of the three Habima founders had significant theatrical experience, and none of them knew how to create the theatre. According to the Russian scholar Vladislav Ivanov (1999: 18), the vision itself was a vague sensation in the heart of one of the founders—The Habima's director Nahum Zemach. Zemach felt that the new theatre must be the Theatre of Tragedy. It should be capable of expressing the epic history of the Jewish nation—from its Talmudic origins, to the recent tragedies of the Pogroms.

Zemach sensed that the Hebrew Theatre should be the Theatre of the Talmud, myth and legend, and the theatre of elevated feelings. Only such a theatre, in Zemach's mind, was capable of revealing the grandeur, richness, and melodiousness of the Hebrew language.

---

1 The theatrical model created by Vakhtangov was historically unprecedented. At the start of the twentieth century, Hebrew Theatre did not exist, as an institution, in Russia, or elsewhere.

Zemach also knew that the new theatre must be of the highest artistic caliber, if it were to beat the odds and, in the long run, establish itself in Palestine. This is why Zemach was seeking no other directors and teachers for his group than those from the Moscow Art Theatre.

Stanislavsky had proven to be sympathetic to the cause;[2] to begin with, he arranged for his best teacher, Vakhtangov, to lead The Habima toward mastering the art of acting. At this point, Vakhtangov pronounced Habima a Studio; he ordered it to abandon a grand building they received from the state and move into a much more intimate space. There, under Vakhtangov's guidance, regular acting classes began.

Theatre as a higher calling

None of The Habima founding members had any doubt about their final destination. Palestine was where the National Jewish Theatre, performing in Hebrew, eventually belonged. This was more than The Habima's goal; this was its mission and its higher calling. The three founders even gave the vow of chastity: they were not to start families before The Habima stepped onto Palestine soil. Many of the Jewish actors answered The Habima founders' call, and took a dangerous trip to Moscow at a time of economic turmoil and political chaos.

One of the factors that brought Vakhtangov together with The Habima was their mutual perception of theatre as the means for a greater and higher goal. The Habima, among other things, aimed at restoring the sense of national identity among the Jews. In the minds of the Studio founders, the creation of the Hebrew Theatre was meant to strengthen the cultural consciousness of the scattered and persecuted nation.

Vakhtangov also lived with the sense of great mission. His dream of the future theatre, though, was initially as vague as The Habima's vision of the Hebrew Theatre. On April 14, 1916, a year prior to meeting The Habima, Vakhtangov wrote in his diary:

> In our theatre, at the Studio and among my own students, I can feel a need for the uplifting. I can feel their dissatisfaction with a performance depicting "the mundane," even if it aims for the good.

---

2 Besides Stanislavsky and Vakhtangov, other members of the Russian artistic intelligentsia, at different points in time, came to the aid of The Habima, including Fyodor Shalyapin, Vsevolod Meyerhold, and Maxim Gorky.

Perhaps, this is the first step toward "romanticism," toward a turnaround.

I too imagine something ahead.

A kind of festival of feelings, reflected onto the uplifting spiritual realm (what kind of spirituality?), rather than onto the virtuous, so-called, Christian feelings.

We must rise, even if only one foot high, above the earth. For now.
(*Sourcebook* 2011: 235)

One year after the start of his work at The Habima, Vakhtangov's dream about the heroic theatre took a more concrete shape. He prepared to stage Byron's *Cain*; he considered Verhaeren's *The Dawn*. Vladislav Ivanov (1999: 30) suggested that Vakhtangov's plan for adapting the Old Testament for the stage, outlined in his diary entry from October 25, 1918 (*Sourcebook* 2011: 241), was directly connected with The Habima.

Upon Vakhtangov's arrival at The Habima, he was immediately perceived as a theatrical prophet by the entire troupe. The Studio members sensed that they could not fulfill their own mission without Vakhtangov's artistic genius. Both the Studio and Vakhtangov also recognized that, without the highest caliber of artistry, The Habima would never reach its final destination—Palestine. This is why each actor at The Habima fulfilled Vakhtangov's every direction "persistently and implicitly, believing in his every note and happy about their work" (Podgorny 1984: 401).

The hard work was not in vain—as soon as Vakhtangov's production of *The Dybbuk* opened at The Habima in 1922, the company found itself on the theatrical map. They graduated from having to fill an empty theatre with their own members, to permanently sold-out houses. *The Dybbuk* eventually secured The Habima's triumphant journey through Europe and the United States to the land of their ancestors.

Challenges of *The Dybbuk*

On October 8, 1918, The Habima officially opened with *The Genesis Performance*, an evening of one-act plays, directed by Vakhtangov.[3] For the most part, it consisted of pieces depicting the everyday life of the shtetl. How far these works were from the original vision of the Theatre

---

3 *The Genesis Performance*, directed by Vakhtangov for The Habima opening, consisted of four one-act plays: *The Elder Daughter* by Shalom Ash, *The Fire* by Isaac Leib Peretz, *The Sun! The Sun!* by Itzhak Katzenelson, and *The Pest* by Isaac D. Berkowitz.

of the Tragedy, the Theatre of the Talmud! It was understood, however, that the works by the contemporary Jewish authors provided necessary realistic training material for the inexperienced Habima actors. Vakhtangov's *The Genesis Performance* was meant to serve as a school for the young actors, who needed to start their life in theatre by developing the feeling of truth—a foundation for their inner technique.

It is in this naturalistic mode that Vakhtangov began to work on the play, entitled *The Dybbuk, or Between the Two Worlds.*

The Dybbuk was written by an extraordinary man with the Russian penname Semyon Akimovich An-sky. His real name was Shloyme Zanvl Rappoport, and he was a folklorist, dedicated to gathering accounts of the Jewish tradition, myth, legend, and ritual. At the same time, An-sky was a mystic, a fact that accounts for the second title of his play: *Between the Two Worlds.* Finally, An-sky was a well-known social revolutionary and populist figure, who welcomed the Russian bourgeois Revolution in February 1917. The play, written in Russian, was presented to Stanislavksy, who for several years actively considered it for the First Studio of MAT.[4]

In 1917, a wealthy philanthropist bought the play for the emerging Habima under the condition that the great Jewish poet Hayim Nahman Bialik [1873–1934] create a Hebrew translation. Bialik's Hebrew version surpassed the original; An-sky himself called it "pure music." Vakhtangov, who, despite popular belief, did not stand behind the commission of the Hebrew translation, nevertheless, considered Bialik "a major poet," "powerful and vehement" (Vendrovskaya and Kaptereva 1984: 271).

Like Vakhtangov, populist An-sky believed that archetypal images that live within the people must be extracted and artistically formed. Using Vakhtangov's terminology, "An artist crystallizes and completes images and symbols previously kept in the popular art" (*Sourcebook* 2011: 162). An-sky spent three years in Jewish *shtetls*[5] collecting the myths and legends, fairy-tales and rituals of the Jews. *The Dybbuk* became an artistic summary of this work.

Like Vakhtangov, An-sky believed the creative impulse born in the people must be *returned* to them in an artistically shaped form. People

---

4 At different points, Sulerzhitsky and Sushkevich were supposed to direct the piece with Khmara and Michael Chekhov acting. Vakhtangov, it seems, was not involved until after the play was passed onto The Habima. Both Sulerzhitsky and Stanislavsky contributed to the rewrites of the play.

5 An-sky was accompanied on this trip by the musical folklorist and the future composer for Vakhtangov's *Dybbuk*, Joel Engel.

must be given an opportunity to experience *in a creative way* those passions, both ugly and beautiful, that live in their collective soul. Otherwise, the locked-up impulse would manifest itself in a non-creative, ugly shape, fraught with historical cataclysms. When An-sky transformed his research into a play, he must have relied on the theatre's power to implement a *live popular act*. Vakhtangov, in his turn, managed to make *The Dybbuk* an actual reenactment of the deepest desires, sorrows, yearnings that live in the people's soul as legends, rituals, or myths.

An-sky's play is based on a popular Jewish myth about the spirit of a dead man—*dybbuk*. Moreover, the play is built around three rituals. Its first act features study and prayer at the synagogue. The second act is built around the wedding feast and, finally, its third act contains a trial, and an act of exorcism—both carried out in the prayer room of the holy man.

The play tells the story of Channan, a young Talmudic scholar, and Leah, the daughter of the rich merchant Sender. Leah and Channan were betrothed by their fathers at birth, but Sender defaulted on the agreement. He promised his daughter's hand to the son of a wealthy man. Desperate Channan goes against the faith of his ancestors. To win back his beloved Leah, he resorts to the power of the Kabbalah. While Channan's fellow Batlanim[6] recite traditional chants in the synagogue, Channan calls upon the spirit of the Kabbalah to prevent Leah's wedding with the rich man. Channan's incantations produce no effect. At the end of the first act, the young man falls dead at the news that Leah's wedding day has been set (see Figure 24.1).

The day of Leah's wedding has arrived. Prior to the ceremony, the bride attends the *shtetl* cemetery and invites the dead Channan to the festivities. Beggars at Leah's wedding swirl the bride in a violent dance, thus making her susceptible to Channan's spirit. The spirit of the dead man, or *dybbuk*, possesses Leah's body. Overpowered by the *dybbuk*, Leah refuses to go on with the wedding.

Leah's father takes the bride to the local *tzaddik* (Hasidic sage), who exorcizes the spirit. No sooner than the *dybbuk* exits Leah's body, she crosses the boundary of the magic circle, drawn by the *tzaddik*. "I come to you, my fiancé"—says Leah to the spirit of her beloved Channan, as she falls dead (see Figure 24.2).

---

6 Batlanim, or "men of leisure"—in the Jewish religious tradition, learned men, unencumbered with worldly things. Batlanim are at leisure to study Torah and take care of the affairs of the synagogue.

Figure 24.1 Finale of Act 1 of *The Dybbuk*, 1922. Courtesy of Vakhtangov Theatre Museum.

Figure 24.2 Finale of Act 3 of *The Dybbuk*, 1922. Aleksandr Prutkin (Karev) as the Messenger, Hannah Rovina as Leah. Courtesy of Vakhtangov Theatre Museum.

The theme of the dead and the living worlds, the classical Vakhtangovian theme, was literally turned upside down in *The Dybbuk*. The real, live world of the play included the bride's family and relatives, who were portrayed as heavy and spiritless. The beggars at the wedding ceremony were also rendered as ghostly and dead. In Vakhtangov's interpretation, the world of the living revealed its nightmarish quality—it appeared as pointed entirely into the past.

The "dead world" in *The Dybbuk* included the otherworldly love of Channan and Leah, Channan's mystical dreams, and his life beyond the grave—both in the world of the dead, and in Leah's body. Vakhtangov endowed the dead world with tremulous, vibrant qualities. This world appeared in the production as powerful and spiritually alive. When Leah spoke in Channan's voice, she appeared passionate and agitated as never before. Her own love for Channan, so timid in the real world, was finally liberated in the realm of the otherworldly.

Life—beautiful and mysterious—appeared to be *on the other side* of the earthly threshold. Such a reversal may have been due to Vakhtangov's sense of the line he himself was about to cross. In the eyes of his students and colleagues, Vakhtangov was overcoming death through his final creative act. His Channan and Leah were freed from the *earthly* world of the dead—the world of materialism and dogma that had no place for their love.

The Gesture of the composition

What expressive means did Vakhtangov use to make the ancient language, that few people in Moscow spoke, understandable to all? What artistic devices did he utilize to tell the story of the two worlds— the dead and the living? Why did Vakhtangov's *The Dybbuk* win audiences over in Russia, Europe, US, Egypt, and Palestine? What was the secret of its universal power?

The answer to all these questions lies in the device of the Archetypal Gesture, utilized by Vakhtangov in *The Dybbuk*. In this production, the actor's body and hands, as well as the principle of the dynamic speech, became Vakhtangov's major means of expressiveness.

In *Erik XIV*, Vakhtangov exposed an atmosphere and rhythms of the murky and tremulous revolutionary times, consonant with any time of turmoil. In *The Dybbuk*, Vakhtangov revealed the gesture of the cataclysm, of the destruction—the universal gesture of the bloody twentieth century. The story of Channan and Leah, separated by the dead world of the rich, seemingly has nothing to do with the communist purges, or war and Holocaust—be it a "miniature" Holocaust of the *pogrom*, or the machine of mass destruction set forth by Adolf Hitler. Nevertheless, throughout its 40-year performance history, the famous beggars' dance from the second act of *The Dybbuk* became permeated with all the horrors of the bloody century.

Parallels between the beggars' dance and Bialik's 1903 poem *City of the Killings* have been drawn by the Vakhtangov scholar Smirnov-Nesvitsky (1987: 209). As mentioned earlier, Vakhtangov was familiar with the poem, and considered it Bialik's masterpiece:

> And if you rose early tomorrow and went to the crossroads
> you'd see many bits of men all groans and sighs,
> swarming the windows of the rich and hanging about their doors
> crying aloud their wounds as a hawker does his goods;
> who has a cracked skull, and who a hand-cut and a bruise
> and every one puts forth a grimy paw and bares a broken arm,
> with eyes, the eyes of beaten slaves, to the hands of their masters
> to say: I have a broken skull, I a "martyred" father—pay me for
> them!
>
> (Bialik 2000: 8)

As if echoing Bialik's poem, Vakhtangov told his actors, as he directed the beggars' dance:

> You have a limp, you are not comfortable dancing. Go ahead, dance. You are blind, you can't see a thing, you don't know how to dance, you are not even supposed to be dancing. All the same— go ahead, dance. I need a protest-dance, a scream-dance.
>
> (Karev 1959: 417)

The gesture of protest, the essence of the beggars' dance, was also present in the story of Leah and Channan's love, as retold by Vakhtangov. In Vakhtangov's production, the union of Channan and Leah was seen by the audience as a *rebellious act* of liberation achieved beyond life's threshold. The couple's challenge to the world of the living dead read as a breaking with the heavy and powerful tradition of the ancestors. In the rigid traditions of the Hasidic world, Channan and Leah's gesture of defiance did amount to a revolutionary act.

Overall, Vakhtangov's production was filled with powerful gestures bypassing the audiences' rational mind and going straight to their psyche.

Vakhtangov's composition of the beggars' wedding dance, for example, was a many-leveled gestural structure. Nikolai Volkov, a specialist in dance and ballet, saw it better than any of his contemporaries:

> Upon the white, red and green background of Sender's house [see Plate 17], in the atmosphere, permeated with the bright sunlight, [Vakhtangov] creates a number of dissonances. Directorial harmonization becomes more and more complex. The world of the dead is being molded not through one,[7] but through three different techniques. [Firstly,] Vakhtangov applies a statuary style to the group of three festively dressed and overly made up women. Their frozen puppet-like figures create a stagnant, lifeless and standoffishly foolish sensation. [Secondly,] Vakhtangov utilizes the monotony of fixed movements to convey the characters of Sender himself, the groom, his teacher, and the matchmaker. For each of these characters he finds several strictly defined small gestures. They are using these regardless of what the content of their inner emotional experience might be at a given moment. In an amusing way, Vakhtangov disunites the soul and the body. He draws his comic effect from the violation of the human psychophysical parallelism. Finally, the crowd of the beggars, invited to the wedding feast, is elaborated by Vakhtangov in the manner of exaggeration. These monstrous faces, deformed bodies and contorted movements, look as if they are taken from the caricatures by Leonardo [see Figure 24.3]. If one remembers the *bas-relief* of the beggars from *Erik XIV*, the enormity of the distance traveled by Vakhtangov between these two productions becomes obvious.
>
> (Volkov 1922: 19–20)

Volkov's analogy between *Erik* and *Dybbuk* can be continued. The device of disintegration of body and soul was used by Vakhtangov in *Erik* to tragic effect. The same device is fulfilling comedic purposes in *The Dybbuk*. Statuary immobility belonged in Vakhtangov's *Erik* to both the courtiers, and to the common people at the King's wedding feast. In both cases, the immobility was supposed to produce a threatening effect upon the audience. The immobility device in *The Dybbuk* was applied to the portrayal of the three women. These women

---

7 As in *Erik XIV* where the beggars were rendered as an immobile *bas relief*.

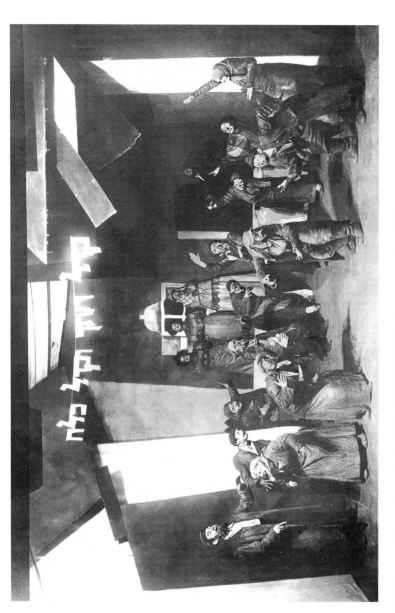

Figure 24.3 Beggars' dance from Act 2 of *The Dybbuk*, 1922. Courtesy of Arsis Design.

appeared as if they had stepped out of a primitive folk picture. They also somewhat related to the folklore drawn commoners in *Erik*. Finally, the swarming, dynamic group of the beggars created yet another counterpoint to the immobile women and to the broken up puppets of the groom's company.

Out of the three wedding groups, the group of the beggars appears, of course, most alive. Vakhtangov's sympathies rest with this group. Ugly and grotesque in their execution, the beggars overall fulfill a positive function in the play. By swirling the bride in a crazy dance, they weakened Leah—therefore making her susceptible to Channan-the-*dybbuk* (Yzraely 1970: 73) (see Figure 24.4). Cruelty and ugliness, according to Vakhtangov's moral compass, suddenly become equated with justice and beauty.

The cruelty of Vakhtangov's talent was mentioned by critics and artists continuously, since his First Studio of MAT directorial debut in *The Festival of Peace*. Vakhtangov's gift of unmasking his characters, traveling to the darkest corners of their psyche, as well as his talent for revealing "the beauty of ugliness" (Volkov 1922: 20) caused some Vakhtangov scholars (Ivanov 1999: 95–6) to suggest that his final masterpieces *practically* anticipated Artaud's theory of the Theatre of Cruelty.

The Gesture of the design—Chagall vs. Altman

At the start of Vakhtangov's work on *The Dybbuk*, nothing pointed to the new methods. The avant-garde artist and designer Marc Chagall, whom Nahum Zemach invited to attend a rehearsal, found it to be in the best Moscow Art Theatre's traditions. If things were to continue this way, An-sky's play would become a faithful illustration of the life of the Hassidim, a tribute to the ancestors.

The play itself yielded to such an interpretation, as it featured traditional rituals. A less common act of exorcism was, nevertheless, a part of the not so distant past (see Figure 24.5). Throughout the rehearsal, Marc Chagall, whose characters did not walk, but flew, kept wondering why Zemach thought him a likely designer for *The Dybbuk*. Vakhtangov himself did not welcome the visitor; the director made it clear that Chagall's "deformations are foreign to him, that the Stanislavsky method is the right one" (Chagall 2003: 166).

The turning point in the creation of *The Dybbuk* was, nevertheless, connected with Vakhtangov's choice of a designer. Having rejected Chagall, the director suddenly accepted radical and non-naturalistic designs, proposed by another avant-garde artist—Natan Altman.

Figure 24.4 Hannah Rovina as Leah (right) pulled into the dance by the beggars, scene from Act 2 of *The Dybbuk*, 1928. © The Israel Goor Theatre Archives and Museum (non-profit organization).

Vakhtangov's choice today seems a mistake, especially through the eyes of the Western cultural consciousness. Who is Altman, and who is Chagall? Nevertheless, Vakhtangov made an accurate choice for *The Dybbuk*.

Chagall's designs of the 1920s were too full of *joie de vivre* to ever agree with the tragic *Dybbuk*. The overall gesture of Chagall's art was not nearly as radical as Altman's. Chagall's crooked, bent, and curved lines are acrobatic in nature: they come from the Jewish wedding jester (*badkhonim*), from the circus, from harlequinade, even from *commedia dell'arte*. Chagall's gesture does not cut into the space, it does not overcome it. Like a circus acrobat, Chagall juggles with the space.

Altman's gesture attacks the space, battles with it and transforms it—it is a pure Archetypal Gesture (see Plates 11–16). Chagall's suggestion that, in the end, Vakhtangov found an artist to design *The Dybbuk* after Chagall is baseless. Altman's set for *The Dybbuk* can be, perhaps, compared to some of Chagall's theatre works of the period—for example, to his set for the Sholem Aleichem-based *Mazel Tov*, staged by the director Granovsky at the State Jewish

Figure 24.5 Scene from Act 3 of *The Dybbuk*, exorcism scene, 1922. Courtesy of Vakhtangov Theatre Museum.

Theatre in 1921. And yet, Altman in *The Dybbuk* uses a very different play of colors; he creates a different space, and ultimately a different world . . .

There is nothing from the expressionism, or from the theatrical aestheticism in Altman's set of *The Dybbuk*. Altman's set radiates condensed atmosphere, without even a hint of aesthetic beauty. In fact, it is bordering on ugliness. Altman's set does not pretend to be ugly and rough, as often happened with other designers of the early twentieth-century Jewish Russian Theatre. Altman's is a pure, artistically treated austerity (see Plate 17).

With designer Ignaty Nivinsky, who was responsible for the costumes and sets of Vakhtangov's *Erik XIV* and *Princess Turandot*, one can recognize some creative quotations. His works "paraphrase" Dürer, Bruegel, etc. Altman's chief source of inspiration is life—condensed, or theatrically transformed life. This too united him with Vakhtangov.

Altman's graphic distinctness is Vakhtangov's distinctness, as Vakhtangov too is graphic in his approach to theatre. Vakhtangov's works are not decorative; he is a master of the clear line, of black and white, of pure light and shadow. As a theatre artist, Vakhtangov avoided the richness of an oil painting—his richness lay in the structure of graphic contrasts.

Altman's sketches for *The Dybbuk* are also harmonious with Bialik's poetry. Vakhtangov's description of Bialik as "a powerful, vehement artist" can be applied to Altman. Each beggar sketch is a masterpiece of theatrical grotesque—in the Meyerholdian sense. Animal and bird archetypes stand behind these beggars: a beggar woman is a toad (see Plate 13), one beggar is a crow (see Plate 16), another a wolf.[9] Defective, crippled, warped faces, truncated people (see Plate 15), sick with tuberculosis (see Plate 12) . . .

Most importantly, Altman's work is pure gesture. Next to the zigzag of a broken line, we encounter straight, parallel, and perpendicular lines. Next to them, we see twisted, warped, and skewed lines. (Only the sketch of Leah has a graceful curve in it.) Some of Altman's sketches are reminiscent of Vakhtangov's marionette, Tackleton, from *The Cricket on the Hearth*. Altman's beggar palette consists of black, gray, white, and pale beige colors. It is similar to the palette of the artist Remisoff, who created Psychological

9 See *Sourcebook* (2001: Plate 4).

Gesture sketches for the 1946 Russian version of Chekhov's book, *On the Technique of Acting*.[10] The incorporeal quality of Altman's designs also united them with Michael Chekhov's concept of the Psychological Gesture.

In *The Dybbuk*, Vakhtanov and Altman "bared" the Archetypal and Psychological Gestures, thus openly exposing the pure essence of every character or event. The creator of the Psychological Gesture technique, Michael Chekhov, considered it a predominantly internal phenomenon. At the same time, Chekhov believed that Psychological Gestures could be revealed onstage, in an extreme moment—Vakhtangov's *The Dybbuk* was such an extreme, from beginning to end.

Unlike the beggars, Altman's sketches of Leah's family and friends use bright colors (red, purple, blue, lilac); their shapes are traditional—these characters are realistically "recognizable." Unlike the beggars, they have weight, roundness, and volume. At the same time, these sketches are executed with a touch of cubism. They too resemble puppets; if the beggars are pivot-hinged marionettes, or perhaps stick puppets, Leah's family resembles the traditional folk dolls (see Plate 14). The groom's family appears in Altman's sketches as genre puppets. They too are grotesque, but this grotesque is bordering on parody, on the burlesque.

Altman's sketches of the religious scholars—of the Batlanim and Channan—are erased, faded, and ghostly (see Plate 11). In Vakhtangov's production, this group of characters appeared *literally* as though they did not live "by bread" but "by every word that proceedeth out of the mouth of God." While directing the synagogue scene, Vakhtangov suggested that the Batlanim were perpetually starving and substituted spirited religious discussions for food (Yzraely 1970: 123–24). The moment Vakhtangov offered this image, the starving Habima actors knew exactly how to play the synagogue scene.

The character of Channan was treated by Vakhtangov as a pure spirit, already a living ghost at the start of the play. His entire being was filled with unearthly love for Leah, and with the striving to restore justice through the mysterious power of the Kabbalah.

All these different artistic textures, or techniques, introduced by Altman in his character sketches, *were actually incorporated by Vakhtangov in his production*. The director discovered a corresponding variety of textures in movement and acting techniques

---

10 Chekhov had this book printed at his own expense in the US.

that fit in with the sketches. It is hard to tell if the idea of multiple expressive techniques applied to *The Dybbuk* characters belonged to Vakhtangov or Altman. Chronologically, Vakhtangov preceded Altman in his *Erik* and *The Miracle of Saint Anthony*; however, both of these works were rehearsed in parallel with the gradually developing *The Dybbuk*. In any case, the *conceptual* use of multiple principles of "characterization," within the parameters of the same performance, were unprecedented in the Russian theatre of the time.

The Gesture of the acting

Vakhtangov did not speak Hebrew, but he did study the language. During one of Vakhtangov's frequent stays at a rehabilitation resort, his Jewish roommate taught him some Hebrew words. When Vakhtangov could not remember one of the words, the roommate made a very characteristic (if not to say archetypal) gesture, "moving his palms apart, with a slight smile, gently" (Karev 1959: 418). This gesture of gentle wonder, or even reproach ("How could you forget?"), became for Vakhtangov the gesture of *The Dybbuk*. Numerous variations on this gesture were played out in *The Dybbuk* physically—from gentle wonder, to resignation, astonishment, shock, indignation, etc.[11] Moreover, the gesture became the atmosphere, the through-line, or, better still, the Archetypal Gesture behind *The Dybbuk*. Just as the master's hands of the electrician helped Vakhtangov to interpret the meaning of the proletarian revolution, the hands of his Jewish roommate helped him to resolve *The Dybbuk*.

The Dybbuk cast member Karev (1959: 418) considered this gesture of the upward palms moving apart a foundation for the "national form of the production." There is plenty of wonder in the fate of the Jews. The eternal Jewish irony and self-irony are also contained in this gesture. In fact, as a true Psychological Gesture, it can endlessly reveal new shades of psychological meaning, depending on the emotional quality with which it is endowed. The gesture of wonder before the unknown realms, or before life beyond the threshold, permeates *The Dybbuk*.

With each of the actors, Vakhtangov searched for their character's hands. The character of the Messenger, whose sudden appearances framed every act, represented a prophetic figure. This character,

11 See the Batlan at the utmost right of Figure 24.1 for an illustration of the gesture.

capable of foretelling the future, was suggested to An-sky by Stanislavsky. For the Messenger, Vakhtangov discovered the gesture of
perpetual movement. Even as the Messenger stopped, the position of
his body indicated an interrupted movement. "Lift your right shoulder
a bit, move it forward" (Karev 1959: 419), Vakhtangov would say to
the actor.[12]

A hungry beggar woman with greedy, crooked, and rheumatic
hands owned the gesture of grabbing; Sender, the wealthy merchant
with his open, puffy, content palms—the gesture of satiety, of plenty.
Depending on the group of characters, on the complexity of their
psychological texture, their gestures could be grotesque, or archetypal
(beggars, Leah's family), or psychological (the Batlanim, Leah,
Channan).

To demonstrate his idea of the "Psychological Gesture", Vakhtangov
once got up onto the stage and spoke to his Habima actors about the
well-known portrait of Tolstoy, painted by the artist Ilya Repin:

> Tolstoy stands in his long peasant shirt, his hands tucked behind his
> belt. This is how he lived his life, his hands tied. The form told us
> about it: his hands are tied by the traditions of his class. He dreamt
> of justice and truth. As he was approaching the end of his life's
> path, he tore this cursed belt with his hands. (Vakhtangov shows
> how Tolstoy freed his hands.) He tore himself free—and died.
>
> (Karev 1959: 418)

The speech in *The Dybbuk* was also turned into gesture by Vakhtangov.
The director knew that he could not rely on the literal meaning
of the text, on its content, as an audience member would seldom know
Hebrew. He had to concentrate on the melody, intonation, subtext,
or rather—the hidden gesture behind the speech. The words had
to become graphic, vivid, distinct, and visible. The speech also had
to ring as organic, sincere, and be deeply felt by the actors.
In order to help his actors personalize heightened emotion and an
elevated manner of speech, Vakhtangov used the numerous methods
in his arsenal.

One of the devices utilized by Vakhtangov in order to achieve the
heightened musicality of speech could be called "emotional subtext."
The director would find a short, emotionally charged line, and lay it

---

12 See the Messenger in the center of Figure 24.1.

under a passage of text, thus transforming it from the inside. Vakhtangov's technique, essentially, introduced the idea of an emotional archetype present behind a textual bit.

An entire monologue could be said with a single psychological "lining" expressed in the phrase: "I curse the day I was born!" A line like that naturally has a melody to it—it cannot be pronounced "flat." The gesture of the line would begin to live in the monologue, emotionally justifying its heightened, musical quality. At The Habima, Vakhtangov used this approach to invent the very melody of the *spoken* Hebrew, and to discover its universal musicality. There was truly no precedent, or a legitimate model Vakhtangov could follow—in Russia and Europe the Hebrew language had not been spoken in everyday life for centuries. In this sense also, Vakhtangov was creating a model for the Hebrew Theatre.

In his memoir, *The Path of the Actor*, Chekhov recalls how Vakhtangov worked to make *The Dybbuk* accessible to all audiences, regardless of their knowledge of Hebrew. The director would invite a non-speaker, like Chekhov, to a closed rehearsal, and ask his actors to play out a newly rehearsed scene. Vakhtangov would then quiz his spectator on what exactly he gathered from the scene.

The life of the scene was so expressive, the enthusiastic Chekhov would claim that he understood it all. Upon Vakhtangov's request, Chekhov would then proceed to retell the content of the scene—*as he perceived it*—in the smallest detail. On such an occasion, Vakhtangov would usually turn back to his actors and pronounce his sentence: since Chekhov did not get several important nuances, the entire scene is to be "dismantled" and recreated anew (Chekhov 1995 vol. I: 142).

According to Sinel'nikova (interviewed in Khersonsky 1940b: 158), in 1920 Vakhtangov shared with his students a dream of "staging a performance where people would speak utterly obscure words, and yet everything would be clear." In *The Dybbuk*, Vakhtangov fulfilled the task of discovering a universal theatrical language. *The Dybbuk* found its place in theatre history as a performance that overcame language barriers. At the core of this achievement lies Vakhtangov's belief that the language of theatre, at its best, must be based in an Archetypal Gesture.

The Archetypal Gesture represents life at its quintessential; in that it is akin to the life of the artist's fantasy. The Archetypal Gesture moves like a great statue of antiquity. These movements are harmonious—the statue moves just as we do in life, when our life is completely free and creative. As Vakhtangov put it during the final talk with his students: "A play can be directed naturalistically, or using the method of fantastic realism. And the latter will be the strongest, because a sculpture is intelligible to every nation." (*Sourcebook* 2011: 156).

25 *Princess Turandot*

The threshold of creativity, or the making of a new man

Gozzi's manifesto

Vakhtangov—The Habima prophet—often arrived to *The Dybbuk* rehearsals in the middle of the night, and he continued the work through the early morning. The Habima troupe patiently awaited their director for as long as it took. Upon Vakhtangov's arrival, they greeted him ecstatically, despite the hour. In the meantime, at Vakhtangov's own Studio, a group of his students rehearsing Gozzi's *Princess Turandot* waited impatiently for their director. They were jealous of The Habima.[1]

At first glance, Gozzi's play is a mere trifle. Its leading man—brave, if not reckless Prince Calaf (see Figure 25.1)—fell in love with the proud Turandot—the princess of China. To win the princess' hand in marriage, Calaf agreed to solve the three riddles Turandot puts to her contenders. Calaf's life is at stake, as the unlucky contenders, who fail to solve even one riddle, have their heads cut off.

Calaf immediately wins the sympathies of Turandot's father Khan Altoum, and of the courtiers, who are weary of the princess' cruelty. Turandot's lady in waiting, young and naïve Zelima, begs her mistress to give "easy riddles" to Calaf. Turandot herself is partial to Calaf, but her pride drives her to go forth with the contest. Having solved all three riddles, Calaf unexpectedly frees the proud princess from her obligation to marry him—on one condition. Turandot must solve Calaf's own riddle: the princess must guess his name and heritage. (Calaf is incognito in China—a refugee, in flight from the enemies who invaded his kingdom.) According to the new pact, Turandot would be free from her obligation to marry Calaf, providing she can identify him.

---

1 As the legend goes, on one occasion the Third Studio actors even showed up at The Habima determined to "collect" their leader.

Figure 25.1 Yuri Zavadsky as Prince Calaf in *Princess Turandot*, 1922.
Courtesy of Andrei Malaev-Babel.

The curious courtiers, one by one, try to force Calaf to confess his name and heritage, but in vain. Turandot's slave woman Adelma (herself a princess in exile) is secretly in love with Calaf. In her attempt to prevent Calaf from marrying her rival, she betrayed his secret to Turandot. The princess obtained the answer, but, instead of sending Prince Calaf away, she married him all the same. Thus, in the play's finale, the now loving Turandot overcame her pride.

The eighteenth-century Italian playwright Carlo Gozzi wrote his play in the style of *commedia dell'arte*. The plot of his cruel fairy-tale is enveloped in the buffoonery of the four traditional *commedia* masks: Tartaglia, Pantalone, Brigella, and Trufaldino. For Carlo Gozzi, his *Turandot* was not a mere trifle, but a challenge, and a manifesto.

Gozzi's entire body of work served to defend the Italian popular tradition of *commedia dell'arte* against the realist playwright Carlo Goldoni. According to Gozzi, Goldoni "deprived the Italian theatre of the charms of poetry and imagination" (Simonde 1823 vol. II: 369).

What Goldoni was trying to do with his own plays, such as *The Servant of Two Masters* and *The Mistress of the Inn*, was to *reform* the Italian *commedia dell'arte*. He aimed to introduce psychologically drawn characters instead of masks, and transpose *commedia* plots from the imaginary theatrical world (resembling Shakespearian *Illyria*) into the contemporary Italian society. In addition to that, Goldoni forced his actors to abandon improvisation and strictly adhere to the written text.

Gozzi won his dispute with Goldoni—the Venetian audience went with him, literally driving Goldoni out of the country. Historically speaking, however, the victory was Goldoni's—throughout the nineteenth and twentieth centuries, theatre continued developing in a predominantly realistic and non-improvisational vein, while the art of the Italian *commedia* slowly became an obscurity. Nevertheless, throughout the history of the modern theatre, the *commedia dell'arte* heritage periodically attracted theatre practitioners' attention—not only in Italy, but worldwide.[2]

Improvisation in *Turandot*

The texture of the improvisation in Vakhtangov's *Turandot* was varied. It included traditional *commedia dell'arte* improvisational techniques used by the actors playing the Italian masks. The four traditional masks present among fairytale characters improvised some of their lines anew at every performance. Throughout the rehearsal period, the four masks went through the school of improvisational training.

Special rehearsals were organized by Vakhtangov for the four actors playing the mask. The entire studio sat in the audience at these rehearsals. The four actors had to improvise comedic dialogues and businesses (*lazzi*) in front of a live audience—without any preparation. The spectators were not supposed to play along, but rather be honest in their appraisals of the actors' work. They could appear bored, if the improvisations were such, or loudly express their disapproval, if the masks' acting was bad, etc. Vakhtangov personally set the tone for

2 See the discussion of *commedia*'s influence on Vakhtangov and his contemporaries on pp. 136–40.

the audiences' reactions. In these rehearsals, Vakhtangov practically implemented the requirement for a *commedia* performer, formulated in Meyerhold's magazine *Love for Three Oranges* (Solovyov 1914: 65) as "absence of fear of the audience."

The zest of this school was in developing the freedom and courage to move on to the next bit, and *carry on as if nothing had happened* when a given improvisation failed to reach the audience. Eventually, many of the jokes and *lazzi* played out by the four *Turandot* performers were prepared in advance. Its originality was less important to Vakhtangov than the task of developing an actor's self-confidence and boldness.

Turandot also included the contemporary equivalent of the *commedia* improvisation, attributed by Vakhtangov to those actors playing Gozzi's fairy-tale characters. The actors performing the parts of Turandot, Calaf, Adelma, Zelima, etc., did not actually improvise their lines, or their actions. According to Vakhtangov, these actors needed to learn how to "play with the improvisation" (Zakhava 1930: 143). This play required from the actors the kind of lightness and ease that produced an *illusion* that everything an actor says and does onstage is happening for the first time.

The improvisational quality in Vakhtangov's *Turandot* was nevertheless not entirely an illusion. It was achieved by the fact that the *subtle nuances* of the characters' behavior and interactions (the so-called "adaptations") were improvised by the actors anew every night. The spirit of improvisational creativity became a certain threshold Vakhtangov's actors were supposed to cross in *Princess Turandot*.

Four thresholds of *Princess Turandot*

The question of the creative threshold occupied Vakhtangov for some time. He searched for the path towards "instant" inspiration. Stanislavsky's concept of "artistry," or the desire to act, intrigued Vakhtangov. In October 1916, he promised his student-actors: "As time goes by, we will learn, without preparation, to meet the challenges of the most passionate moments of the role" (*Sourcebook* 2011: 110).

Around 1919, however, Vakhtangov admitted that the Stanislavsky System does not provide an answer on the source of artistry, or immediate access to creativity. Moreover, Vakhtangov insisted that the problem of artistry was not the only major problem unresolved by Stanislavsky:

There are three unresolved elements in the system:

1   *Artistry* is the means to immediately become inspired by the material offered by the author. How to reach an ability to become inspired on command is unknown.

2   *Kernel*: this is the kind of starter that creates the character. The character is created when an actor discovers the kernel. The discovery of the kernel is something we do not know. What is cast into the actor's inner world, no one knows.
[. . .]

3   How to allow oneself onstage to strive to fulfill the tasks, to avoid pushing and wait for this striving to come—that is unknown.

(*Sourcebook* 2011: 100)

In his account of elements unresolved in the System, Vakhtangov enumerated three basic thresholds an actor must cross in order to enter the space of inspiration, or the creative space. The first threshold separates the actual theatrical space from the imaginary world of the play, created by the author. For actors, expressing themselves in full harmony with this fantastical environment requires full faith in the imaginary circumstances.

The second threshold is the one between the actor and their character, or mask. Stanislavsky tried to solve the problem of this crossing using the biblical term of the "kernel."[3] Vakhtangov had always considered this term "questionable," as to him it only solved the problem of characterization, without resolving the issue of the character's spiritual essence.

The third is the *audience* threshold—it is the border that separates the performer from the audience. The main factor that prevents an actor from being able "to avoid pushing and wait for this striving to come" is the presence of the watching, "expectant" audience. Vakhtangov clearly distinguished between the desire to act in the solitude of one's own home, and the desire to act publicly. He insisted that "the art of theatre consists of an ability to awaken a feeling and infect the audience with it" (*Sourcebook* 2011: 87), or, as he put it on another occasion—"the art of expressing ourselves, our very souls, before the audience" (*Sourcebook* 2011: 172).

The division into three thresholds is, of course, purely theoretic. This is true of any division applied to the indivisible organic process.

---

3 Vakhtangov's relationship toward the Stanislavskian concept of the character's "kernel" is discussed at length in *Sourcebook* (2011: 22, 90–91, 106–9).

In practice the three thresholds, and the three unresolved problems of creativity, are deeply connected. The crossing of even one of these thresholds, in practice, would immediately result in the crossing of the other two. Only when all three thresholds have been crossed can an actor transcend the culminative threshold—the threshold of creativity.

In the Stanislavskian "fourth wall-type theatre," the crossings of all three thresholds (and the creative challenges they bring) culminate at the moment when the curtain is drawn, or when an actor enters the stage from the wings. The actor's meeting with the mask of the character, with the imaginary reality, and with the audience—all happen at once, often causing a shock to the actor. At such a moment, the stakes are incredibly high. An inexperienced actor intuitively *senses* this challenge and tenses up, while an experienced actor *knows* this challenge, and also grows tense. Experience does not necessarily help to solve this particular problem, as even experienced actors are seldom equipped by Stanislavsky (or anyone else) with a concrete technique that would help them to cross all three thresholds at once.

Vakhtangov's principle of crossing the threshold of creativity was deeply rooted in the workings of the actor's subconscious. This principle is included in Vakhtangov's concept of organic technique.[4] Organic technique was practiced by Stanislavsky, "on occasion," and it was masterfully developed by Nikolai Demidov. In Vakhtangov's formulation of this technique, the secret of entering the creative realm, or crossing the creative threshold, lies in the device Demidov later defined as psychological "non-alteration" (Demidov 2007: 11). Around 1919, Vakhtangov supplied the following description of this technique:

> The first state an actor experiences onstage is the one he just experienced in life. One needs great courage not to betray this experience.
>
> One must surrender entirely to the power of one's artistic nature. It will do all the necessary things. Don't impose any solution upon yourself in advance. The quality to develop in an actor is courage.
>
> (*Sourcebook* 2011: 99)

But how does an actor develop this courage? In Vakhtangov's view, the Stanislavsky System did not provide an answer.

---

4 For more details on the organic technique see *Sourcebook* (2011: 10–11).

Theatrical "truths" that kill an actor's creativity directly apply to the problem of the three thresholds. The first truth has it that the world of the stage is made of fabric, paint, wood, and metal—rather than of what it is supposed to be made of, according to the reality of the play, etc. The second truth contains the fact that people onstage are, indeed, dressed-up and made-up actors, and not really the characters from the play. This truth brings actors to realize that they do not really want or need any of the things their characters want or need. The third truth consists of the fact that the audience is watching.

At the same time, Vakhtangov understood that all these theatrical "truths" can serve as a source of inspiration for the actors, and the greatest stimulus for their imagination—as long as the actor perceives them *correctly*. In other words, instead of perceiving theatrical "truths" as a lie, according to the everyday reality, actors must train to develop a special sense of theatrical truth. This sense is based in a deep understanding that the unnatural (from the standpoint of everyday life) theatrical environment is nothing but a special atmosphere of the stage, or, as Vakhtangov would put it, a "special stage air" (Zakhava 1930: 130), conducive to an actor's creative life.

The special atmosphere of theatre—if perceived correctly—instead of intimidating actors, will make them freer, more imaginative, sensitive, emotionally available, impressionable, responsive, and therefore expressive physically and vocally, etc. Natural-born actors always perceive the theatrical environment creatively, while actors deprived of this special instinct must develop it through training.

Vakhtangov, who was occupied with the task of discovering the secret of "instant" inspiration, could not accept Stanislavsky's approach of putting a blinder on actors and carrying them over the creative threshold with their eyes closed. Merely distracting the actor from the disturbing "truths" with the image of the "fourth wall" was not a solution for Vakhtangov. He needed to solve the problem of the crossing once and for all, and he did so in *Princess Turandot*.

The audience threshold

Vakhtangov's preliminary "dreams" about *Princess Turandot* included the dismantling of the fourth wall. At the start of rehearsals, in 1920, he spoke to his actors of erasing the threshold between them and the audience:

> The performance will start with the mutual acquaintance. Everything is open to the audiences' eye. This includes the entire stage.

You are dressed in a regular [actors'] working uniform;[5] perhaps, you are meeting the audience at the lobby stairs . . . Everyone has the right to say hello to you, to ask you how you feel today and even . . . ask you about your affairs of the heart. (Suppose that the other day they saw you at the movies, or in the street, with a charming stranger!) [. . .] Oh, how curious the audience is about the private life of an actor! We should not blame them for that, however. They do love you and want to know everything about you, since they take such an interest in you.

[. . .]

So, the audience arrived at the theater auditorium. After you have seated them, and surrounded them with care, you move up onto the stage.

(Gorchakov 1957: 112–13)

In the final version of *Turandot*, however, Vakhtangov used the *commedia* esthetics to attack the threshold in a much more radical way. The performance started with the actors' parade; performers appeared from behind the curtain—young men wearing tailcoats and young ladies in fashionable evening dresses (see Figure 25.2).[6] They lined up along the proscenium, directly facing the audience, and the four *commedia* masks introduced their colleagues to the spectators. The *Turandot* cast was introduced to the audience *as actors about to perform the play*.

The four actors playing *commedia* masks—Tartaglia, Pantalone, Brigella, and Trufaldino—were the only *Turandot* performers wearing traditional *commedia* costumes. The leather masks were substituted by makeup that, nevertheless, was styled after traditional Italian masks. The four masks did not openly reveal themselves to the audience as Vakhtangov Studio actors. They remained "in character" during the opening parade, thus posing as the *commedia* performers.

During rehearsals, Vakhtangov put special emphasis on the parade. He did so, as the parade set the laws of creative play for *Turandot*. A special document was circulated among the Studio members, outlining these laws:

5 During the early rehearsals Vakhtangov considered dressing his actors in Meyerholdian *prozodezhda* (a sack-like jumpsuit used for both men and women alike and designed in constructivist style). Vakhtangov eventually discovered a different "uniform" for his actors.

6 In the Moscow of 1922, at the time of "military communism," this was an extremely brave move of Vakhtangov's.

Figure 25.2 The actors' parade at the start of *Princess Turandot*, 1922. Courtesy of Vakhtangov Theatre Museum.

1 Utmost composure.
2 Complete confidence in myself as an actor, creator, artist. This begets self-respect coupled with complete modesty.
3 No show of false modesty whatsoever, and nothing ostentatious. I am your servant, and I am proud, endlessly proud of being a servant of the people.
4 Clarity and purity in everything: thought, word, diction, voice, movement.
   [. . .]
7 I, Vakhtangov, am in charge of (and inflict penalty for) the parade!
                        (*Sourcebook* 2011: 144–45)

Vakhtangov's rules of creative play in *Turandot* eliminated the audience threshold. The director was not forcing this threshold, but erasing it altogether. He was establishing, once and for all, *the equal relationship* between the audience and the actor[7] (this being the only type of

---

7 "I am your servant, and I am proud, endlessly proud of being the servant of the people."

relationship specific theatrical conditions can naturally support). Thus Vakhtangov's *Turandot* crossed the audience threshold using theatrical means, rather than the non-theatrical device of the fourth wall.

The threshold of the creative space and time: transforming the theatrical reality

At the end of the parade, the four masks opened the curtain, and the cast of *Princess Turandot* dashed onto the raked deck of Nivinsky's set. The actors picked up fabrics and objects lying on the deck. Light, colorful fabrics and improvised props soared in the air. The actors proceeded to make rhythmical movements, throwing and catching the objects in the rhythm with the music (see Figure 25.3).

The music for *Turandot* was composed by Nikolai Sizov. It was filled with improvisational lightness and mischief. The Vakhtangov Studio member, Kozlovsky, collaborated with the composer. In addition to that, Kozlovsky conducted the "improvised" orchestra, also consisting of Studio members.

The unusual music with its "swimming sound" intrigued and delighted Stanislavsky. Following the dress rehearsal for *Turandot*, he demanded that the backstage orchestra be brought onto the stage to perform all of the *Turandot* musical numbers again. When the orchestra entered the stage, it was revealed that, besides regular musical instruments (which were few), the core of the orchestra consisted of the young Studio members "playing" hair combs, wrapped in cigarette paper. These improvised "musical instruments" were responsible for the "swimming" sounds of the *Turandot* score.

Turandot music resembled the nasal-sounding fifes of the traditional Russian jesters of the Middle Ages and Renaissance period—*skomorokhi*. Consciously or subconsciously, Vakhtangov brought his *commedia* performers close to their Russian brothers and sisters.

The actors' play with fabrics and props created "a firework," a "whirlwind of colorful patches" (Gorchakov 1957: 159) onstage. In the audience's eyes, the actors were no longer just members of the Vakhtangov Studio; they were virtuosi of rhythm, plasticity, and movement—actors-creators and masters, transfiguring the theatrical space. A different, creative dimension opened for the audience—the theatrical space and time were artistically transformed. Vakhtkangov's own talent of merging with the props, breathing life into objects was immediately recognizable in the *Turandot* device.

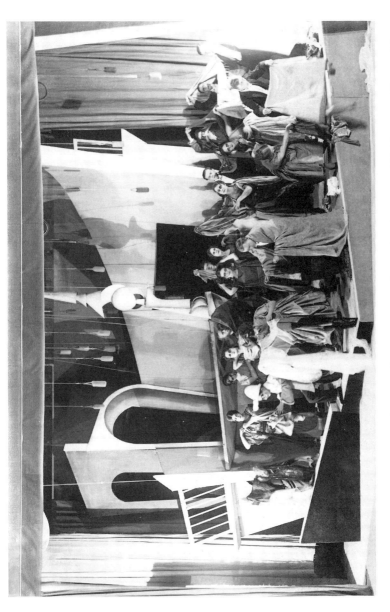

Figure 25.3 Actors putting on costumes at the start of *Princess Turandot*, 1922. Courtesy of Vakhtangov Theatre Museum.

Every element of the *Turandot* performance was creatively transfig-
ured. This included Nivinsky's set. In 1921, Vakhtangov wrote:
"Every kind of performance calls for its own form of stage platform:
Shakespeare, Molière, Gozzi, Ostrovsky, etc." (*Sourcebook* 2011:
127). In Vakhtangov's view, every type of theatre has its unique
creative psychology and aesthetics—they dictate a different spatial
configuration for each of the types. This configuration is dictated,
among other things, by the nature of the relationship between the
actor and the audience.

The traditional theatrical platform of the *commedia dell'arte*
performance was erected in a town square. Before the performance,
actors mingled with the crowd. In the course of the performance, those
actors not participating in a given scene could be found sitting on the
steps of the platform, watching their colleagues perform. At times,
they enter the crowd. The platform contains no sets, just a simple
backdrop, usually depicting an urban street. Similarly, furniture
and props are scarce—the *commedia* master-performers are self-
sufficient—they use their psychology, body, voice, and imagination to
create the world of the play.

Vakhtangov's concept of the stage platform was successfully realized by *Princess Turandot*. The function of Nivinsky's set was not
reduced to supplying the places of action. Vakhtangov formulated
Nivinsky's task as creating a special *theatrical environment* harmonious with the content of the production. Moreover, the theatrical set
was to amount to an artistic image, a symbol, an archetype—also
harmonious with the production's content.

The unchangeable element of the Nivinsky set was its raked platform (see Plate 18). It resembled a ship deck. The steep deck tipped
toward the house, thus creating a further illusion of the connection
between the performer and the spectator. Moving upon the raked
deck of the set required months of special training for the actors. In
the long run, the raked deck helped the actors to expressively mold
their bodies in the space. This skill was essential for a *Turandot* actor,
who was to appear as a master-creator to the audience.

Throughout the performance, *zanni* would unroll stage curtains and
attach them to the fly system ropes. The *zanni* looked like sailors,
tying the sails. They pulled on the ropes, curtains flew up, and the
image of the ship was complete. Like most of Vakhtangov's images, it
was not literal, but rather associative, or subliminal. The audience did
not immediately *recognize* the ship, but they received the *sensation* of
sailing. At the same time, different sets of sails *represented* different
places in the fairy-tale action: Peking city gate (see Figure 25.4), the

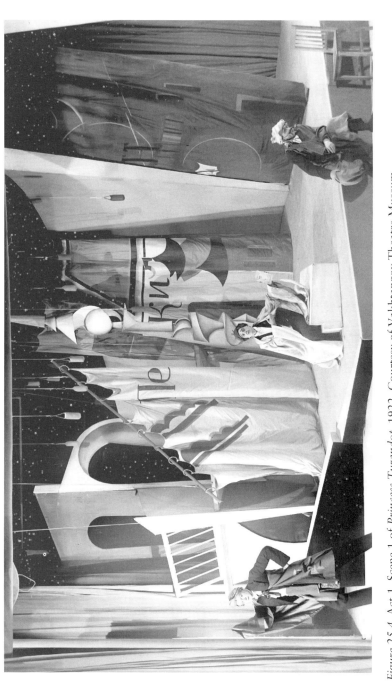

Figure 25.4 Act 1, Scene 1 of *Princess Turandot*, 1922. Courtesy of Vakhtangov Theatre Museum.

throne room in the palace of Khan Altoum (see Figure 26.1), a room in the palace harem (see Plate 19), etc.[8]

Russian theatre critic Fyodor Stepun was among those in the *Turandot* audiences who were able to decipher Vakhtangov/ Nivinsky's ship imagery. He wrote in his article on *Turandot*:

> There is a deep spiritual kinship between the motif of the ship deck and the melody of the artist's soul. Truly: what can be closer and dearer to the dichotomous, wandering souls of an artist, who eternally plays with his own destiny? What can be closer to it than a ship deck? This exterritorial (in relation to the solid, mundane way of life), unsteady and treacherous space darts somewhere between the two chasms—the high and the low. It is tossed between the two shores—the one abandoned and the one yet to be gained, and between the two temptations—the temptation of death, and the temptation of a far expanse.
>
> (*Printsessa Turandot* 1923: 60)

Fyodor Stepun's decryption of the *Turandot* meaning is echoed by Vakhtangov's apprentice Nikolai Gorchakov. At the end of his book about his master, Gorchakov (1957: 187) wrote that Vakhtangov's *Turandot* was an improvisation "on the theme of *an actor's [stage] life* being a unique *life of a man*—just as in Leoncavallo's opera *Pagliacci* it is sometimes difficult to distinguish where the drama of the play turns into an actor's drama."

The threshold between the actor-creator and the character

Both Gorchakov and Stepun recognized the essential and ultimately tragic layer of Vakhtangov's production. They saw that *the actors and their story* (rather than *the characters with their story*) constituted the true content of *Turandot*. Early in the rehearsal period, Vakhtangov told his actors that, instead of performing Gozzi characters, they are to play actors, members of the imaginary Italian *commedia* troupe. These unusual "characters" were indeed developed by Vakhtangov's actors—in accordance with the Stanislavsky school of experiencing.

Every traveling company is, in fact, a family. Love and hate, friendship and betrayal—these feelings are closely interwoven within the troupe. Vakhtangov's imaginary troupe was not an exception. For

---

8 On *Turandot* set design principles, see *Sourcebook* (2011: 296–98).

example, the tragic actress playing the role of Adelma (Turandot's slave and rival, according to the play) in Vakhtangov's imaginary reality happened to be the wife of the company manager, in love with the leading man (who played the part of Prince Calaf). When this actress fought with Turandot for Calaf, her emotions were *real*.

Such imaginary biographies and relationships were created, in Vakhtangov's production, for each member of "the Italian troupe." The border between the imaginary company, the actual Vakhtangov Studio company, and the group of characters in the play was fluid— three different layers of relationships (and realities) created the rich tapestry of the *Turandot* world. Yuri Zavadsky, the performer of the role of Calaf, wrote in his memoir:

> Vakhtangov strived to achieve from me a "double," or even a "triple" life onstage. I, Yuri Zavadsky, felt myself an Italian actor, who enthusiastically uses his mastery to create the character of Calaf. As an Italian actor, I perfectly comprehend all the naivety and comicalness of my character's situation; as Yuri Zavadsky I, at the same time, convey the stilted style of the Italian actor's performance, and sense its symbolic nature.
>
> (Zavadsky 1975: 200)

At any point in the production, a *Turandot* actor might exist on any of the three levels composing the structure of their role (but more often on two, or even three levels at once). As evident from Zavadsky's testimony, the layers of each *Turandot* role consisted of:

1   Gozzi character/*commedia* mask (this layer required an actor's emotional identification with the character or mask);
2   Vakhtangov Studio actor—creator and master;
3   Italian actor—*commedia* troupe member.

The effect the character structure produced on actors' creativity was significant, but, perhaps, equally significant were the possibilities it opened for the audience. At any given moment in the performance, a *Turandot* audience member was engaged in a unique creative *transformation*. Prior to Vakhtangov's *Turandot*, the right to transform was reserved exclusively for an actor. An audience member could transform by identifying themselves with the character; however, they did not have a distinctive role *of their own*.

At any point in the performance, a *Turandot* audience member assumed one of the three identities. Just as the *Turandot* character structure was complex, the *Turandot* audiences' identities were also many-layered. The layers of a *Turandot* audience member's "role" were:

1   member of the Vakhtangov Studio audience;
2   member of the crowd at the *commedia* performance in an Italian town square;
3   active participant in the *Turandot* plot (by emotional identification with the Gozzi characters).

Finally, the texture of the *Turandot* creative space also appeared to be many-layered. It included the following three artistic dimensions:

1   the Vakhtangov Studio in Moscow on Arbat Street;
2   *commedia* performance in an Italian town square;
3   Gozzi's China.

The structure of the *Princess Turandot* imagery was such that it ensured the audience's creative collaboration with the performers. The spectators were put into the position where they were naturally co-creating, transforming the reality and their own selves, together with the actors. This process of collaboration between the audience and the stage anticipated the future theatre, as Vakhtangov saw it. The relationship between an audience member and an actor, as described in Vakhtangov's note to his actors,[9] was also modeled on the director's vision of the future society where free and equal individuals will *creatively collaborate* with each other.

In 1911, Vakhtangov wrote down the following words by Stanislavsky: "The divide between the stage and the audience makes them grow closer, as the audience draws toward the stage on its own accord" (Ivanov 2011 vol. I: 223).

Stanislavsky insisted that the trust of the audience must be won by creating a complete illusion of life onstage. He claimed that the audience will never play a creative role in theatre, unless the stage is separated from the audience by the imaginary "fourth wall." Vakhtangov, on the contrary, won his audiences' trust by destroying the theatrical illusion. He boldly unmasked the machinery of the stage in the audiences' eyes and—most importantly—he demystified the sacred act of the actors' transformation.

9 See p. 223.

At the end of the *Turandot* parade, the actors suddenly began to clad themselves in improvised costumes, using the very same fabrics and props they artfully juggled in the air. These elements of costume were put on top of actors' basic "uniform"—tailcoats and evening dresses (see Figures 20.1, 20.2, and 25.1). As they did so, fabrics and objects continued to dance in their hands. The actors were *transforming into characters* before the audience's eyes. This unprecedented act of *public* transformation strengthened the bridge between the audience and the stage. Vakhtangov trusted the audience to enter the Holy of Holies—the secret backstage life of an actor.

Impromptu character costumes were originally improvised in rehearsals by each actor, in collaboration with the *Turandot* designer Nivinsky. These costumes were constructed out of everyday objects and fabrics found in the studio storage. Wiseman headgear could be built out of woven bread baskets, soup spoons, photography trays, linen napkins, etc.—Khan Altoum's headgear was made out of a lampshade; a kickball was used as a symbol of royal power, and a tennis racket as a scepter.

When the actors' transformation was complete, the *zanni*, also known as the "servants of the proscenium," dressed up the stage.[10] In doing so, *zanni* revealed the simple "secrets" of theatrical machinery, traditionally kept from the audience. This gesture of revealing the backstage theatrical secrets to the spectator further strengthened the trust between the stage and the house; moreover, it anticipated the crossing of the final theatrical threshold.

The final threshold

In part because the master died three months after the opening of *Turandot*, the theme of threshold reoccurred incessantly in some of the most profound responses to his final work. These responses were written by people who knew and understood Vakhtangov. Nikolai Volkov wrote in his posthumous monograph on Vakhtangov:[11]

> [. . .] Vakhtangov associated his name with the honorable title of the juggler of Our Lady. The gates of heaven are open for Our Lady's juggler. Vakhtangov will enter them.
>
> (Volkov 1922: 11)

---

10 See pp. 226, 228.
11 In addition to the first Vakhtangov monograph, Volkov was also responsible for the one and only extensive two-volume study of Meyerhold's works published in the director's lifetime.

Natalia Bromley, the First Studio actress and author, wrote one year after Vakhtangov's death:

> Vakhtangov stands between us and the future; this future is the golden age that will arrive by means of transcending tragedy. The first step on this path is Vakhtangov's *Turandot*. Did he not himself personify the transgression of tragedy? Death lived in him for years and breathed through his breath, and yet the vivifying life came wherever he stepped, across every threshold he crossed. What permeates the emptiness beyond the thresholds he abandoned last?[12] I hear the dance of this emptiness whistle and play,— who will fill it?—it is so densely filled with him.
>
> *Turandot* resounds in the emptiness beyond *the last* threshold he crossed in his life,[13]—this is his last victory on earth; he played this victory to the end in his dialogues with his last partner—death . . .
>
> (Bromley 1923: 35)

Vakhtangov is described in these passages as a person possessing special knowing—the kind that comes to those capable of glancing beyond the final threshold. Michael Chekhov, another person close to Vakhtangov, reported on Vakhtangov's final performance in the role of Fraser in *The Deluge*:

> His acting was magnificent. All of his partners marveled at him, literally. But all of them kept thinking in their heads that this was the last performance with Vakhtangov. And this is how it was— Vakhtangov performed for the last time. Why did he act so magnificently? Because he was asserting his *life*. . . . *Life*, the feeling of *life* begot the creative state. Is it true that we, artists, are

---

12 Bromley is still referring to the earthly thresholds: probably the ones of the First Studio, Third Studio, and The Habima Studio where Vakhtangov staged his three final productions.

13 The last threshold Bromley refers to is the threshold of death. In order to comprehend Bromley's spatial orientation, one has to imagine himself outside of all the spaces Bromley is referring to, but still on this earth. The emptiness beyond the last thresholds abandoned by Vakhtangov is the painful emptiness of his personal absence left in the earthly spaces he visited last. The emptiness beyond his last threshold, however, is the cosmic emptiness; it is filled with the joyful atmosphere of *Turandot*.

only capable of feeling life when it is in danger, or when it is fading away forever? Would we ever break through to the feeling of life, while we are still healthy and strong?

(Chekhov 1995 vol. I: 98–99)

Was it truly the closeness to the final threshold that is responsible for Vakhtangov's creative breakthrough as both director and actor, or was it an artistic ability Vakhtangov *acquired* in his final years? Vakhtangov kept growing until the end. On another occasion, Chekhov mentioned that shortly before his death, Vakhtangov developed an ability "to grasp any theatrical situation, any stage idea as easily as taking a book off the shelf" (Chekhov 1995 vol. I: 74).

The anticipation of close death may have caused the special knowing in Vakhtangov. Is it also possible that approaching this special knowing caused the early death? One fact remains: Vakhtangov's tragic demise at the age of 39 became an actual *artistic* factor in the most joyful and optimistic of his productions. Another close associate of Vakhtangov's, the First Studio director and actor Sushkevich said in his speech on Vakhtangov:

> One theme rings out to me in *The Dybbuk* and in *Princess Turandot*. This is the theme Vakhtangov perceived with a special acuteness,—the one of a man who perishes, but feels himself as a victor of death. This is the theme of *The Dybbuk*—in it love defeats death. The same theme is present in *Turandot*—the victory of life over death. These performances were created by an artist who knew that he was leaving life forever. In one case [*The Dybbuk*], the content was cast into the form of the highly condensed tragic conflict, in the other [*Turandot*]—in the form of the most wondrous witticism. Behind this witticism, however, we heard the fanfare of the victor of death. This is how all of us perceived *Turandot* at the dress rehearsal, when we first saw it.
>
> (Sushkevich 1959: 369)

This tragic content was the first to evaporate from the production, as the new performers, who had never worked with Vakhtangov, assumed the roles in the play. The Vakhtangov Theatre's artistic director Ruben Simonov revived Vakhtangov's *Turandot* in 1959, some 37 years after its premiere and almost 20 years past the last time an original *Turandot* cast member entered the stage in this production. At the time of the revival, Simonov told the new generation of Vakhtangov actors that they should appear in front of the audience during the opening parade experiencing what he called "Ridi, Pagliaccio!" (Laugh, Pagliaccio!).

The main character of Leoncavallo's opera *Pagliaccio*, clown Canio, is surviving a personal tragedy, and yet he has to go on performing, entertaining the audience. In his famous aria ("Ridi, Pagliaccio!"), Canio sings of the torturous psychological split—having to be merry onstage, while his heart is torn with anguish. This psychological phenomenon occupied Vakhtangov since his youth. Around 1902, Vakhtangov authored a sketch, titled *Street Clown*, dedicated to this phenomenon (Ivanov 2011 vol. I: 62–63).

How seemingly remote is this formula of living onstage from Vakhtangov's psychological non-alteration. This is a process of force-fully altering one's inner life, of forcing oneself to experience something completely alien to one's actual feelings. The cursed psychological split, characteristic of presentational theatre, was justified by Vakhtangov in the vein of the theatre of experiencing. This was done despite the fact that an actor's life in the theatre of experiencing is based on psychological oneness, sincerity, and non-alteration.

Vakhtangov achieved this result by substituting the content of the fairy-tale with the content of the Italian actors' life. In a typical Vakhtangov approach, he provoked his student-actors into life on the threshold of laughter and tears. Most of his students knew that their master was dying of cancer while rehearsing *Turandot*. Even those younger actors from whom Vakhtangov's terminal condition was kept secret could not help but notice that Vakhtangov was rehearsing through excruciating pain. And yet, they witnessed Vakhtangov at the peak of his artistic powers, creating his most joyful, lighthearted, and optimistic masterpiece.

When Vakhtangov's disciple Simonov (see Figure 25.5) revived *Turandot* in 1963, after having played the role of Trufaldino in 1922, he also tried to recreate this powerful psychological effect. During the rehearsals for the parade, he called his actors to hide their everyday-life pain and tears behind the joyful mask. For the original *Turandot* actors, who knew that they were losing their teacher, this was a natural and easy psychology they did not need to master. This tragic content, however, eluded the later generations of Vakhtangov actors who performed *Turandot*. It is no wonder that Peter Brook (1995: 16), when he saw this revival of *Turandot* in Moscow, thought that it had "no more than an antiquarian interest." Without its tragic spirit, Vakhtangov's *Turandot* was deprived of its essence.

Figure 25.5 Ruben Simonov as Trufaldino in *Princess Turandot*, 1922. Courtesy of Arsis Design.

Conclusion
Turandot and the Theatre of the Eternal Mask

As an artist of the Russian avant-garde, Vakhtangov was as much concerned with the new forms of life as he was with the new forms of art. Non-separation between artistic forms and the forms of life was Vakhtangov's trait since his first steps in theatre. Vakhtangov always saw Theatre as a prerequisite to the new, more beautiful, and sophisticated forms of life.

The Bolshevik Revolution of 1917 created an illusion that, in the new society, popular masses would be exposed to arts and culture—both as spectators and artists. Stanislavsky's dream "to cover Russia with a web of studios" (Ivanov 2011 vol. I: 430) was literally coming to life. Hundreds of new theatre studios were opening throughout Russia during the first years of the Revolution. Regular people felt the necessity to engage in creative play. Theatres were filled with people who, prior to 1917, could never attend a theatrical performance. Theatre art was promising to become a major force in the spiritual life of the nation.

In a way, the Soviet regime fulfilled this promise, with one major stipulation. Shortly after Vakhtangov's death, arts and culture in the Soviet Union were subjected to heavy censorship by the regime. Moreover, Stalin's doctrine of Socialist Realism led Soviet theatre in the direction contrary to the path indicated by Vakhtangov.

In the meantime, like many of the Russian avant-garde artists of the 1920s, Vakhtangov was working toward freeing the human spirit—by enriching it with creativity. He saw the future of mankind as a community that will introduce a new man—a perpetual creator. When such a new man appears, the Stanislavskian formula of theatre art—recreating "life of the human spirit" (Ivanov 2011 vol. I: 223) onstage—would be realized, as the human spirit and the creative spirit will be one.

Vakhtangov believed that, in its present condition, however, the human spirit is not creative; it is not free to fully express itself and, therefore, it is not fully alive. According to Vakhtangov, such a spirit cannot be communicated in a beautiful "artistic form," as Stanislavsky (2009: 19) suggested, but only through the very form it is granted in life—the one of the physical characterization. This form in life, just as on the stage, is meant to imprison every free and spontaneous movement of the human soul. It is meant to encase, and ultimately bury the contemporary man's spiritual strivings.

Vakhtangov's vision of the contemporary man's life, therefore, was deeply tragic. This tragic perception of life created an invisible layer in Vakhtangov's *Princess Turandot*. At the same time, Vakhtangov's production proclaimed that creative human beings (actors) can overcome the tragedy of their daily existence through their creative act. Actors, who can evoke the spirit of creativity in their acting, according to Vakhtangov, can achieve inner and outer freedom and approach the beautiful sphere of Higher Reason.[1]

Vakhtangov believed that in the society of the future, where the human spirit will become perpetually creative, every human being will possess the gift of an artist. This belief of Vakhtangov's was at the foundation of his vision of the Future Theatre. Vakhtangov saw the theatre of the future as a kind of forum where any audience member, at any point in the performance, could step onto the stage, and take up a role in a play. The future society will allow everyone's artistic gift and free creative spirit to flower in whatever way it demanded. Those of the future society, whose artistic gift is more inclined toward acting, will act. This is how Vakhtangov himself explained his idea of the Future Theatre to one of his students:

> The time will come when theatre will be an ordinary event of our life. Theatre will simply be in a square. Everyone, who feels himself capable, will act. Theatre will be free of charge—there will be no admittance fee, or a performance honorarium. It will be a free art for free people. Narrow professionalism will disappear, all naturally talented actors will play.
>
> (Leonid Volkov, interviewed in Khersonsky 1940b: 67)

The future of the theatre art was closely connected for Vakhtangov with the search for the Eternal Theatrical Form. Vakhtangov suggested that in *Turandot* he discovered the formula for the Contemporary Form, and he gave the following explanation of the *Turandot* success:

---

1 On Vakhtangov's philosophy of life and art, see *Sourcebook* (2011: 38–39).

> Why is [Princess] Turandot being received? Because in it we discovered harmony. The Third Studio performs the Italian fairy tale by Gozzi on January 22, 1922. The expressive means are both contemporary and theatrical. The content is in harmony with the form, like a single chord. This is fantastic realism; this is a new direction in theatre.
>
> (*Sourcebook* 2011: 157)

Nevertheless, Vakhtangov did not consider the discovery of the Contemporary Form as his final task. In that respect, Meyerhold (1984: 447) was true in suggesting that everything Vakhtangov discovered in theatre must be seen as a "preliminary act." During Vakhtangov's last talk with his students, the director made the following statement on the future of his creative search:

> A perfect work of art is eternal. Only a work in which the harmony between the form, content, and material has been discovered can be called a work of art. Stanislavsky only found harmony with the sentiments of the Russian society of the time, but not all that is contemporary is eternal. All that is eternal, however, is contemporary without fail. Meyerhold never sensed "today"; he only sensed "tomorrow." Stanislavsky never sensed "tomorrow"; he only sensed "today." Ideally, one should sense "today" in the day to come and "tomorrow" in the present day.
>
> When the revolution came, we all felt that things in art cannot remain the same. We did not yet know the form—the real, appropriate form [. . .] The next stage of our work will be dedicated to the search for the eternal form. [. . .] In time, the means we have chosen will cease being theatrical. We must find the true theatrical means. We must find the eternal mask.
>
> (*Sourcebook* 2011: 152–53)

Vakhtangov's Contemporary Form was capable of expressing the given theatrical collective in the given time. In order to do so, this form often had to reshape the work of the author (the play), to reduce it to a mere pretext for the theatre ensemble's creativity. In order to realize his productions, Vakhtangov often had to create a new "scenario" out of a play—such was the case with *The Dybbuk* and, ultimately, such was the case with *Turandot*. Vakhtangov even prepared a "scenario," based on Shakespeare's *Hamlet*, where the bard's texts were "reconstructed" with the boldness of a contemporary "conceptual" director.

By often choosing unfinished (sketchy) or weak dramatic material, even if by a classical author, Vakhtangov made sure that his "surgical" approach to the play was somewhat justified. But he finally could not justify creating a "scenario" out of an eternal play.

Vakhtangov's Contemporary Form serves as a foundation for the conceptual theatre of today. In our contemporary theatre, plays are often transposed into different time periods, or—better yet—different time periods are mixed within the space of the same play. Often classical plays are set in contemporary times, thus turning larger than life characters (heroes) into mediocre contemporary "average people." Plays are stylized after popular movies, TV shows—all other kinds of liberties are taken with them. These devices are usually justified by the fact that they make the classical plays more accessible to the contemporary audiences. In actuality, however, such "creative" transpositions are usually motivated by the fact that a particular theatrical company is simply incapable of staging a classical play (and approaching classical characters) as they are written by dramatic geniuses.

Vakhtangov fully understood the limitations of the Contemporary Form. He was aware of its tendency to tailor the play to the limited capacities of the ensemble. In most of his productions, Vakhtangov, striving to express the individuality of the creative collective, had to change the content of a play. He did so in order to make this content fit with the one of the collective. For example, the story of *Turandot* was turned into a story about actors, performing *Turandot*, etc.[2] Having discovered the formula for the Contemporary Form, however, Vakhtangov proceeded toward the Theatre of the Eternal Mask.

Contemporary Form, according to Vakhtangov, had to be periodically renewed—in order to remain contemporary. Vakhtangov insisted that, as soon as he got well, he must immediately restage *Turandot*. He felt that the rapid flow of time demanded that the form of the performance evolve. Similarly, in a letter to the First Studio of MAT actress Birman, Vakhtangov wrote: "So, if I have my health—together with those who would want to help me, I undertake to restage all our plays in such a way that they would sound contemporary" (*Sourcebook* 2011: 321).

Therefore, the Eternal Theatrical Form, according to Vakhtangov, would have to be completely free and alive—so that it could renew itself from the inside at any moment of the performance. Subtle adaptations, but also intonations, movements, and entire blockings,

---

2 Perhaps, in this particular case, the alteration was minimal. Carlo Gozzi's main striving *was* to revive the popular Italian theatrical tradition (*commedia dell'arte*) with its tendency to use the plot as a mere pretext for a performance.

would have to be renewed *daily* in Vakhtangov's Theatre of the Eternal Mask—not once or twice a month, as in the case with the Contemporary Mask.

This is why, in Vakhtangov's mind, the Eternal Form was connected with the renewed human of the new society, who was to be absolutely free—both in art and in everyday life. This new human of the Golden Age—"the society of equal, content, well-fed people" (*Sourcebook* 2011: 153)—was anticipated by all of the representatives of the Russian avant-garde. Such was the world anticipated by Vakhtangov's euphoric *Turandot*. Vakhtangov's resolve to search for the Eternal Mask, however, was not just a vague anticipation of the new form. Vakhtangov possessed the keys to the inner and outer technique of the Theatre of the Eternal Mask.

What is preventing an actor from possessing the technique of living every moment of the performance as if it was an entirely new moment? Actors' imperfection consists of their lack of absolute psycho-physical freedom, coupled with inner necessity to confine this freedom within the given circumstances of the performance. According to Vakhtangov's disciple Zakhava, the principle of improvisation in *Turandot* already contained the seed of the resolution of this eternal theatrical conflict—the conflict of freedom and discipline:

> Vakhtangov's [formal] requirements made the actor exceptionally responsible for the slightest manifestation of their life onstage. To express one's inner life as it expresses itself was no longer possible; everything was set and cast into clear and chiseled form. Only when everything [the form of the performance] was prepared, has the actor *regained* his right to improvise (movements, gestures, intonations), according to those requirements dictating the form of the performance. Thus the actors received their right to improvise "adaptations" only when there was a guarantee that they became so firmly grounded in the principles of acting in a given performance that their improvisation won't leave the boundaries established by these principles.
>
> The actors' ability to improvise "adaptations" while sensing full responsibility for these adaptations, i.e. subjecting adaptations to the requirements of the form and mastery of acting, is called by Vakhtangov "feeling of the stage."
>
> (Zakhava 1930: 130)

The question of improvisational freedom resolved itself, as soon as the laws of the improvisation—its strict principles, intrinsic to the given performance—became an organic necessity for an actor. At the same time, the form of Vakhtangov's final productions cannot be considered a definitive prototype for Eternal Form. Vakhtangov's Eternal Form—inwardly alive, evolving and renewing itself with every performance—is the only form, suitable for the realization of the formula, defined by Stanislavsky during his 1911 talk with the MAT youth as "refined realism." "This is no longer the former realism of the mundane, and of the external truth"—Stanislavsky said to his young colleagues of his and Sulerhitsky's search for new realism. "This realism is externally simplified, down to a minimum, for the sake of spiritual deepening" (Ivanov 2011 vol. I: 223).

The Eternal Form—vibrant, fluid, and yet monumental—would remain completely free within the boundaries of precise discipline. Needless to say, such a form would ask for a new actor, capable of filling in. Vakhtangov had faith in the possibility of cultivating an actor, who is an ultimate artist. Actors of the Eternal Form, according to Vakhtangov, would possess a refined, ultrasensitive inner and outer instrument. In order to do this, actors would need to develop extrasensory powers—all of their senses would need to be cultivated to the capacity that is unknown to today's science. Vakhtangov's belief in the infinite powers of the human spirit and body were on par with the philosophy of the Russian avant-garde.

The culture of Russian theatrical avant-garde of the early twentieth century is underexplored. Enough has been said of the formal search, conducted by the theatre artists of the avant-garde, such as Meyerhold, Tairov, and Eisenstein. Not enough, however, has been said of the philosophy and final goals of the avant-garde movement. As for the creative *psychology* of the avant-garde—this theme is still waiting to be uncovered.

The avant-garde movement was not confined to theatre—it existed in music, visual art, architecture, literature, poetry, etc. At the heart of the avant-garde philosophy lies the forward-looking belief in the infinite possibilities of the human being. Russian avant-garde artists believed that all of the human being's faculties—sight, hearing, physical body, etc., but also their spiritual or creative faculties (thought and imagination) carry infinite possibilities. In short, human capacity, as we know it today, according to avant-garde philosophers, is only a small, limited part of the actual human potential.

A noted artist of the Russian avant-garde, Mikhail Matiushin, for example, claimed that artists of the future will possess "panoramic" vision. He insisted on that, and he taught his students how to see with the back of their head, or sideways. He sat his students with their backs turned toward St. Petersburg's Neva River, and made them paint the riverscape. On one occasion, a respected painter-academician passing by almost fainted at the sight of Matiushin's students (Tilberg 2003: 157).

For Vakhtangov, as the avant-garde thinker, theatre art was the means of practically *transforming* both the artist and the audience into a new creative body—social and spiritual. This transformation is achieved in theatre by inspiring, in the ensemble and the audience alike, a hitherto unknown, infinite level of creativity. According to the philosophy of the avant-garde, the liberating effect of the art—both psychological and social—is meant to transform the genetic makeup of the nation, thus engineering a new breed of man.

The new men of the avant-garde thinkers are fully free in their artistic expression, and their creative abilities are limitless. The cultivation of the new men, in Vakhtangov's mind, was achieved in theatre through improvisational play. In Vakhtangov's theatre, audiences and actors together practiced in modeling innovative theatrical forms. By doing so, these audiences and actors trained in creating refined resolutions to life's old tasks.

Vakhtangov and his fellow avant-garde thinkers believed that life and art will become synonymous in the society of the future. Vakhtangov predicted that creativity and freedom will be the chief qualities bred by the new society of men—the society where "everyone, who feels capable, will act" (*Sourcebook* 2011: 72). Such a suggestion may be considered utopian. As every futuristic thinker, Vakhtangov was impatient; however, it may only be a matter of time before his predictions come true.

Figure 26.1 Scene of the riddles from *Princess Turandot*, 1922. Courtesy of Vakhtangov Theatre Museum.

Glossary of terms

actor cultivation (*vospitaniye aktyora*) "Actor cultivation must consist of enriching the actor's subconscious with varied abilities: freedom, concentration, seriousness, stage intelligence, artistry, activity, expressiveness, gift of observation, quickness to adapt, etc. . . . The subconscious, equipped with such a supply of means, will forge a near perfect creation from the material it receives (*Sourcebook* pp. 118–19). [. . .] [Common] actor cultivation . . . allows an actor to merge with the collective; its absence creates a division between the actor and the troupe" (*Sourcebook* p. 87).

adaptation (*prisposobleniye*) An actor's unique way of resolving their creative task (*see* "task"). Vakhtangov considered an actor's creative *how* (an expression of their creative individuality) the leading component of the creative task and a reason that brought the audience to the theatre. According to Vakhtangov, actors should improvise their adaptations anew at every rehearsal or performance. "Emotion can be expressed externally. This expression is called 'adaptation'; adaptations are characterized by the performer's talent; the more talented the actor, the more different forms of adaptation he gives, the more varied the fulfillment of tasks" (*Sourcebook* p. 252).

archetypal gesture (*arkhetipichnyi zhest*) Artistic term and device developed by Michael Chekhov, and inspired by his work with Vakhtangov. Symbolic, universal, larger-than-life inner gesture that lies at the essence of every theatrical phenomenon—character, speech, a single moment in a play, performance as a whole. Vakhtangov utilized this device in his productions of the early 1920s, openly manifesting it onstage. Both form and content of these productions were universally archetypal. (*See also* "psychological gesture.")

artistry, a desire to act (*artistichnost*') Artistry is an actor's ability to sense himself or herself as creative artist with their individual artistic mission, or theme. A sense of artistic mission (Vakhtangov, after Sulerzhitsky, called it "what for") begets an actor's desire to create. All elements of the Vakhtangov system are harmoniously connected with each other. The reader will sense the coalition between artistry and creative passion that arises from perceiving the essence, festivity, etc.

atmosphere (*atmosfera*) The actual term "atmosphere" was rarely used by Vakhtangov. According to the MAT practice, Vakhtangov used the term "mood." In contemporary theatrical vocabulary, however, "mood," or "emotional mood" has been substituted by "atmosphere." A certain psychological sensation or overtone that conveys from the stage to the audience through multiple expressive means—such is the contemporary definition of atmosphere. This is why, throughout the *Vakhtangov Sourcebook*, the term "mood" is translated as "atmosphere." This translation also helps distinguish atmosphere from the emotional life of the characters. (According to Michael Chekhov, characters in a given scene can live with different moods or emotions and nevertheless be united by a common atmosphere. This atmosphere, as it conveys to the audience, becomes a common "mood" uniting the actors with the audience.)

Vakhtangov denied the presence of artistic atmosphere in the MAT naturalistic productions. During his final discussions with the students, Vakhtangov insisted that naturalistic works produced by the MAT affected the audience with their bare content, or plot. Presented in the forms of life, these productions broke out of the artistic realm, turning an audience member into a witness to actual events. These events, presented as actually happening events, could depress, horrify, gladden the audience, but they could not radiate an artistic atmosphere. In Vakhtangov's view, festivity should substitute atmosphere in a theatrical performance, while MAT's interpretation of atmosphere as "emotional mood" was incorrect. Vakhtangov exclaimed, "Only joy should exist in the theatre, and no atmospheres." (*Sourcebook* p. 151.) (*See* "festivity.")

attention, concentration of attention (*vnimaniye*) "The second prerequisite of the creative state is concentrated attention, in brief—concentration" (*Sourcebook* p. 176). (*See also* "outer (muscular) freedom.")

audience (*publika*) A prerequisite for the specific (public) creative process of a theatre artist. In Vakhtangov's view, audience serves both as a source of artistic impulses for the actor as well as a creative collaborator in the formation of the performance's image.

Vakhtangov was asked how his suggestions as a director were embodied in the play in a manner that was inevitably "conveyed" to the audience. His answer was, "I never direct before an empty audience room. From the first rehearsal, I imagine the theatre filled with the audience. When giving my suggestions or demonstrating to the actor this or that passage, I 'hear' and 'see' clearly the reaction of the imaginary audience and reckon with it. Very often I quarrel with the imaginary audience and insist upon my point of view" (Chekhov 1991: 21). (*See also* "image," "character," and "circle of attention.")

breath (*dykhaniye*)   Breath is the prototype of the musical measure, the ancestor of rhythm. Breath implies an ability to transform time and impart our soul with a sensation of rest, of the stoppage in time (Lussy 1884: 3; cited in Volkonsky 1912: 148).

No evidence of Vakhtangov's concepts of breath survived. Sergei Volkonsky, who worked with the Vakhtangov Studio students on movement and speech, had the following philosophy of breath:

> To receive and to give: these are the two life functions that belong to everything living on this earth. Breath continually repeats these two functions—from a newborn's first breath that begins the human's process of accumulation, to the "last breath," in which man returns to nature what he no longer needs. Inhale and exhale is a microcosm of our existence: inhale—birth, exhale—death . . . The principle of polarity that acts in this world, with all its manifestations—height and depth, strength and weakness, darkness and light, woe and joy—finds its expression in the rising and lowering of the chest. With this movement, a man takes from nature and gives back the air he took from her.
>
> (Volkonsky 1913: 32)

> Breath consists of two movements—inhale and exhale. The first movement is an action, while the second is rest. Because of this, the psychological meaning of both functions, as well as the general character of the spoken word, is determined by the stress placed on each of the functions. Inhale is heard in excitement, and exhale—in calm. All emotions can be divided into "inhaling" and "exhaling"; the first group is the one of suffering, the second group is the one of joy.
>
> (Volkonsky 1912: 148)

Breath exercises offered by Volkonsky were based in deep observation of life and nature; nevertheless, these exercises were external, or mechanical. When it came to mechanical exercises, Vakhtangov always advised his students to dive deeper into an exercise, in order to penetrate the very soul, or the essence of the technique. In other words, Vakhtangov insisted that his students use intuition to internalize external technique. By doing so, a student could gain a deep experiential understanding of breathing—the one inherent in the essential principles, as described in Volkonsky's philosophy of breath.

The two master teachers Vakhtangov employed at his Studio as voice teachers, Volkonsky and Pyatnitsky, insisted on the so-called "diaphragmal" breathing. Pyatnitsky, a self-taught man, practiced a more organic approach than Volkonsky. Here is an example of a Pyatnitsky approach to diaphragmal breathing that leads to a genuine emotional experience, as described by Nikolai Demidov:

Speak a monologue, or a verse and, instead of following the lines, follow the stomach walls as they rise (with inhale) and fall; at the same time, he [Pyatnitsky] recommended not to inhale until all of the air was used up (until all of the air was squeezed out). And, instead of breathing with one's chest, to breath with one's stomach [diaphragm]!

With time, less and less concentration will be needed for the mechanical work per se, and the spare concentration will move onto the lines. Little by little, the lines will begin to captivate and then emotionally move the actor.

(Demidov 2009: 252)

character, image of the character (*obraz*)   The word *obraz* in Russian has multiple meanings. In the artistic vocabulary, it means two things: image and character. Vakhtangov's approach towards character was essentially the same as in music, visual art, and literature. Theatrical character, according to Vakhtangov, is not a living, breathing human being but *an image of the character*, created by the living, breathing creative artist. Vakhtangov's concept of the character image is similar to his concept of theatrical reality. The artistic image of the theatrical production cannot equal life; it is a new artistic reality that does not duplicate nature and everyday life. At the same time, this reality is governed by the essential creative rules present in life and nature.

characterization (*kharakternost'*)   *See* "kernel" and "transformation."

circle of attention (*krug vnimaniya*)   "The circle of attention is a concentrated state, distinguished by free muscles and faith in the importance of what happens onstage. This circle can be expanded or contracted. An ability to swiftly shift the boundaries of the circle is one of an actor's very important qualities" (*Sourcebook* p. 180).

In a "fourth wall"-type production, an actor's artistic world is "restricted by the circle of the stage characters" (*Sourcebook* p. 247). During the type of production Vakhtangov defined an *actor's performance*, when actors communicate directly with the audience, the actor's circle of attention (or artistic world) includes the audience.

clarity (*chyotkost'*)   An intrinsic quality belonging to every great work of art. Everything a theatre artist does on stage should be done with clarity and distinction. Vakhtangov speaks of the distinction of character drawing, distinction of bits in the role and the play, etc. He insisted that even "blurring" of movements, qualities, bits, and textures onstage should be done with clarity.

contemporary form (*sovremennaya forma*)   The contemporary form, discovered by Vakhtangov for his final productions, was the form of grotesque (*see* "grotesque"). In Vakhtangov's views, this form was harmonious with the rhythms and forms of the revolutionary life. In fact, such a form can be contemporary to any period of a historic cataclysm. Contemporary form, according to Vakhtangov, requires a periodic renewal—throughout the life of the performance—in order to stay contemporary. Following his experiments with the contemporary form, or the form of grotesque, Vakhtangov was planning to work on discovering the eternal form (*see* "eternal form").

creative individuality (*tvorcheskaya individual'nost'*)   A unique creative mission of an artist constitutes their creative individuality (*see* "festivity"). Full expression of an actor's creative individuality implies an actor's ability to live onstage as an improviser and "fantasize" their adaptations. Therefore, according to Vakhtangov, an actor can only practice their individuality by the means of spontaneous subconscious creativity. No matter how "stage savvy" or experienced an actor might be, intellectual expressive means and choices do not distinguish their creative individuality. Any other actor could arrive at the same choices, and the skill of manipulating the audience's attention onstage can be learned by anyone. "One can learn the means; as for the form—it should be created, it should be fantasized" (*Sourcebook* p. 158).

creative spirit (*tvorcheskiy dukh*) In Vakhtangov's philosophy, the highest force obtainable by human beings on earth. Evoking the creative spirit is the ultimate goal of Vakhtangov's method and theatre.

creative state (*tvorcheskoye samochustviye*) An actor's self-experience, grounded in festivity. According to Vakhtangov, the creative experience of every artist is based in festive joy, but it also varies, based on the creative individuality and the artistic laws of the given performance. In other words, there is no "generic" creative state, as there is no "generic" theatrical truth. Both the creative state and the feeling of truth need to be rediscovered anew in every production and in every role.

cultivation (*vospitaniye*) *See* "actor cultivation."

definition (*chyotkost'*) *See* "clarity."

discipline (*distsiplina*) An actor's sense of responsibility for the form of the performance. When engaged in a performance, based in the contemporary form, or in the form of grotesque, an actor is supposed to discover a special kind of creative freedom, based in the rigid discipline of the pre-established form. In Vakhtangov's philosophy, the category of discipline is closely connected with the actor's feeling of the stage. (*See also* "freedom.")

dynamics (*dinamika*) The laws of movement and gesture, outlined by François Delsarte (*see* "gesture"). In Vakhtangov's philosophy: continuous inner (psychological) movement of the performance, accompanied by alternations between external (physical) movement and stillness. (*See* "rhythm" and "immobility.")

essence (*suschnost'*) In Vakhtangov's philosophy, essence is the creative spirit, invested by the artist-creator into the creation. Out of this spirit, the play and the role can grow organically. As long as a theatre artist preserves the sense of the play's or the character's essence, the artist is able to live creatively onstage—from the essence. The essence of an artistic work resides within the subconscious realm, and, therefore, it cannot be fully defined intellectually. The essence of the artistic work is absorbed as the artist receives their first spontaneous (intuitive) impression from the work. (*See* "spirit," "subconscious.")

eternal mask, eternal form (*vechnaya maska, vechnaya forma*) The form of theatre that always remains contemporary, as it evolves and renews itself in *every* performance.

étude In theatre training practice, an *étude* is an improvisational exercise with a simple plot.

everyday life/the mundane (*byt*)   "Resolving the mundane elements of life artistically onstage," according to Vakhtangov, is one of the most difficult theatrical tasks. In his letter to Nemirovich-Danchenko, Vakhtangov wrote that in his production of *The Dybbuk* he "had to find a theatrical, contemporary treatment for [depicting] the mundane onstage" (see *Sourcebook* p. 327).

faith/gaining faith (*vera*)   An actor's belief in the seriousness of their artistic mission awakens their creative passions and allows them to "gain faith" in the artistic reality of the stage.

fantasizing (*fantazirovaniye*)   An *active* psycho-physical life of a theatre artist's imagination, instrumental to the theatre artist's creative process at all of its stages—in development and execution of a theatre work.

fantastic realism (*fantasticheskiy realizm*)   A creative method, formulated by Vakhtangov and utilized in the creation of Vakhtangov's final productions, such as *The Miracle of Saint Anthony, Erik XIV, The Wedding, The Dybbuk*, and *Princess Turandot*.

"Naturalism in theatre should not exist, and neither should realism. Only fantastic realism should exist. Rightly discovered theatrical means give an author a true life onstage. One can master the means; as for the form, it should be created, it should be fantasized" (*Sourcebook* p. 158).

feeling of the stage (*stsenizm*)   An actor's ability to experience his or her body and psychology as an instrument for creating stage forms and theatrical textures and his or her movements and voice as an expressive means within the space and time of the performance.

Vakhtangov's close colleague, Michael Chekhov, had this to say about the feeling of the stage:

The sense of stage space is . . . unfamiliar to the actor. He does not distinguish the right side from the left, he does not distinguish in all its fullness the proscenium from the back of the stage, the straight and curved lines in which he is walking . . . An actor's eyes are his means of maximum expressiveness, although they will only be truly expressive when the whole of the actor's body, imbued with will, is drawing forms and lines in the stage space . . . The body in space and rhythms in time—these are the means of an actor's expressiveness.

(Chekhov 2005: 59–60)

Zakhava (1930: 130) described this principle thus:

Only when everything [the form of the performance] was prepared, has the actor *regained* his right to improvise (movements, gestures, intonations), according to those requirements dictating the form of the performance. Thus the actors received their right to improvise "adaptations" only when there was a guarantee that they became so firmly grounded in the principles of acting in a given performance that their improvisation won't leave the boundaries established by these principles. The actors' ability to improvise "adaptations" while sensing full responsibility for these adaptations, i.e. subjecting adaptations to the requirements of the form and mastery of acting, is called by Vakhtangov "feeling of the stage."

The "feeling of the stage" is an actor's ability to live and act in the environment of "stage air." Vakhtangov taught that the "stage air" differs from the one we usually breathe. Just as one cannot feel and act the same in water as on earth, one also cannot feel the same on the stage as in everyday life. As one finds himself in water, one ought to adapt to the new environment. He becomes responsible for his behavior, and he ought to subject his every movement to the environment's demands. In order to stay in the water, one must learn to *swim*. So must the actor adapt. As he finds himself on the stage, he must learn how to "swim" in the stage environment. Without such ability he will "drown." The slightest movement on the stage does not equal its life equivalent; the slightest movement on the stage is of great consequence, as *the audience sees it*.

Vakhtangov scholar Natalia Smirnova (1982: 33) provides the following definition of Vakhtangov's term:

Vakhtangov staged a production and simultaneously taught his actors how to model a blocking; he developed in them a skill of seeing themselves from the side, being able to sense themselves in the space, drawn in a blocking. This cannot be achieved without developing "in an actor the sense of his own material, as well as the sense of the stage air as a condensed environment. According to Vakhtangov, an actor was supposed to feel himself in this environment, like in water. He had to develop a different way of calculating his movements, and a special sense of responsibility for every movement he makes" (Zakhava 1930: 130).

(Smirnova (1982: 33)

festival/festivity, joy (*prazdnik, rados't*)   The essence of the theatre process, every theatrical situation, as well as the essence of creativity.

> There are moments in a man's life when he wants to live more than ever and when he joyfully feels himself belonging to everything living. He becomes vigorous, and both his good and bad seeds express themselves with special vividness.
>   In such moments a man becomes inspired, his eyes light up festively, and he fills up with vigorous desires and a thirst for activity. This is a festive moment.
>   It is the same for an actor.
>
> (*Sourcebook* p. 108)

freedom (*svoboda*)   An actor's ability to freely follow their creative impulses onstage. (*See* "organic technique, crossing the creative threshold.") "The entire teaching is a device, the means to achieve something. This 'something' is an absolute freedom!" (*Sourcebook* p. 99).

freeze   *See* "full stop."

full stop (*tochka*)   An expressive device used to prepare and sustain rhythmical bits in performance. A full stop usually comes at the end of a play/role bit, to separate one bit from another and, thus, achieve definition and clarity of rhythmical division. (*See* "immobility" and "clarity.")

gesture/laws of the gesture (*zhest*)   If rhythm is meant to transform and organize space and time, then gesture is the most powerful device an actor has at their disposal in order to execute their rhythmical patterns and create the image of character, or performance. A man's relationship to space and to self is expressed in gesture.

> "Gesture is an expression of a human being's inner self by the means of his external self. Gesture is a process of self-modeling that constantly evolves both in terms of a man's relationship to self and to his surrounding world. Each human being is a center of his own cosmos, and his every movement causes a shift of all the relationships. An arm is a beginning of an endless radius; its end touches an invisible and seemingly nonexistent periphery of the universe" (Volkonsky 1912: 16).
>   The size of the glossary does not allow outlining all laws of gesture. Here are a few of those especially important for Vakhtangov:

- Gesture is connected with the thought behind the words, rather than with the literal meaning of the words.
- The spirit of the gesture should permeate an actor's entire being and affect their psychology, body and speech.
- The gesture will only be theatrical and beautiful, when it is inwardly purposeful.
- Theatrical gesture requires a physical and esthetic balance.

Delsarte's law of opposition in gesture implies interdependent positions and responsive movements of the different parts of the human body. "When the limbs follow the same direction, they cannot be simultaneous without injury to the law of opposition. Therefore, direct movements should be successive and opposite movements simultaneous" (Delsarte; quoted in Stebbins 1902: 262).

Theatrical gesture must be fully executed. "A gesture, when discovered, should be executed *in its completeness* (except for those cases when the psychology of the character requires the gesture to be incomplete)" (Volkonsky 1912: 34–35).

According to Delsarte, "There are nine laws that govern the significance of motion in the human body, namely: 1. Attitude; 2. Force; 3. Motion; 4. Sequence; 5. Direction; 6. Form; 7. Velocity; 8. Reaction; 9. Extension" (Stebbins 1902: 257). Other fundamental laws of gesture and movement outlined by Delsarte are the laws of trinity, evolution, and correspondence.

The types of gesture used in theatre are numerous. We distinguish between historical gesture, national gesture, descriptive gesture, "automatic," or reflexive gesture, gesture of the individual characteristic, archetypal gesture, psychological gesture, etc. Vakhtangov used all of the gestures mentioned above as his acting and directorial expressive means. For example, in Vakhtangov's production of *The Dybbuk*, several characters had their own gestural "*leitmotif*," a repeated gesture that expressed their psychological and social essence. According to Vakhtangov, a gesture he observed from a Jewish accountant, his ward mate at the health rehabilitation resort, served him as an inspiration for the form of *The Dybbuk*.

grimace (*grimassa*)   A physical mask of the character. Vakhtangov utilized it for those characters, executed in the manner of condensed characterization, or grotesque. Vakhtangov the actor used the grimace for the facial mask of his character of Tackleton from the First Studio of the MAT production of *The Cricket on the Hearth*. Tackleton's facial mask featured lips pursed in disgust and one eye permanently screwed.

grotesque (*grotesk*)   A kind of the theatrical art that allows an artist to create a form that expresses the quintessence of the object being depicted or to emphasize its particular aspects. Several definitions of grotesque exist in Russian theatrical practices, given by such different artists as Meyerhold and Stanislavsky. Vakhtangov's definition of grotesque is featured in Nikolai Gorchakov's book *Vakhtangov's Directorial Lessons*:

> Grotesque is a method that allows an actor and director to inwardly justify the content of the given play in a dramatic and condensed way. Grotesque is the limit of expressiveness, a rightly discovered form that manifests the deepest, innermost essence of the play's content. In the art of the director, grotesque is the conclusion of his creative search expressed through the harmonious, organic combination of the performance's form and content.
>
> (Gorchakov 1957: 41)

Another definition of Vakhtangov's art of grotesque is given by the Vakhtangov scholar Natalia Smirnova. In her book on Vakhtangov (Smirnova 1982), she writes of Vakhtangov's tendency to introduce satirical elements to a character after it has been thoroughly developed by an actor, in accordance with the school of psychological realism. In other words, after such an actor "justified" his or her character, Vakhtangov asked them to condense some of their character's psychological or social traits to the form of the tragic-comic grotesque: "From the collision and struggle of two opposing forces—lyricism and satire, psychological element and a tendency toward 'mask-like characterization'—an entirely new quality was born, endowed with sudden tragic overtones" (Smirnova 1982: 32).

hands (*ruki*)   "Hands are the eyes of the body" (Ivanov 2011 vol. II: 532). Vakhtangov considered hands the most expressive part of an actor's body. In his productions, such as *The Miracle of Saint Anthony* and *The Dybbuk*, the expression of the actor's inner life culminated in their hands.

> In terms of expressiveness, legs and feet play a supporting part, while arms and hands play the leading part; legs and feet bind us to the earth while arms and hands lift us up from the earth. The unbendable law of gravity acts upon our legs and feet. Our arms and hands are permeated with an upward striving; our legs and feet ground us, while our arms and hands free us from the earth and lift us up.
>
> (Volkonsky 1912: 155)

image (*obraz*)   In the Vakhtangov method, an archetypal (symbolic, grotesque) image behind the entirety of the performance. The original source of the archetypal imagery, according to Vakhtangov, is myth—a creation of popular consciousness. The image of the performance is formed gradually, throughout the entire performance. It is formed within the audience's subconscious mind and does not reveal itself to the audience in its entirety until after the performance is over.

image of the character   *See* character.

immobility (statuary immobility) (*statuarnost'*)   A stopping in the physical movement of the performance that implies continuous inner movement. Interrupted movement is a powerful means of attracting the audience's attention to the essence of the stage bit, character, etc. Vakhtangov's principle of statuary immobility develops Delsarte's principles, such as the law of opposition, harmonic poise, and statue-posing. (*See* "gesture.")

joy (*rados't'*)   *See* "festivity."

justification (*opravdaniye*)   "What should one do in order to gain . . . faith? In order to do it, one should discover a justification, that is the cause of every given action, situation, sensation, etc." (*Sourcebook* p. 177).

Vakhtangov distinguished between the Stanislavskian psychological justification that originates from the private life of an actor and *artistic* justification. When Stanislavsky justified theatre according to everyday life (What would I do, how would I behave if, in my real life, I was put in a similar situation?), Vakhtangov justified theatre according to the creative life of an actor. The question Vakhtangov actors asked of themselves differed from Stanislavsky's formula. According to Lee Strasberg (1988: 85), this question was, "The circumstances of the scene indicate that the character must behave in a particular way; what would motivate you, the actor, to behave in that particular way?" Overall, Vakhtangov's take on justification is closely connected with an actor's ability to sense the seriousness of their mission, as well as with festivity, artistry, passion that arises from perceiving the essence, and other concepts of the Vakhtangov technique featured in this glossary.

During his work on *Princess Turandot*, Vakhtangov coined the term "theatrical justification" (*teatral'noye opravdaniye*). According to this term, and device, the life of *Turandot* characters received justification in a specific reality of a theatrical performance—as opposed to the everyday reality.

kernel (*zerno*)   An inner sensation that causes actors to assume the character's external characterization and express themselves as characters, both physically and psychologically. Realistic characterization, as one of the theatrical textures, and as one of the techniques of drawing the image of the character, was preserved by Vakhtangov. Vakhtangov did, however, abandon the inner technique of the "kernel." The image of the character, according to Vakhtangov, does not originate from the character's kernel. It is conceived when the creative spirit of the author fertilizes an actor's (theatre artist's) creative spirit. (*See* "transformation.")

mastery (*masterstvo*)   An actor's ability to *consciously* express themselves onstage according to the requirements of the external technique, as dictated by the form of a particular performance. (Vakhtangov's master also inwardly justifies the fixed form of the performance, however complex it might be.) An actor who possesses the feeling of the stage, however, can subconsciously improvise according to the *principles* of the required form. (*See* "subconscious expression.")

modeling (*lepka*)   An actor's ability to model their body, speech, and psychology. (On modeling, see Vakhtangov's rehearsals of Pushkin's *Feast During the Plague* in Part VII of the *Sourcebook. See also* "plasticity" and "feeling of the stage.")

molding   *See* "modeling."

motivation/motive (*tsel'*)   In the realm of the play's circumstances, a pretext that motivates character to enter the stage and engage in their actions. Since these pretexts are fictional in a theatre performance, Vakhtangov believed that true motives of an actor's creative passions lie in his or her subconscious artistic mission.

mundane, the   *See* "everyday life."

mystery (*misteriya*)   In Vakhtangov's philosophy, the Theatre of Mystery evokes the presence of a higher force, or a higher being, and unites the audience and the actors in this act. Vakhtangov's final productions achieved the synthesis of the Theatre of Mystery and the Popular Theatre, thus signifying a new type of performance. In Vakhtangov's theatre, the audience and the actors united in evoking the creative spirit.

organic technique, crossing the creative threshold   Practicing organic technique requires an actor's courage to trust that whatever he or she actually experiences while crossing the threshold of the stage will apply to the fulfillment of his or her creative task. According to Vakhtangov, an actor does not need to alter his or her experience upon entering the stage; it is individual and unique, and, therefore, valuable. An actor's creative nature will incorporate this experience into the equation of the creative task; this subconscious nature will eventually create the needed artistic effect out of the actor's initial experience. An actor's job is not to interfere with his or her creative impulses and yield to them fully onstage. In other words, an actor should allow himself or herself full freedom to do what he or she truly feels like doing onstage. The creative subconscious will take care of the "required" artistic result.

outer (muscular) freedom and control (*vneshnyaya (muskul'naya) svoboda i kontrol'*)   An actor's ability to spend a *sufficient* amount of muscular energy for every activity. Overspending or underspending muscular energy would lead to physical and psychological tension and interfere with an actor's creative process. Therefore, Vakhtangov called muscular freedom the first prerequisite of an actor's creative state.

"Muscular freedom and concentration closely depend on each other. When you are concentrated, you are necessarily free, however, a lack of muscular freedom won't allow you to concentrate your attention. This is why, first of all, you must destroy tension, as far as possible, and then discover an object for your attention. The remaining trace of tension will then disappear" (*Sourcebook* p. 176).

plasticity (*plastichnos't'*)   An essential artistic quality that implies complete physical and psychological freedom, harmony, flexibility, and naturalness. According to Vakhtangov, plasticity is a natural phenomenon, and, therefore, a theatre artist must absorb it from nature. (*See* Vakhtangov's notes on plasticity, *Sourcebook* p. 120.)

"Actors should engage in long and diligent work to consciously *cultivate* the habit of plasticity, so that later they can unconsciously *express* themselves in a plastic way. This applies to their ability to wear a costume, adjust the volume of their voice, achieve physical transfiguration (through a visible external form) into the form of the character they portray, allocate their muscular energy efficiently, and model themselves into anything in gesture, voice, or musical speech. Actors should also be able to achieve plasticity in the logic of their feelings" (*Sourcebook* p. 120).

point of view (*otnosheniye*)   A property of the theatre artist's imagination, capable of creating a new artistic or creative reality of the performance. Vakhtangov had this to say about the point of view in theatre:

Creative play in theatre is a play of the new points of view. One cannot believe literally. One must have an ability to take lies for truth, using the power of one's creative imagination; one must know how to instigate a new point of view on what happens onstage[. . .]

Adults lose the naivety of a child. When a child is tired of play, it means that he is tired of creating new points of view. A child is naive, which is why he creates new points of view so seriously.

To be serious means to know that I am doing an important work. An actor, creating new points of view seriously, becomes naive.

(*Sourcebook* p. 89)

Vakhtangov distinguished between the creative point of view of the author and that of the theatrical collective. (This collective includes the director, actor, designers, composer, etc.). Many productions staged by Vakhtangov presented reality from a particular character's point of view—usually from the point of view of those characters possessing the popular consciousness or those who transgressed their social masks.

As a teacher of theatre, and director, Vakhtangov utilized the technique of shifting an actor's point of view on object, place, partner, and fact. On Vakhtangov's use of these techniques, see rehearsal records for *The Lanin Estate* (*Sourcebook* p. 248).

Popular Theatre (*narodnyi teatr*)   The kind of theatre where the reality is presented through the prism of the popular consciousness. (*See also* "mystery.")

Presentational Theatre/School of Acting (also known as Theatre of Symbolism, Expressionism, Futurism and the Fantastic; School/ Theatre of Presenting the Part, Non-Psychological Theatre) (*Predstavleniye*)   A trend of theatre where the theatrical collective copies the form of the role and the performance night after night. This form of theatre does not imply a creative emotional experience, transformation, as well as the working of the subconscious "creative nature." It relies on highly polished external technique (voice, speech, movement, gesture) to copy, or approximate the portrayed reality. In opposition to it, the School of the Emotional Experience calls for the stage reality to be recreated anew in every performance.

Vakhtangov is often credited with marrying the presentational school of acting with the school of experiencing. The reason Vakhtangov was able to achieve this merger is that he significantly redefined Stanislavsky's concept of experiencing. By doing so, he was able to place the numerous expressive means, usually associated with the presentational art, in the hands of the "experiencing" creative artist.

psychological gesture (*psikhologicheskiy zhest*) Psycho-physical technique, developed by Michael Chekhov, and inspired by his work with Vakhtangov. Psychological Gesture technique is based in a concept that every character, stage moment, atmosphere, production as a whole—in fact every artistic phenomenon— carries within itself an elaborate, living, breathing dynamic. Having grasped this dynamic both physically and psychologically—by executing an artistically formed gesture—an actor can absorb the psychological essence of a theatrical phenomenon, and express it in powerful and vivid form.

public solitude (*publichnoye odinochestvo*) According to Vakhtangov, a circle of attention, assumed in front of the audience, constitutes public solitude. This process, when executed right, creates the following sensation in an actor: "In front of an audience I (we) am (are) busy with what is important, necessary and interesting to me (us)" (Ivanov 2011 vol. II: 359).

rhythm (*ritm*)   In a work of art, rhythm signifies harmony of its separate parts that arises from an artist's ability to embrace the entirety of the work. The idea of stage rhythm also implies uninterrupted internal movement of the performance. On the performance external side, it is paralleled by an alteration between movement and stillness. (*See* "immobility," "dynamics," and "full stop.")

Vakhtangov applied his concept of rhythm to every aspect of the performance, be it actor's movement (gesture) and speech, character development, or the overall composition of the performance. Vakhtangov approached rhythm as the life stream of an artistic creation. If in life, rhythms can be arbitrary, in theatre they need to be harmonious. In theatre, as in other forms of art, rhythm serves as a force that organizes a performance. It is also the essential creative means of an actor. The artistic image, and the overall artistic reality of the performance, according to Vakhtangov, is created through the use of rhythm.

In his letter to the Gunst Studio movement class, Vakhtangov refers his students to Sergei Volkonsky's book *A Man on the Stage* (1912). To follow are the guiding principles of rhythm outlined in Volkonsky's book:

Space and time are the forever present conditions a man is placed under; they cannot be escaped. Physical conditions of space and time affect every single perception and action, and every single creation, spiritual or physical. He, who wants to create, must place space and time under his command; in order to do so, he must develop appropriate skills—the physical means of perception and expression that allow him to act within the boundaries of space and time.

The means of perceiving the space is vision; the means of perceiving time is hearing.

The means of expression in space is body, in time—voice.

The method of training the actor for the space is plasticity of movement, for the time—speech.

The means of merging the two is rhythm—correspondence of image and sound, of plasticity of movement and speech, of the categories of space and time.

Only through such a merger will the entire, complete human (actor) be able to affect the entire, complete human (spectator).

(Volkonsky 1912: 179–80)

According to Vakhtangov, every nation, every character, every activity or action has its own rhythm that belongs to them by nature. An actor must be able to assume this rhythm.

spirit (*dukh*)   An artistic spirit of the character, play, or performance is the creative spark, invested in it by the artist-creator. It is this spirit of the work of art (play, character) a theatre artist must perceive from the author. When the spirit of the artistic work "inseminates" the spirit of the theatre artist, it is then that a theatrical work of art is born. (*See* "essence.")

stage object (**object of attention**) (*stsenicheskiy obyekt (obyekt vnimaniya)*)   "By sending our attention in some direction we are going to create a center of attention. It is clear that we cannot have two centers of attention at the same time; one cannot at the same time be reading a book and listening to a conversation in the next room. At any given moment, you can only concentrate your interest upon one object. Such an object we call *an object of attention*. A sound, a physical object, a thought, an action, your own emotion or your partner's emotion can all become an object of your attention.

"How can we attract our interest to one particular object? We can concentrate our five senses either on some object, or on a sound (hearing), our thought power upon some thought, and inner feelings upon a feeling, be it our own feeling or our partner's. *Every second of his existence on the stage an actor must have an object of attention.* Otherwise, an actor won't be able to experience the required feelings at his own will" (*Sourcebook* p. 176). (*See also* "attention" and "outer (muscular) freedom.")

stage platform, a place of (theatrical) action (*stsenicheskaya ploschadka*) Physical organization of theatre space is essential to the theatrical nature of the given production. A stage platform creates a necessary environment that supports the method of acting and the nature of communication with the audience utilized in the given performance. In addition to that, the stage platform contributes to the performance imagery. In his 1921 diary entry (*Sourcebook* p. 127), Vakhtangov points out that "every kind of performance calls for its own form of stage platform." He continues by naming four theatrical personalities, whose names signified an epoch in the development of theatre: Shakespeare, Molière, Gozzi, Ostrovsky. Vakhtangov's thought is easy to transcribe: every great theatrical epoch introduced a new principle of the stage platform that did not change from one performance to the next. It might have been "dressed" differently for a different production, but its overall architecture remained the same.

Vakhtangov's concept of a stage platform that can serve several performances of the same type contradicted the "progressive" principles of stage design, introduced by his contemporary directors and designers. For example, the MAT prided itself in creating a unique set for every new performance. Vakhtangov, on the contrary, put the emphasis on discovering a *new method of actors' existence onstage* for every type of theatre. As for the overall architecture of the stage platform, he considered that a contemporary version of the stage platform should be discovered for every type of theatre, once and for all. On Vakhtangov's principle of stage platform for the contemporary version of the *commedia dell'arte*, see accounts of *Princess Turandot* rehearsals published in Part VII of the *Sourcebook*.

subconscious, subconscious perception and expression (*podsoznaniye, podsoznatel'noe vospriyatiye i vyiavleniye*) An actor's ability to instantaneously grasp and express the essence, or the entirety of an artistic phenomenon—be it an object of observation, a character, a play, a theatrical situation, etc. "A couple of empty hints" (*Sourcebook* p. 131) or details of the phenomenon coming to such an artist's attention allow the artist to synthesize the phenomenon at hand.

"A genius actor . . . immediately, at once, embraces the character in its entirety, thus finding himself instantly at its apex. It is from this place that he perceives the details" (*Sourcebook* p. 105). (*See also* "essence," "spirit.")

"He who consciously feeds his subconscious and expresses the results of its work in a subconscious way is a talent.

"He who subconsciously feeds his subconscious and engages in a subconscious expression is a genius.

"He who expresses consciously is a master" (*Sourcebook* p. 112).

task, creative task (*zadacha, tvorcheskaya zadacha*)   In every particular instance of the performance, be it plot, artistic form, or character psychology, a theatre artist is meant to resolve a particular creative task. The way by which the task is resolved (creative means, or actors' adaptations) constitutes the aspect of the performance perceived by the audience. Through these means or adaptations the audience receives the overall image of the performance. Therefore, if the task is resolved consciously, and adaptations are calculated, the image of the performance will not affect the audience's creative core. In order to do so, according to Vakhtangov, the resolution of the task should be fulfilled creatively: in other words, it should be spontaneous, improvisational, and imaginative.

According to Vakhtangov, a stage task consists of five elements:

1   Action, Physical and Verbal (What do I do?)
2   Motive (Why do I enter the stage?)
3   Desire (Why do I want to fulfill my motive?)
4   Adaptation (How do I fulfill my motive?)
5   Subtext (What do I truly mean by what I say?)

The fourth element of task, adaptation, is its leading element, a measure of the actor's talent and his or her ability to affect the audience's creative nature.

temperament (*Temperament*)   Creative passion, or emotional individuality of an artist.

texture   See "theatrical texture."

Theatre of Experiencing/School of Experiencing (also known as Experiencing, School of Living the Part, Theatre of the Emotional Experience, Psychological Theatre, Theatre of Psychological Realism, Representational Theatre/Acting) (*Perezhivaniye*)   A school of theatre that develops an actor's ability to awaken emotional experience at every performance. Experiencing is tightly connected with the process of an actor's transformation; in fact, one cannot happen without the other.

For Vakhtangov, experiencing signified an actor's ability to relive an emotional experience onstage without any external motivation. In Stanislavsky's opinion, the emotional life of the actor is motivated by the actor's faith in his or her character's given circumstances. Vakhtangov considered it both impossible and anti-artistic for an actor to literally believe in the fictitious circumstances. In Vakhtangov's opinion, such a literal belief would either be a sign of naivety or sick hallucination. According to Vakhtangov, an actor's faith was motivated by their imagination as well as their self-realization as a creative artist.

"An actor must awaken his passion *without any external motivation* for creative passion; to achieve this, an actor must work in rehearsals chiefly to make everything that surrounds him, according to the play, his own atmosphere and to make his role's tasks his own; this will cause his passion to speak 'from the essence'" (*Sourcebook* p. 141).

In other words, every creative individual, according to Vakhtangov, needs to discover a unique atmosphere and the essence of every stage event, situation or object. Such an individual atmosphere is the atmosphere of this particular artist's private artistic mission or theme; it awakens in them a sense of creative festivity. Only this personal creative mission, as refracted in the events, objects, and situations on the stage, is capable of arousing this individual's creative passion. In many instances, an actor's very realization, or a sensation of having such a theme, or mission, is sufficient to produce the desired effect.

Theatre of Mystery   *See* "mystery."

theatrical form and theatrical content (*teatral'naya forma i teatral'noye soderzhaniye*)   The two were inseparable for Vakhtangov, as, to his mind, a theatre artist is supposed to fantasize a form that would fully express (or exhaust) the performance's content.

theatrical texture (*teatral'naya faktura*)   The method of an actor's life onstage and their choice of means of expressiveness in creating a stage image. Vakhtangov's concept of theatrical textures is discussed in the *Sourcebook* Introduction.

theatricality (*teatral'nost'*)   Each element of the performance can only be theatrical when it is essential to the unique world of the theatre production and to the essence of theatre at large. In Vakhtangov's mind, any object, blocking, character, set, etc., either "acts," or it does not, based on how fitting and meaningful it is in the artistic word of the given performance. A play, or a literary work, may be theatrical if it contains in it the essence of theatricality. For Vakhtangov, this essence was expressed in his concept of festivity. (*See* "festivity.")

thought (*mysl'*)   Vakhtangov's concept of thought is thoroughly explained in his October 11, 1917, diary note (see *Sourcebook* pp. 117–18), as well as in his rehearsals for Maeterlinck's *The Miracle of Saint Anthony* (see October 9, 1916, rehearsal record in *Sourcebook* p. 262) and for Pushkin's *Feast During the Plague* (see *Sourcebook* p. 284). Boris Zakhava had this to say on the subject:

> According to various aims behind a question, the thoughts that lie underneath the text of the question ("What time is it?") will differ, while never concurring with the literal meaning of the text. To follow are the thoughts that could lie underneath the question "What time is it?"—"Why are you late?" or "why are you still here?" or "My God, what tedium!" or "Am I late?," etc.
>
> In accordance with various thoughts, lying under the given bit of text, its intonations and gestures would also differ. This is easy to prove by asking the question "What time is it?" while investing it with one or the other of the thoughts indicated above.
>
> This is why Vakhtangov demanded that his students do not speak the words but thoughts. He called an actor's work of discovering the thoughts underneath the words of the text "unsealing the text" (*Sourcebook* p. 193).
>
> Thus, in order to "make the author's . . . words his own" (*Sourcebook* p. 90), an actor must make his own "the thoughts" his character lives with.
>
> (Zakhava 1930: 59)

transformation/transfiguration   (*perevoploscheniye*)   Vakhtangov's actor organically transforms as a creative individual. Transformation makes a creative individual out of the actor's everyday self. Such a creative individual reveals the hidden aspects of his or her inner world to the audience. With such a transformation an actor remains free to use a variety of expressive means, both physical and vocal, using them to create the artistic image of the character.

Between 1913 and 1918, Vakhtangov explored the Theatre of Mystery. At that stage of his work, Vakhtangov denied the art of characterization and insisted that actors must preserve their "God-given face" and "God-given voice." This phase of Vakhtangov's creative search, however, did not signify his denial of the creative transformation. Vakhtangov demanded that an actor must transform "by the power of the inner impulse," or by proceeding from oneself. Between 1918 and 1922, Vakhtangov created his method of fantastic realism, synthesizing the Theatre of Mystery with the Popular Theatre. This innovation, as well as the spirit of revolutionary times, caused Vakhtangov to arrive at a new logical conclusion on transformation. Vakhtangov concluded that an actor who transforms and lives onstage as a creative individual is free to use any theatrical texture (characterization, grotesque, symbolism, futurism, etc.), as long as this texture remains true to the spirit of the work and of the contemporary times.

truth of the passions (*istina strastei*)   "The moment of passion within the theatrical creative state, when an actor almost forgets that he is onstage, is the moment of faith, the moment of truth" (*Sourcebook* p. 92).

Bibliography

Bachelis, Tatyana (1983) *Shekspir i Kreg* [*Shakespeare and Craig*], Moscow: Nauka.

Barakcheyev, Sergei (1939) "Stenogrammy besed s Sergeyem Barakcheyevym [Transcripts of Conversations with Sergei Barakcheyev]," in Vladislav Ivanov (ed.) (2011), *Yevgeny Vakhtangov, Dokumenty i svidetel'stva* [*Yevgeny Vakhtangov, Documents and Evidence*], vol. I, Moscow: Indrik, p. 478.

Bialik, Hayim Nahman (2000) *Songs from Bialik: Selected Poems of Hayim Nahman Bialik*, edited and translated by Atar Hadari, Syracuse, NY: Syracuse University Press.

Blok, Alexander (1960–63) *Sobraniye sochineniy v vos'mi tomakh* [*Collected Works in Eight Volumes*], vol. VI, Moscow-Leningrad: Khudozhestvennaya literatura.

Bromley, Nadezhda (1923) "Turandot Vakhtangova [Vakhtangov's Turandot]" in *Printsessa Turandot* [*Princess Turandot*], Moscow-Petrograd: Gosudarstvennoie Izdatel'stvo.

Brook, Peter (1995) *The Empty Space*, New York: Touchstone.

Butkevich, Mikhail (2002) *K igrovomu teatru* [*Toward the Theatre of Players*], Moscow: GITIS.

Chagall, Marc (2003) *My Life*, London: Peter Owen Ltd.

Chekhov, Anton (1974–1983) *Polnoye sobraniye sochineniy v 20-i tomakh* [*Complete Works in 20 Volumes*], Moscow: Nauka.

—— (1997) *The Plays of Anton Chekhov*, Paul Schmidt (translator), New York: Harper Collins Publishers.

Chekhov, Michael (1991) *On the Technique of Acting*, New York: Harper Collins.

—— (1995) *Literaturnoie nasledie* [*Literary Heritage*], 2nd edn, vol. II, Moscow: Iskusstvo.

—— (2002) *To the Actor*, London and New York: Routledge.

—— (2005) *The Path of the Actor*, London and New York: Routledge.

Demidov, Nikolai (2004) *Tvorcheskoie nasledie* [*Creative Heritage*], vol. I, book 1: *Iskusstvo aktyora v ego nastoyaschem i buduschem* [*The Art of the*

Actor: Its Present and Future] and book 2: *Tipy aktyora* [*Actor Types*], St. Petersburg: Giperion.

—— (2007) *Tvorcheskoie nasledie* [*Creative Heritage*], vol. III, book 4: *Tvorcheskiy khudozhestvennyi protsess na stsene* [*Creative Artistic Process Onstage*], St. Petersburg: Nestor-Istoriya.

—— (2009) *Tvorcheskoie nasledie* [*Creative Heritage*], vol. IV, book 5: *Teoria i psikhologia aktyora affektivnogo tipa* [*Theory and Psychology of the Affective Type Actor*], St. Petersburg: Baltiyskie Sezony.

Deykun, Lidiya (1984) "Iz vospominaniy [From Memoirs]," in Lyubov Vendrovskaya and Galina Kaptereva (eds.) (1984), *Yevgeny Vakhtangov*, Moscow: VTO, pp. 355–56.

—— (2011) "Nezabyvaemoe. Vospominaniya. [The Unforgettable. Memoirs]," in Vladislav Ivanov (ed.), *Yevgeny Vakhtangov, Dokumenty i svidetel'stva* [*Yevgeny Vakhtangov, Documents and Evidence*], vol. I, Moscow: Indrik, pp. 162–63.

Dikiy, Aleksey (1957) *Povest' o teatral'noi unosti* [*Novel of My Theatrical Youth*], Moscow: Iskusstvo.

Dostoyevsky, Fyodor (1922) *The Brothers Karamazov*, transl. Constance Garnett, New York: The Macmillan Company.

Efros, Nikolai (1984) " 'Studiya' i eyo 'Potop' ['Studio' and its 'Deluge']" Kievskaya mysl', February 8, 1916, reprinted in Lyubov Vendrovskaya and Galina Kaptereva (eds.), *Yevgeny Vakhtangov*, Moscow: VTO, pp. 146–47.

Giatsintova, Sofia (1989) *S pamyatiu naedine* [*One on One with My Memory*], Moscow: Iskusstvo.

Gorchakov, Nikolai Mikhailovich (1957) *Rezhissyorskiye uroki Vakhtangova* [*Vakhtangov's Directorial Lessons*], Moscow: Iskusstvo.

—— (1959 probable year) *The Vakhtangov School of Stage Art*, Moscow: Foreign Languages Publishing House.

Gorky, Maksim (1954) *Polnoye sobraniye sochineniy* [*Complete Works*], vol. XXVIII, Moscow: Molodaya gvardiya.

Gromov, Viktor (1970) *Mikhail Chekhov*, Moscow: Iskusstvo.

Gurlyand, Arseniy (Ars. G.) (1904) "Iz vospominaniy o A.P. Chekhove [From Memoirs on Anton Chekhov]," *Teatr i iskusstvo*, No. 28 (July 2011), pp. 520–22.

Ivanov, Vladislav (1999) *Russkiye Sezony Teatra Gabima* [*The Russian Seasons of the Habima Theatre*], Moscow: Artist.

—— (ed.) (2011) *Yevgeny Vakhtangov, Dokumenty i svidetel'stva* [*Yevgeny Vakhtangov, Documents and Evidence*], vols I, II, Moscow: Indrik.

Karev (Prutkin), Aleksandr (1959) "Vesyolyi, neuyomnyi khudozhnik [Merry, Persistent Artist]," in Lyubov Vendrovskaya (ed.), *Yevg. Vakhtangov, Materialy i statyi* [*Yevgeny Vakhtangov, Materials and Articles*], Moscow: VTO, pp. 416–22.

Khersonsky, Khrisanf (1940a) *Vakhtangov*, Moscow: Molodaya gvardiya.

—— (ed.) (1940b) *Besedy o Vakhtangove* [*Conversations About Vakhtangov*], Moscow-Leningrad: VTO.

Lussy, Mathis (1884) *Le Rythme musical*, Paris: Heugel.

Luzhsky, Vasily (1959) "Slovo ob uchenike [A Word About My Student]," in Lyubov Vendrovskaya (ed.), *Yevg. Vakhtangov, Materialy i statyi [Yevgeny Vakhtangov, Materials and Articles]*, Moscow: VTO, pp. 362–64.

Macrae, David (1870) *The Americans at Home (Pen-and-ink Sketches of American Men, Manners and Institutions)*, Edinburgh, Edmonston and Douglas.

Malaev-Babel, Andrei (ed.) (2011) *The Vakhtangov Sourcebook*, London and New York: Routledge.

Markov, Pavel (1923) "Printsessa Turandot i sovremennyi teatr [Princess Turandot and the Contemporary Theater]," in *Printsessa Turandot [Princess Turandot]* (1923) Moscow-Petrograd: Gosudarstvennoie Izdatel'stvo, pp. 41–51.

—— (1925) "Pervaya studiya, Sulerzhitsky-Vakhtangov-Chekhov, 1913–22 [First Studio: Sulerzhitsky-Vakhtangov-Chekhov, 1913–22]," in *Moskovskiy khudozhestvennyi teatr vtoroi [Moscow Art Theatre II]*, Moscow: Izdaniye Mosk. Khud. *Teatra 2-go*, pp. 65–176.

Meyerhold, Vsevolod (1984) "Pamyati Vozhdya [Remembering the Leader]," *Ermitazh [Hermitage]*, No. 4. June 7–11, reprinted in Lyubov Vendrovskaya and Galina Kaptereva (eds.), *Yevgeny Vakhtangov*, Moscow: VTO, p. 447.

Nemirovich-Danchenko, Vladimir (1984a) "Zapis' v knige pochyotnykh gostei [Entry in the (Vakhtangov Studio) Honored Guests' Ledger]", in Lyubov Vendrovskaya and Galina Kaptereva (eds.), *Yevgeny Vakhtangov*, Moscow: VTO, pp. 426–27.

—— (1984b) Speech Before the Vakhtangov Memorial Performance, quoted in Yuri Sobolev, "Den' Vakhtangova [Vakhtangov's Day]," *Teatr i muzyka*, No. 10. December 5, 1922. Moscow. Reprinted in Lyubov Vendrovskaya and Galina Kaptereva (eds.), *Yevgeny Vakhtangov*, Moscow: VTO, pp. 452–54.

Podgorny, Vladimir (1984) "Otryvki iz memuarov [Excerpts from Memoirs]," in Lyubov Vendrovskaya and Galina Kaptereva (eds.), *Yevgeny Vakhtangov*, Moscow: VTO, p. 401.

Polyakova, Yelena (ed.) (1970) *Leopold Antonovich Sulerzhitsky*, Moscow: Iskusstvo.

—— (2006) *Teatr Sulerzhitskogo [Sulerzhitsky's Theatre]*, Moscow: AGRAF.

Printsessa Turandot [Princess Turandot] (1923) Moscow-Petrograd: Gosudarstvennoie Izdatel'stvo.

Pyzhova, Olga (1974) *Prizvaniye [An Artistic Calling]*, Moscow: Iskusstvo.

Rybakova, Yu (1994) *V. F. Komissarzhevskaya: Letopis' zhizni i tvorchestva [Chronicle of Vera Komissarzhevskaya Life and Art]*, St. Petersburg: Institut istorii iskusstv.

Simonde, Jean-Charles-Léonard (1823) *Historical View of the Literature of the South of Europe*, vol. II, London: Henry Colburn and Co.

Smirnova, Natalia (1982) *Yevgeny Vakhtangov*, Moscow: Znanie.

Smirnov-Nesvitsky, Yuri (1987) *Yevgeny Vakhtangov*, Leningrad: Iskusstvo.

Solovyov, Vladimir (1914) "*K istorii stsenicheskoi tekhniki commedia dell'arte* [*On the history of Commedia Dell'arte Stage Technique*]," in *Lubov' k tryom apel'sinam* [*Love for Three Oranges*], St. Petersburg. 1914. No. 4–5.

Speranskaya, Yuliya (1987) *Bratya Adel'geim* [*The Brothers Adelgeim*], Moscow: STD.

Stanislavsky, Konstantin (1953 probable year) *Moya zhizn' v iskusstve* [*My Life in Art*], Moscow: Foreign Language Publishing House.

—— (2008) *An Actor's Work*, London and New York: Routledge.

—— (2009) *An Actor's Work on a Role*, London and New York: Routledge.

Stebbins, Genevieve (1902) *Delsarte System of Expression*, New York: E. S. Werner.

Strasberg, Lee (1988) *A Dream of Passion: The Development of the Method*, New York and Scarborough, Ontario: Plume Werner.

Sushkevich, Boris (1959) "Vstrechi s Vakhtangovym [Encounters with Vakhtangov]," in Lyubov Vendrovskaya (ed.), *Yevg. Vakhtangov, Materialy i statyi* [*Yevgeny Vakhtangov, Materials and Articles*], Moscow: VTO, pp. 365–71.

Tilberg, Margareta (2003) *Coloured Universe and the Russian Avant-Garde*, Stockholms Universitet.

Vakhtangova, Nadezhda (1959) "Vladikavkaz i Moskva [Vladikavkaz and Moscow]," in Lyubov Vendrovskaya (ed.), *Yevg. Vakhtangov, Materialy i statyi* [*Yevgeny Vakhtangov, Materials and Articles*], Moscow: VTO, pp. 331–43.

Vakhtangova, Nadezhda, Vendrovskaya, Lyubov and Zakhava, Boris (eds.) (1939), *Vakhtangov: Zapiski. Pis'ma. Statyi* [*Vakhtangov: Notes. Letters. Articles*], Moscow and Leningrad: Iskusstvo.

Vendrovskaya, Lyubov (ed.) (1959) *Yevg. Vakhtangov, Materialy i statyi* [*Yevgeny Vakhtangov, Materials and Articles*], Moscow: VTO.

Vendrovskaya, Lyubov and Kaptereva, Galina (eds.) (1984) *Yevgeny Vakhtangov*, Moscow: VTO.

Vinogradskaya, Irina (ed.) (1971) *Zhizn i tvorchestvo Stanislavskogo. Letopis'.* [*Stanislavsky's Life and Art. Chronicle*], Moscow: VTO.

Volkonsky, Sergei (1912) *Chelovek na stsene* [*A Man on the Stage*], St. Petersburg: Izdanie "Apollona".

—— (1913) *Vyrazitel'noe slovo* [*Expressive Word*], St. Petersburg: Tipografia Sirius.

Volkov, Nikolai (1922) *Vakhtangov*, Moscow: Korabl'.

Vygotsky, Lev (1936) "K voprosu o psihologii tvorchestva aktyora [On the Creative Psychology of an Actor]" in Pavel Yakobson, *Psikhologiya Stsenicheskih Chuvstv Aktyora* [*Psychology of an Actor's Emotions Onstage*], Moscow: Goslitisdat, pp. 197–211.

Yablonsky, Sergei (1984) "Studiya Khudozhestvennogo teatra. 'Prazdnik mira' [Art Theatre Studio. *Festival of Peace*]," *Russkoe slovo*, November 24, 1913, reprinted in Lyubov Vendrovskaya and Galina Kaptereva (eds.), *Yevgeny Vakhtangov*, Moscow: VTO, pp. 126–28.

Yeryomenko, Nadezhda (1959) "Ego unos't' [His Youth]," in Lyubov Vendrovskaya (ed.), *Yevg. Vakhtangov, Materialy i statyi [Yevgeny Vakhtangov, Materials and Articles]*, Moscow: VTO, pp. 344–51.

Yzraely, Yosef (1970) "Vakhtangov Directing *The Dybbuk*," unpublished doctoral dissertation, Carnegie-Mellon University's Department of Drama.

Zakhava, Boris (1930) *Vakhtangov i ego studia [Vakhtangov and His Studio]*, 2nd edn, Moscow: Teakinopechat'.

Zavadsky, Yuri (1959) "Oderzhimost' tvorchestvom [Creative Possession]," in Lyubov Vendrovskaya (ed.), *Yevg. Vakhtangov, Materialy i statyi [Yevgeny Vakhtangov, Materials and Articles]*, Moscow: VTO, pp. 278–305.

—— (1975) *Uchitelia i ucheniki [Masters and Students]*, Moscow: Iskusstvo.

Zograf, Nikolai (1939) *Vakhtangov*, Moscow-Leningrad: Iskusstvo.

Supplementary Reading

Amaspiuriants, Abri (1996) *Turandot-63*, Moscow: Folio.

Barba, Eugenio (1995) *The Paper Canoe: A Guide To Theatre Anthropology*, London and New York: Routledge.

Barba, Eugenio and Savarese, Nicola (2005) *A Dictionary of Theatre Anthropology: The Secret Art of the Performer*, London and New York: Routledge.

Ben-Ari, Raikin (1957) *Habima*, London and New York: Thomas Yoselof.

Black, Lendley C. (1987) *Mikhail Chekhov as Actor, Director and Teacher*, Ann Arbor, MI: UMI Research Press.

Brecht, Bertolt (1964) *Brecht on Theatre: The Development of an Aesthetic*, ed. and trans. John Willett, New York: Hill & Wang.

Brestoff, Richard (1995) *Great Acting Teachers and Their Methods*, Lyme, NH: Smith and Kraus.

Bromley, Nadezhda (1959) "Put' iskatelia [Seeker's Path]," in Lyubov Vendrovskaya (ed.), *Yevg. Vakhtangov, Materialy i statyi [Yevgeny Vakhtangov, Materials and Articles]*, Moscow: VTO, pp. 322–30.

Chamberlain, Franc (2004) *Michael Chekhov*, London and New York: Routledge.

Chekhov, Michael (1984) *Michael Chekhov's To the Director and Playwright*, New York: Limelight Editions.

Clurman, Harold (1997) *On Directing*, New York: Fireside.

Craig, Edward Gordon (1939) "Habima's Achievement," in *Habima*, English Publication of *Bama*, Theatre Art Journal of Habima Circle in Palestine, Tel-Aviv, August.

Gorchakov, Nikolai (1957) *The Theater in Soviet Russia*, New York: Columbia University Press.

Gordon, Mel (1987) *The Stanislavsky Technique: Russia*, New York: Applause Theater Book Publishers.

Hethmon, Robert H. (ed.) (1991) *Strasberg at the Actors Studio: Tape-Recorded Sessions*, New York: Theatre Communications Group.

Hodge, Alison (ed.) (2000) *Twentieth Century Actor Training*, London and New York: Routledge.

Leach, Robert and Borovsky, Victor (eds.) (2006) *A History of Russian Theatre*, Cambridge: Cambridge University Press.

Levy, Emanuel (1979) *The Habima: Israel's National Theater, 1917–1977*, New York: Columbia University Press.

Marowitz, Charles (2004) *The Other Chekhov*, New York: Applause Theater Book Publishers.

Moore, Sonia (1984) *The Stanislavski System: The Professional Training of an Actor*, London: Penguin.

Parke, Lawrence (1985) *Since Stanislavski and Vakhtangov: The Method as a System for Today's Actor*, Hollywood, CA: Acting World Books.

Rudnitsky, Konstantin (2000) *Russian and Soviet Theatre: Tradition and the Avant-Garde*, London: Thames & Hudson.

Rzhevsky, Nicholas (ed.) (1999) *The Cambridge Companion to Modern Russian Culture*, Cambridge: Cambridge University Press.

Schmidt, Paul (ed.) (1996) *Meyerhold at Work*, New York: Applause Theatre & Cinema Book Publishers.

Shikhmatov, Leonid (1970) *Ot studii k teatru* [*From Studio to Theatre*], Moscow: VTO.

Simonov, Ruben (1969) *Stanislavsky's Protégé: Eugene Vakhtangov*, trans. Miriam Goldina, New York: DBS Publications.

Slonim, Mark (1961) *Russian Theater: From the Empire to the Soviets*, Cleveland, OH: The World Publishing Company.

Vakhtangov, Yevgeny (1947) "Preparing for the Role: From the Diary of E. Vakhtangov," in Toby Cole (ed.), *Acting: A Handbook of the Stanislavski Method*, New York: Lear Publishers, pp. 116–24.

—— "Fantastic Realism [Two Final Discussions with Students]" in Toby Cole and Helen Krich Chinoy (eds.), *Directing the Play*, Indianapolis, IN: Bobbs-Merrill, pp. 160–65.

Vendrovskaya, Lyubov and Kaptereva, Galina (eds.) (1982) *Evgeny Vakhtangov*, Moscow: Progress Publishers.

Worrall, Nick (1989) *Modernism to Realism on the Soviet Stage: Tairov-Vakhtangov-Okhlopkov*, Cambridge: Cambridge University Press.

Zagorsky, Mikhail (1984) "Gadibuk (Studiya Gabima) [The Dybbuk (The Habima Studio)]," *Teatral'naya Moskva*, 1922, no. 25, reprinted in Lyubov Vendrovskaya and Galina Kaptereva (eds.), *Yevgeny Vakhtangov*, Moscow: VTO, p. 400.

Zakhava, Boris (1935) *Vzaimodeistvie mezhdu aktyorom i rezhissyorom* [*Interaction Between Actor and Director*], Moscow: TS K RABIS.

—— (2010) *Vakhtangov i ego studia* [*Vakhtangov and His Studio*], 3rd edn, Moscow: ArsisBooks.

Index

Page numbers in *italics* refer to illustrations.

www.routledge.com/performance

Related titles from Routledge

The Vakhtangov Sourcebook

Edited by **Andrei Malaev-Babel**

'Scrupulously translated and skilfully translated by Andrei Malaev-Babel, *The Vakhtangov Sourcebook* ... provides the most comprehensive addition to English readers' knowledge of the philosophy, pedagogy, and legacy of Vakhtangov.' – *Modern Language Review*

Yevgeny Vakhtangov was the creator of fantastic realism, credited with reconciling Meyerhold's bold experiments with Stanislavsky's naturalist technique. *The Vakhtangov Sourcebook* compiles new translations of his key writings on the art of theatre, making it the primary source of first-hand material on this master of theatre in the English-speaking world.

Vakhtangov's essays and articles are accompanied by:

- unpublished diary and notebook excerpts
- his lectures to the Vakhtangov Studio
- in-depth accounts of Vakhtangov's methods in rehearsal
- production photographs and sketches
- extensive bibliographies
- director's notes on key performances.

An extensive introductory overview from editor Andrei Malaev-Babel explains Vakhtangov's creative life, his groundbreaking theatrtical concepts and influential directorial works.

March 2011: 216x138: 368pp
Hb: 978-0-415-47268-5
Pb: 978-0-415-48257-8
Ebk: 978-0-203-85291-0

For more information and to order a copy visit
www.routledge.com/9780415482578

Available from all good bookshops